Relational Approaches in Gestalt Therapy

Lynne Jacobs and
Rich Hycner, Editors

••••••••••••••••••

Foreword *Erving Polster*

•••••••••••••••••••••••••••••••••••••••

Relational

Approaches

in

Gestalt

Therapy

A GestaltPress Book

published and distributed by
Routledge, Taylor & Francis Group
New York

Copyright 2009 by: GestaltPress
127 Abby Court
Santa Cruz, CA 95062

and   165 Route 6A
Orleans, MA 02653

Email: gestaltpress@aol.com, gestaltpress@comcast.net

Distributed by: **Routledge, Taylor & Francis Group**
270 Madison Avenue
New York, NY 10016

Sculpture in cover image: "Centered," 2008 by Syd Harris
Cover design: Elena Sidorova

Library of Congress Cataloging-in-Publishing Data
  1. relational Gestalt therapy, 2. psychology, 3. field theory,
  4. relational process, 5. intersubjectivity, 6. Dialogue ,
  7. Rich Hycner, 8. Lynne Jacobs

ISBN: 978-0-415-87931-6.

for Gordon Berger,
always encouraging me.
Lynne Jacobs

and

for Brynne,
my daughter,
who gives me so much joy and aliveness,
and who, along with Dorothy and Bryce,
has been so understanding of me
working on my projects.
Rich Hycner

Contents

••••••••

Section 1 — Overview and Explorations

Section 2 — The Crucible of the Consulting Room

Section 3 — A Wider Embrace: Groups and Organizations

Foreword

••••••••••

Any therapy theory requires continual elaboration of its most hallowed principles. Hycner and Jacobs have been doing just that in their writings: expanding Gestalt therapy's fundamental concept of "contact" into its larger potential, the more socially pertinent concept of "relationship." Relationship has long been a term everybody uses but only as a diffuse statement of people engaged with each other. The concept of contact, in contrast, had revelatory effect because it was a focal statement, a recognition of the elemental, finely directed and universal entry power of people meeting each other, each moment to the next. Now, having successfully addressed the power of the elemental contact experience, there is a surging renewal of Gestalt therapy's humanistic perspective in accentuating contact as the springboard to *relationship*, a transformation wherein *implied* relationship becomes *described* relationship, organized in all of its complexity and its personal empowerment. Laughing, crying, planning, loving, giving, wondering: everything the person does with the people in the enveloping world is grist for the Gestalt exploration.

People don't just meet moment to moment; they are in a joined endeavor, building a union that trumpets the reality that me and thee make we. In this augmentation from simple experience into the larger humanity of engagement, Jacobs and

Hycner have created a rendezvous of minds sharply attentive to the indivisibility between self and other and to the security that comes with knowing that never, ever is anybody alone in this world.

Many people do experience themselves to be alone because of the individualistic impediments to feeling the "we" in their lives. However, in the deepest understanding of life's gifts, there is a silent undercurrent of appetite for storyline, continuity and belonging. To this end, *Relational Approaches in Gestalt Therapy* is a new contribution, a human scale portrayal showing that people may transcend their prejudices about each other and enjoy the communal entity that houses all of us.

September 2008   Erving Polster
                                                    LaJolla, CA

Preface

◆◆◆◆◆◆◆◆◆◆◆◆◆◆◆◆◆◆

For a long time, both of us sensed a void. That void was that there was no single compilation of authors actively exploring how to apply a relational approach in Gestalt therapy. We felt that it was time to draw together some of the many voices engaged in developing the relational perspectives in Gestalt therapy. Each of the included authors has a unique contribution to add to the development of the relational approach. We wanted to have a mix of some of the well established leading proponents of this approach and some who were coming from a fresh and emerging understanding of relationality. We are acutely aware that this work is in no way inclusive of all Gestalt practitioners writing about the relational approach. We regret that it could not even begin to approach that ideal. Consequently, many other interesting authors could not be included. However, we hope that this collection furthers the dialogue that will encourage other emerging voices. If this work, in some small way, supports those emerging voices, and contributes to the dialogue exploring this approach, we will consider the work a success.

July 2008

Lynne Jacobs
Los Angeles, CA

Rich Hycner
Encinitas, CA

Acknowledgments

•••••••••••

First and foremost, our fellow authors deserve appreciation for their generosity with their ideas, time, and patience.

A major impetus for this edited book emerged from experiences with colleagues and students who have attended the Pacific Gestalt Inst. Residential program over the years. The emotional courage and intellectual excitement of the participants has been a major source of inspiration for me. Of course without students and patients to teach us, we would have nothing to say.

Robert Lee has provided steadfast and clear support as a representative of GestaltPress.

July 2008   Lynne Jacobs
                                                                   Los Angeles, CA

I appreciate that Lynne has always pursued the relational approach with depth and rigor — and I appreciate her for persevering with this project. I am immensely grateful to the many participants in the workshops I have conducted and the clients I have seen over the last thirty-five years, who have taught me about the relational. I very much value that each of the included authors has presented a unique perspective on applying the relational approach. I also want to thank Robert Lee and Gordon Wheeler for their help in getting this book published.

July 2008   Rich Hycner
                                                                   Encinitas, CA

The Editors

◆◆◆◆◆◆◆◆◆◆◆

Lynne Jacobs, Ph.D. is co-founder of the Pacific Gestalt Institute. She is also a training and supervising analyst at the Institute of Contemporary Psychoanalysis. She is particularly interested in relational processes in therapy. She co-authored, with Rich Hycner, *The Healing Relationship in Gestalt Therapy: A Dialogic — Self-Psychology Approach*. She has written numerous articles and teaches internationally.

Rich Hycner, PhD, is the author of *Between Person and Person: Toward a Dialogical Psychotherapy*; and co-author with Lynne Jacobs of, *The Healing Relationship in Gestalt Therapy: A Dialogic — Self-Psychology Approach.* He has been profoundly influenced by Martin Buber's philosophy of dialogue and Erving and Miriam Polster's creative utilization of Gestalt therapy. He is especially interested in the relational dimensions of the therapeutic relationship as a nexus for healing.

The Contributors

••••••••••••••••

Marie-Anne Chidiac, BEng, MBA, MSc (Gestalt Psychotherapy), works as an organisation consultant and psychotherapist. As an experienced coach and consultant, she has over
14 years experience in mobilising management teams to lead
new ways of working, and delivering better performance. Marie-
Anne has experience of a wide variety of industries within the
private and public sectors. She currently runs her own consulting company specialising in organisational change and
leadership development. She works as a primary tutor on the
Gestalt Psychotherapy Masters programme at Metanoia Training Institute in London, where she is also joint course director
on the Organisational Gestalt programme.

Sally Denham-Vaughan, DPsych, works as a Clinical,
Counselling and Coaching Psychologist and Gestalt Psychotherapist. She holds a senior managerial position in a large
National Health Service Trust in the UK that provides mental
health services for over 500,000 people. She also works as a
primary tutor on the Gestalt Masters programme at Metanoia
psychotherapy training institute in London, and is joint course
director of the Organisa-tional Gestalt Diploma/Certificate
programme there. She is a member of the Editorial Advisory
Board of the British Gestalt Journal, International Faculty
Associate at the Pacific Gestalt Institute and Organisational
Faculty at The Relational Center in Los Angeles.

Mark Fairfield, LCSW, BCD, (Board Certified Diplomate in Clinical Social Work), holds an MS in Social Work from Columbia University and completed four years of post-graduate clinical training leading to certification in Gestalt Therapy. He has served as a faculty member at the Pacific Gestalt Institute, Clinical Director for Common Ground in Santa Monica, and is currently the Executive Director for The Relational Center. Mark's private practice is in two locations, one on the West side of L. A. and the other in the Miracle Mile area. Mark has trained and presented internationally and has published in journals and books primarily on the subject of groups, dialogue, harm minimization and deconstructing individualism.

Robert G. Lee, PhD, a psychologist in private practice in Newton, MA, has written extensively and presented widely on shame and belonging as regulator processes of the relational field. He is co-editor of *The Voice of Shame: Silence and Connection in Psychotherapy*, editor of *The Values of Connection: A Relational Approach to Ethics*, and author of *The Secret Language of Intimacy: Releasing the Hidden Power in Couple Relationships*. His current book project is co-editing *Relational Child, Relational Brain*. Robert is a faculty member of The Gestalt Institute of Cleveland, teaches nationally and internationally, and is an editor at GestaltPress.

Judith Matson, PhD, is a licensed psychologist with a private practice in San Diego, California. As a certified member of the Pacific Gestalt Institute and an active participant in the PGI trainings for the last decade, Judith has been mentored by Lynne Jacobs, Jan Ruckert and Gary Yontef. She is thankful to them, and to her colleague in San Diego, Rich Hycner, for their emphasis on dialogue and the relational; this emphasis has become a touchstone for her work as psychotherapist and in her on-line teaching for Pacific Oaks College.

Leanne O' Shea works as a psychotherapist and is based in Melbourne, Australia. Since 2000, she has been on the faculty of Gestalt Therapy Australia. She studied the Gestalt approach in Melbourne and London, and more recently the relational approach to Gestalt Therapy at the Pacific Gestalt Institute (USA). She is also a faculty member of The Relational Center, a Los Angeles based organization whose mission is to promote greater diversity within the helping professions. She is also interested in creating greater awareness of and sensitivity to our relational responsibility, and is particularly passionate about the place of sexuality and the erotic within the therapeutic relationship. She is well published and is an inaugural co-editor of the new Gestalt Journal of Australia and New Zealand.

Margherita Spagnuolo Lobb, psychologist, licensed psychotherapist, is Founder and Director of the Istituto di Gestalt H.C.C. Italy, a Psychotherapy post-graduate School approved by the Italian Minister for Universities, since 1979. She is an international trainer and a Full Member of the *New York Institute for Gestalt Therapy*. Has been President of the *European Association for Gestalt Therapy* (EAGT) from 1996 to 2002, of the Italian Federation of Associations of Psychotherapies (FIAP) during the years 2003-2005. She edits the Italian Journal *Quaderni di Gestalt* (since 1985) and – together with Dan Bloom and Frank Staemmler – the International Journal in English language *Studies in Gestalt Therapy: Dialogical Bridges*. She authored many chapters and articles published in various languages and is editor, among others, of *Psicoterapia della Gestalt. Ermeneutica e clinica* (Angeli,

2001, translated into Spanish by Gedisa and French by L'Exprimerie) and, with Nancy Amendt-Lyon, *Creative License. The Art of Gestalt Therapy* (Springer, 2003, translated into German by Springer, French by L'Exprimerie, and Italian by Angeli).

Frank-M. Staemmler, PhD, Dipl-Psych, born in 1951, is a psychologist and Gestalt therapist, who lives in Wuerzburg, Germany. He has been working as a Gestalt therapist in private practice since 1976, and as a supervisor and trainer since 1981. He has written about seventy articles and book chapters and six books and has (co-)edited six other books. He teaches internationally and is a frequent presenter at conferences in Germany and abroad. He was editor of the *International Gestalt Journal* from 2001 to 2006, and co-editor of the *Studies in Gestalt Therapy: Dialogical Bridges* from 2007 to 2009.

Stuart Stawman, MGT, is a practicing psychotherapist informed by Gestalt and Relational Psychoanalysis. He has over 20 years of clinical experience working with individuals, couples and groups. Originally from the UK, Stuart now lives on the Northern Beaches of Sydney, Australia, with his wife, son, a cat and a dog.

Carol Swanson, LCSW, Executive Director of PGTI, a therapist in private practice for the last 25 years and a co-founder of the Portland Gestalt Training Institute, has presented at numerous national conferences and was on the planning committee for the first Association for the Advancement of Gestalt Therapy (AAGT) conference. She coordinated and taught at five Portland Gestalt Training Institute European residential programs, and was a guest trainer at the Gestalt Institute in Perth, Australia. Her own teachers/trainers have included Isadore From and Philip Lichtenberg. She studied at the Gestalt Therapy Institute of Los Angeles, and has studied extensively with Lynne Jacobs, integrating the influences of self-psychololgy and contemporary analytic thinking with Gestalt therapy.

Gary Yontef, PhD, FAClinP, Fellow of the Academy of Clinical Psychology and Diplomate in Clinical Psychology (ABPP) has been a Gestalt therapist since training with Frederick Perls and James Simkin in 1965. Formerly on the UCLA Psychology Department Faculty and Chairman of the Professional Conduct Committee of the L.A. County Psychological Association, he is in private practice in Santa Monica. He is a co-founder and faculty member of the Pacific Gestalt Institute (PGI). He is a past president of the GTILA and was longtime chairman of the faculty. He has been on the editorial board of the International Gestalt Journal (formerly The Gestalt Journal), the Gestalt Review, and editorial advisor of the British Gestalt Journal. He wrote *Awareness, Dialogue and Process: Essays on Gestalt Therapy*, which is published or in press in five languages in addition to English. His bibliography includes sixty articles and chapters on Gestalt therapy theory, practice, and supervision.

Relational
Approaches
in
Gestalt Therapy

Section I

• • • • • • • • • •

Overview and Explorations

Introduction

• • • • • • • • • • • •

The three chapters in Section I articulate three overview perspectives. Each represents a unique way of understanding and giving voice to a relational approach. Rich Hycner is evocative, experiential and inspirational. Stuart Stawman's wry story-telling narrative is historical/ developmental. Gary Yontef's love of interweaving theory and practice shines through his schematic of a relational approach.

The section begins with Hycner's poetic evocation of life as a relational practitioner. He invites the reader to taste our reluctance to surrender to relationship as a humbling mystery that challenges our claim to expertise and efficacy. "To study the relational, is like scooping up a handful of sand. For an instant, you can grasp it—it feels like you have something in hand; yet inexorably, what seemed so solid a minute ago slowly slips through your fingers." This is an experience with which we are all familiar, I suspect, and one that you may encounter repeatedly in later chapters of the book.

Next comes Stawman's "theory of evolution of the relational Gestalt therapist species." We describe his chapter with the same sense of play that Stawman weaves into his evolutionary tale. But his chapter is more than an overview of our history. He has written a creation myth. Stawman's chapter is an intriguing analysis of the ground on which relational Gestalt theorizing stands, a critical and richly illuminating perspective on the evolution of relational theorizing to date. He frames it specifically with an eye towards further critique and refinement of what we mean by "relational." He opens the door for all of us to take the next step.

Yontef's chapter closes this section with an overview of the basic theoretical rationale for his conception of the foundational principles that guide his practice. The principles of practice flow seamlessly from his theoretical grounding in field theory, phenomenology and dialogue. If the reader immerses him or herself in the theory, he or she will be changed. That is the point; Yontef, a seasoned practitioner, reminds us that a relational practice is largely an attitude rather than a method, an attitude that leads us to court surprise and humility as cotherapists along the way.

Preamble to a Relational Approach:

A Plea for Existential Fluidity

• • • • • • • • • • • •

Rich Hycner

To study the relational is like scooping up a handful of sand. For an instant, you can grasp it — it feels like you have something in hand, yet inexorably, what seemed so solid a moment ago slowly slips through your fingers.

Alone, none of us is adequate to this task of fully articulating a relational psychotherapy. Even joined with a community, it is a difficult, challenging, and ambiguous exploration. It is fraught with the danger of resorting to gross oversimplification. This is because of our inability to ever see the whole picture. We can become overwhelmed by the relational's infinite richness and ever-shifting contours. Rather than being true to this ever-shifting complexity, our tendency is to overly simplify it by either objectifying or "subjectifying" our relational nature.

Because we are capable of being self-reflective about our relational nature — seemingly able to separate our self from our experience—we too often believe that our truth is the truth. Yet, there is no objective external "platform" from which to study the relational. There is also no ultimate "in-sight" from a privileged subjective viewpoint. All our individual insights need to be validated, as well as mediated and modified, in an open dialogue with others.

Because we are immersed in the relational, of it, (as Merleau-Ponty spoke of "Being"), surrounded by it, we never see it totally from the "outside" — nor from the "inside." We merely have glimpses of it—fleeting moments of illumination. Our overriding task is to immerse ourselves in the fundamental ambiguity of this phenomenon in order to better clarify it. This leaves us with scant security, and the necessity of being courageous in the exploration of the unknown, and the uncertain.

Currently, we are only on the fringes of this exploration. Our present state of knowledge is woefully inadequate. We know so little that our first authentic step is to acknowledge our ignorance: that is however only the beginning, not the ending — and we are always perpetual beginners.

The fundamental impossibility of ever fully achieving what we seek cannot be an excuse for lapsing into unexamined silence or simplistic responses. Rather, we need to take up this task with unceasing curiosity, as well as concurrently with ever-present humility, in the face of that which is much larger than us and which we can never fully grasp. Only then, will our chances of being "true to the phenomenon" be improved.

Our task is not to dispel the fundamental ambiguity of our relational being-with-others (i.e., the interhuman). Rather, it is to articulate as much of its richness as possible, in the short time given to us, and to pass that knowledge on to the next generation. Ironically, each generation must start anew — in order to truly learn about itself, on its own, in its current relational milieu. We must immerse ourselves in the unknown, to discover anew, ourselves-in-the relational and the relational-in-ourselves.

Hopefully these limitations instill humility in us — a recognition that all our knowledge, all our speech, is ultimately limited by that which needs to be spoken about, yet that which can never be fully spoken. That which is hidden about our nature is always far more than that which is revealed — and each revelation merely points to greater hiddenness. Such is our Promethean and Sisyphean task — to constantly speak about the relational, yet to recognize how little we actually "know" of it. It can only have facets of it articulated: it can never be completely mapped out. A working map is helpful, even essential, but is never the territory we experientially live in moment by moment.

Fundamental to this task is to recognize that to articulate the relational is itself a relational endeavor. Any insights we have arise out of our mutual efforts, and are always subject to an ongoing dialogue and corrective. Ultimately, only our dialogue with others can confirm any insights about the relational: it cannot be otherwise. We experience vividly the conundrum that our very study of this phenomenon is subject to the phenomenon we are studying. We struggle constantly with this Gordian knot of our existence.

We begin with mystery: our clinical work is suffused with and infused by this mystery. By dint of our endeavors, hopefully we end with a far richer understanding and appreciation of that mystery. It strikes me as no accident that Martin Buber believed that God dwelled in the "betweeness" of our existence. Ultimately, we end with mystery.

Relational Gestalt: Four Waves[1]

• • • • • • • • • • • •

Stuart Stawman

*I*n the beginning is the relation.

Martin Buber

Preamble

What do we mean by relational and in what ways is Gestalt relational? This chapter will explore how a growing awareness of the relational nature of being, and the reflection of this awareness in Gestalt theory, has evolved in Gestalt discourse. I currently picture this evolutionary process as comprising four phases, which I will be referring to as waves. These four waves:

---

[1] I would like to thank Sally Brooks, Lynne Jacobs, Rich Hycner and Leanne O'Shea for their thoughtful responses to earlier drafts of this paper. A modified version of this chapter appeared in the *Gestalt Journal of Australia and New Zealand, 4* (2), May 2008, 37-55.

"Organism-Environment," "I-Thou," "Intersubjectivity" and "Relational Ground," are not an attempt to accurately reflect history so much as they represent one way of thinking about this topic, a way that will give structure to this exploration.

Before we begin, I want to outline the two ways in which I understand and use the word relational. We can think of these two ways as being "relational in the broad sense," and "relational in the narrow sense."

The philosopher Edmund Husserl, frequently referred to as the "father" of phenomenology, asserted that a basic principle of our existence is that *thought and experience are "directed towards objects."* Awareness, he was saying, is always *of* or *about* something; consciousness is relational. Perls, Hefferline & Goodman's notion of self reflects the same relational dynamic, self is a process of becoming *in relation to something else.* Stated in the language of Gestalt theory, self-process resides in the ongoing resolutions of the organism/environment field. Gestalt is thus relational to the core of its theory. Or, better said, Gestalt theory acknowledges the fundamentally relational nature of being. This is what I think of as the broad sense of the word relational.

Martin Buber's contributions to Gestalt theory were not so much about the self in relation to *something else* as they were about the self in relation to *someone else*; the I in relation to an It or a Thou. Intersubjectivity acted as a bridge between Perls, Hefferline & Goodman's organism/environment field paradigm and Buber's I-It/I-Thou paradigm by merging a finely focused field sensibility with the interplay of subject-subject relating. When our attention is directed solely to the complex interweave of human relationships, then we are in the domain of the "relational in the narrow sense."

The First Wave: Organism-Environment

The definition of an organism is the definition of an organism/environment field . . .

Perls, Hefferline & Goodman 1951/1984, p. 259

Gestalt Therapy: Excitement and Growth in Human Personality (1951/1984) by Perls, Hefferline and Goodman was ahead of its time. Some two decades before Heinz Kohut would attempt to break from the Freudian pack and establish a "Self Psychology," Perls, Hefferline & Goodman were already far outside the psychoanalytic citadel, developing a revolutionary model of self process that remains valid and applicable to this day [*Gestalt Therapy* and its authors are hereafter referred to as "PHG"].

PHG sought to describe an experiential world in which they could locate their evolving theories of human selfhood and therapeutic action. Centuries before them, Descartes had placed a divide between mind and matter, between body and mind. This was a "neurotic dichotomy," according to PHG, who instead declared the boundary of significance as that between organism and environment. PHG proposed that self, which they thought of in process terms, is not *in the mind* but *in* the system of contacts at the boundary between "me" and "not me," between organism and environment. The experience of self, they said, is constituted in the experience of the continually shifting configurations and reconfigurations of the organism/environment field. Self *becomes* in the experienced resolution of relational existence.

This definition, what we might call the *boundary self,* can now be seen as having occurred within a nascent paradigm shift that was increasingly emphasising, in therapeutic thinking at least, that the nature of being is relational. Gestalt was "relational" in that it took the inescapable given of relatedness across the ever-changing boundary between organism and environment as the precondition for experience, and as a primary vehicle for mapping the nature of experience. Still, while they proposed the use of this same map across the differing domains of biology, psychology and sociology, their writings were not particularly relational in the narrow sense of organism-to-organism, let alone subject-to-subject. Their new theoretical map generally pertained to a "single organism" embedded interactively within an environment:

> ... the definition of an animal involves its environment:
> it is meaningless to define a breather without air, a walker
> without gravity ... (PHG, pp. 258-259).

Generally speaking, the environment includes other organisms, but this element was often missing in the language and descriptions of their model. Intrinsically, or as a consequence, their vision had a strong narcissistic flavour; it was a vision in which the organism either derived or failed to derive its survival requirements from the environment.

Falling shy of the dialogical, the pages of PHG are in short supply of *other* selves.[2] It is true that they mention such activities as "satisfying your requirements . . . as a social human being," and there are frequent mentions of society, but their "society" seems to be little more than a community of complex

---

[2] In this author's reading of PHG, the only mention of "actual contact with the other person as a person" (PHG, p. 123) found was delivered in the negative. By this I mean to say that the "actual contact" referred to is being described as something that confluence *avoids*.

(mostly neurotic) animals. In short, the human world they depict lacks the rich possibilities of human-to-human contact. For clues as to why this might have been so, it is tempting to turn to Laura Perls's account of husband Fritz's therapeutic work, "he was not interested in the person as such but in what he could do with her," adding that he "could not carry on the dialogue" (Friedman, 1985, p. 89). Laura, on the other hand, seems to have been far more affected by the ways in which Buber, whom she met in Frankfurt, suggested we engage with other selves.

Laura was not to be the only one to contribute momentum to the building wave of interest in Gestalt toward open human engagement. Another pivotal contribution, albeit couched in different language, came from Arnold Beisser's *Paradoxical Theory of Change* (1970), which advocated that we are most therapeutically useful when we seek only to meet the patient, not to change them (or ourselves).

The Second Wave: I-Thou

... actual contact with the other person as a person.

PHG p. 123

With the gift of hindsight, Martin Buber's philosophy of I-Thou seems the perfect antidote to the narcissistic flavour that infused PHG's portrayal of the organism/environment field paradigm. Buber's interest was in the relationship between subject and subject. His philosophy was an invitation for therapists to shed the role of challenging bystander (Gestalt stereotype) or expert witness (analytic stereotype) and enter the far more sensitive space of genuine relationship. With a growing sense that healing occurs through *meeting* and not, say, through confrontation, the manner in which Gestalt could be considered relational was now more complex, more human.

Laura Perls, we are told, was far less drawn to Buber's thinking and how it could influence her approach to therapy than she was by the way that he actually embodied contact, the way he exemplified moments of meeting (Friedman, 1985). This distinction, between Buber's actual presence and Buber's philosophy, has particular relevance for Gestalt theory. It may well be the case that what is generally intended by the term I-Thou in Gestalt *is* closely related to what actually transpired *between* Laura and Martin when they met. However, it may be equally so that what Gestalt intends by the term I-Thou is far less congruent with the fine print of Buber's stated philosophy. This is not to question Gestalt's formulations concerning the processes of I-Thou relating; it is to question Buber. The work of PHG is frequently questioned and reconsidered in Gestalt literature, often to good effect, but Buber generally seems to have escaped this kind of scrutiny.

A broad review of Buber's work, carried out by Michael Theunissen in his classic work *The Other: Studies in the Social Ontology of Husserl, Heidegger, Sartre, and Buber* (1984) revealed that there are three fundamental characteristics, or traits, attributed by Buber to the I-Thou relationship. These are, "reciprocity," "immediacy," and "common origination from the between" (p. 293). Let us consider each in turn.

Gestalt descriptions of mutuality in the I-Thou experience have always aligned with Buber's first named characteristic, that of reciprocity. This congruence holds despite the qualifications necessitated by the imbalances of the therapist/patient relationship.

With regard to the second characteristic, immediacy, Buber asserts that, "[t]he relation of the Thou is immediate. Between I and Thou there is *no conceptuality, no foreknowledge, and no fantasy*" (Buber, 1954, 15-16:62, cited in Theunnisen, 1984, p. 274, emphasis added).[3] We find here Buber's claim to a capacity for "pristine relatedness" (Donnel Stern, personal communication, Nov 2006) whereby the "I" may experience a "Thou" in a pure way, unaffected by pre-existing "conceptuality, foreknowledge or fantasy."

Buber's immediacy shares an important property with bracketing, a notion that has now been questioned by a number of Gestalt writers (e.g., Sapriel, 1998, Van De Riet, 2001, Staemmler, this volume, O'Shea, this volume). First, however, we should note how these two ideas differ from each other; bracketing is the *active* adoption of a particular attitude whereby one seeks to engage with the given qualities of reality without the colouration of "conceptuality, foreknowledge or fantasy," whereas Buber claims immediacy to be an *unbidden* property of the I-Thou meeting. What the two concepts have in common is their claim to pristine experience.

While bracketing remains an important quality of engagement in a qualified sense (see, e.g., Van de Riet 2001; McConville, 2001), it has been dismissed in the absolute sense of *the environment's pure revelation to consciousness.*[4] The organism is unable to experience the environment "directly" without filtering or shaping the experience in some way,

---

[3] Theunnisen's use of the phrase "no foreknowledge" comes from a translation of Buber by Macann (see Theunisen, 1984). Walter Kaufman's more commonly cited translation of Buber (Buber, 1923/1970) carries the different, but essentially similar, rendition "no prior knowledge."

[4] Heidegger questioned the integrity of Husserl's notion of bracketing, in part by refuting the possibility of "no foreknowledge." It seems strange, therefore, that Buber claimed this capacity in light of his study with Heidegger (Lynne Jacobs, personal communication, May 2007).

whether this is across physical membranes, through complex systems of contextualised expectations accrued through previous experiences (a.k.a.. transference and counter-transference), or a host of other ways. Buber's immediacy is vulnerable to precisely the same critique.

Gestalt's relationship with Buber's third characteristic, "common origination from the between," is probably less clear. By "common origination from the between," Buber conveyed his belief that the genesis of both partners in the I-Thou moment occurs *as a result* of that encounter. Theunissen (1984, p. 280) sets out Buber's position in the following way:

> . . . [T]he fact of the meeting essentially presupposes the fact of those who meet. Instead of the I and the Thou, as already finished beings, bringing the meeting into being, they must, according to the dialogical approach, themselves first spring out of the occurrence of the meeting. Only so can the between be affirmed as more original in contrast to the "sphere of subjectivity," . . .

Buber credits the happening of "the between" as *preceding* the occurrence of an I and a Thou.[5] This notion proves highly problematic when investigated from a philosophical point of view, as Theunissen has done. Indeed, Theunissen suggests that weaknesses such as this one have contributed to the general lack of regard towards Buber from within the discipline of philosophy. The more "Gestalt" approach would be to gauge the merit of this idea experientially.

---

[5] Buber does, at times, put things differently, for example; "I becomes a 'real self' in the meeting with the Thou" (*Eclipse of God*, 1958, cited in Theunissen, 1984). Ultimately though, his position seems to be best represented in his idea that I and Thou are brought into being *purely and simply* in the event of the meeting.

What are the moments that *you* would describe as I-Thou? Most descriptions place I-Thou moments in the dialectical context of a figure/ground relationship with moments of I-It, as Buber did. I-Thou moments are reported to be moments of transformation, moments in which one's sense of self, world and other is transformed. My own leaning is to clothe these experiences in the language of a continuum, which is to say that I would describe experience as moving, moment by moment, along a continuum *away* from I-It *toward* I-Thou, *and vice versa*. This may reflect little more than my own linguistic and conceptual preferences. However, from within this perspective, I conceive I-Thou moments as being *potentially* transformative but, equally, *they may not be*. In fact, they may be relatively ordinary and frequent. By this I am suggesting that I-Thou moments can punctuate, however briefly, the most mundane of days, particularly around loved ones. Within *this* framework, we would be better to speak of being "sustained," or "enlivened" by the between, rather than being "created" by it.

But whatever your experiences of I-Thou may be, and whatever terminologies *you* choose to describe them, the question being asked here remains the same: are these moments in which you sense I and Thou to have been created from the between, as Buber proposed? I cannot presume to answer this question in any general sense but, based on my own experience, my answer would be "no."

This line of questioning invites us to describe our experience of I-Thou moments. Who speaks for the between? This elusive notion, one that courts reification when presented as a noun, permits only partial access in terms of experience or description.[6] Referred to in ways that range from casual to mystical, the between is a "notional space" or "process" that surely remains, to the extent that it exists at all, beyond individual grasp. We might question, therefore, the scope of its utility, particularly within a modality that leans so heavily towards the experiential. "I" can be in relation to "Thou," but I cannot presume to know the between in any direct sense. I can never step outside the realms of "my experience." There are those who disagree with this position, Rich Hycner among them (personal communication, June 2007). It is not my intention to suggest that "restricted access" to the between should silence us on the topic, only to acknowledge our limitations.

Staemmler (2006), speaking to the first wave, has suggested that the "organism/environment field" first articulated in PHG is a "dazzling term" that "lacks the epistemological sophistication . . . encountered in Lewin's writings." He claims a substantial lack of clarity in Gestalt's appropriation of Lewin's term "field." My case relating to the second wave is a little different. I am suggesting that Gestalt has never really claimed total adherence to the small print of Buber's philosophy of I-Thou, but nor has it carefully articulated the ways in which it differs. Buber's ideas, filtered through the works of both Farber and Friedman (e.g., 1968 and 1985 respectively), have undergone steady development within Gestalt theory since his original initiative. The idea of the between has served us well as a kind of "decentering corrective," helping to loosen the grip of the individualist paradigm that infuses our Western culture (see Wheeler, 2000), but it is not without problems of its own, as has been outlined above.

---

[6] The reification effect of the noun "between" could have been avoided, at least in part, by the term "in between" (Lynne Jacobs, personal communication, June 2007).

Third Wave: Intersubjectivity

There is no single function of any animal that completes itself without objects and environment.

PHG p. 228

A third wave arose with the desire to go beyond Buber's detailed descriptions of the I-Thou moment and explore the intricacies of I-Thou process (see, in particular, Hycner & Jacobs, 1995). This was largely facilitated by Kohut's development of Self Psychology (e.g. 1977, 1984) and its elaborations by the Inter-subjectivists (e.g., Stolorow, Atwood and Brandchaft, 1987). Gestalt expanded its horizons by virtue of two models that, to this day, lack a comparable appreciation for the I-Thou.

In effect, Kohut recast the PHG quote cited earlier, and proposed that, *the definition of a self involves its environment: it is meaningless to define a self without selfobjects.* By his cumbersome term "selfobjects" he meant to describe a variety of relational supports that maintain, restore and transform positive self-experience. Kohut was attempting to describe a variety of environmental supports that often occur at the fringes of awareness but which are, nonetheless, central to one's personal sense of wellbeing. In much the same way that oxygen, *crucial to wellbeing*, usually only enters awareness by virtue of its absence or depletion (and even then, it is more likely that *distress* and *restorative actions* will be figural to awareness than the presence or otherwise of actual oxygen molecules), we can see that variations in the availability of these relational experiences may not always figure in awareness per se, but their absence or diminution can be found implicated in processes of human distress and alienation. In other words, their presence supports and enhances both personal wellbeing and intimate relatedness. It was this discovery that started to reveal finer and finer details of how our respective resolutions of the field interact. When these ideas were appropriated by the Intersubjectivists, for whom phenomenology and field-sensitive thinking were paramount, the merit of this thinking became increasingly apparent to a number of proponents of the Gestalt paradigm. The flow-on effect, the fleshing out of these everyday details of subject-to-subject meeting helped offset the "peak experience" quality that dominates many readings of Buber's philosophy, giving weight instead to the ordinary "stuff of life" (see especially, Hycner & Jacobs, 1995).

In the field of psychotherapy, intersubjectivity was an idea waiting to happen. The psychoanalysts were the first to raise the flag, though it could just as easily have been the flourishing neurosciences, or the detailed observations of mother/infant interaction made possible through the advent of video recording. The strange thing is this; Gestalt did not get there first.

The central idea of intersubjectivity is that the extent to which *my* personal, ongoing resolution of the organism/environment field "overlaps" with *your* ongoing resolution of the organism/environment field equates, roughly speaking, to the interactive influence that these two processes of resolution will bring to bear on each other. *To the extent that you and I engage, so does our resolving of the field.* This is intersubjectivity, which was always stated implicitly in the first wave. The Intersubjectivists had put words to something that Gestalt was already "saying."

Perhaps the point to make here is that the implications arising in the alleged wake of Kohut's selfobjects have facilitated an increasingly refined grasp of the contacting processes that manifest in the *"inherent interwovenness of our existence"*

(Hycner in Hycner & Jacobs, 1995, p. 95, emphasis original). In the wake of waves one and two – "Organism/Environment" and "I-It/I-Thou" – the natural progression for Gestalt thinking was to move toward a detailed exploration of the interplay between interweaving "boundary selves" as viewed from a field perspective.

But things have not stopped there; different Gestalt writers have come to make two contrasting uses of the word intersubjectivity. As this can lead to confusion I will describe each usage in turn. As already indicated, the first sense in which the word intersubjectivity has come to be used has it as a recasting of the first wave within the terms of human subjectivity. It is an abstract term referring to a "given" phenomena; whenever two (or more) people meet, their resolutions of the organism/ environment field and, therefore, their subjective experience, are mutually embedded phenomena. This particular usage fits closely with Malcolm Parlett's reflections on field theory (1991) in which he discusses what happens when two people relate together. I mention this in order to note that Parlett approaches this same interweaving of processes perfectly well without recourse to the word intersubjectivity.

The alternative use of the word intersubjectivity (best represented by Gordon Wheeler's writings towards a Gestalt developmental model, e.g., 1998 and 2000), construes it as an acquired capacity. This "intersubjectivity" is the capacity whereby the developing infant/child becomes progressively aware of the existence and nature of personal subjectivity *and* discerns that similar qualities of existence feature in the experiential worlds of others.

By and large, there is an evolving discovery by the child that he or she has sole "admission" to a personal experiential world. This discovery is both paralleled *and facilitated* by the realisation that other individuals are situated at different experiential loci within the environment and, importantly, that each locus is situated at a significantly different "vantage point," one with a different constellation of needs, wishes, motivations, perspectives and so on. Compromises in this capacity for inter-subjectivity equate to different "styles" of resolving the field; there may be varying degrees to which subjectivity privileges the personal vantage point over that of others or, conversely, privileges the vantage point of others over the personal. In such cases, the boundary self can be thought of as having a compromised boundary sense.

This developmental capacity of intersubjectivity can be thought of as a precursor to the possibilities of I-Thou. We are not born such that we fully extend into the realms of human relatedness as denoted by the term "dialogical process." Rather, we are born with formative capacities for "I-It" differentiation (Stern, 1985) and have *the potential* to evolve towards capacities for "I-Thou" experience. If and when we do experience I-Thou, our trajectories surely have passed through the acquisition of intersubjectivity as has been defined in this second, developmental sense.

The study of human development is littered with flawed and partial attempts to describe its processes in linear terms. The Gestalt paradigm seems capable of becoming a home to non-linear, contextual frameworks for understanding development. A rigorously experiential approach can support us in navigating the dangers of moving between generalised abstractions such as intersubjectivity and the specific qualities of a given person's unfolding life. Indeed, there may be scope for Gestalt to expand on the idea that we are born with the potential for growth, (just as Gestalt itself has done), *from* the capacity for "I-It" *toward* capacities that include "I-Thou."

Fourth Wave: The Relational Ground

. . . the men carrying the culture . . . in turn, being shaped by the culture they carry.

PHG, p. 307

We now turn to an aspect of relational existence that operates quite differently from the first three waves. In the first three, we are focused on relational processes occurring *at* or *across* boundaries. In what I will be describing as a potential fourth wave, we attend to relational processes in which we are embedded. A brief, imaginary excursion will help to set the scene.

Imagine you are sitting in the arrival hall of a busy international airport. You are not there to meet anyone, instead you have decided to spend an hour or two watching other people meet. If there was nothing out of the ordinary about the disembarking flights, you would be likely to see a succession of very recognisable patterns of interaction. For example, the range of physical gestures used as people greet each other would usually be quite limited and entirely familiar, with only occasional exceptions. The sorts of things that people would say in the first moments of meeting, or the prosody of their speech, such as rising to a higher than usual pitch, would also generally fall within fairly narrow parameters.

Imagine watching two people joyfully reuniting after a prolonged separation. Their unique, individual experiences of these special moments could be destined to stand out as memorable punctuation marks in the stories of their lives. You, however, might note that you saw a remarkably similar scene unfold when the last Boeing 747 disembarked. And the one before that.

What we see in the arrival hall is, of course, the experiences of individuals being shaped by culture, language and our biological constitution. To take an obvious example, some of the variations you might observe would be readily explained by different planes having travelled from different countries, that is, from different cultures and different linguistic possibilities. Still, the majority of individuals, wherever they had come from, would probably have greeted each other with an open, partial or implied display of their teeth, an activity that most of us start exhibiting between the ages of six to ten weeks. The ubiquitous smile would be one of the many ways in which our biological constitutions, culturally reinforced, could be found shaping events at the airport arrival hall.

Our biological constitutions, our cultures and our languages create what I will be calling the relational ground. Speaking figuratively, this is the ground against which our figural sense of individuality emerges. The individual elements of the relational ground have received varying degrees of consideration by Gestalt writers. My contention is that there is value in re-cognising the profound ways in which they operate together as mutually-embedded phenomena that shape and limit the possibilities through which our individual lives evolve. This central thesis of the relational ground can be restated, metaphorically, in the following way; *our subjectivities emerge from the crucible in which our biological constitutions, culture and language combine, melt and merge with experience, particularly our experience with others.*

The relational ground is not a new idea; see particularly Jacob's discussion of context (2003), or Staemmler's discussion of culture (2005). The ideas that constitute the relational ground can be found permeating the work of phenomenologist philosopher Maurice Merleau-Ponty (see, e.g., 1969 and 1992). In many respects, the relational ground is my own attempt at developing, within a Gestalt framework, particular aspects of the postmodern conception that self is socially constructed within linguistic and cultural contexts. Whether the relational ground amounts to the rising swell of a fourth wave is clearly a moot point. However, from within the confines of this chapter (and echoed in the work of Staemmler and Jacobs, cited above), a key assertion to be made here is that an ongoing exploration of the relational ground's implications would render Gestalt's relational theory more comprehensive.

In contrast to the first three waves, where we are focussed on the nature of the moment-by-moment unfolding of me/not-me relational experience, the fourth wave focuses on preconditions that shape and limit the possible ways in which these moments can occur. Kurt Lewin's concept of the "life space" is helpful here. Lewin's idea of the life space (1951, recently discussed by Staemmler 2005) is a metaphor used to describe the phenomenal field of the individual, a kind of virtual space that is defined and confined by field conditions; a virtual space that embraces the sum total of all the possibilities that a given individual's subjectivity may potentially assume. By the term relational ground I mean to focus attention on those field conditions that craft and limit the possibilities from which individual life spaces emerge. In other words, these three factors – our biological constitution, culture and language – give structural properties to the relational "spaces," so to speak, within which individual life spaces are nested. It is at the intersection between an individual's unique life trajectory and these transpersonal factors that subjectivity arises.

The three elements of the relational ground – our biological constitution, culture and language – are mutually embedded phenomena that do not readily submit to individual examination in any ultimate sense. They are more like three primary colours separated by thought's prism-like capacities for categorisation. In reality, they combine in myriad hues with a complexity that lies beyond the grasp of the individual. With this caveat in place I will now give brief consideration to each in turn.

Biological

It is clear that PHG incorporated a biological viewpoint into their work, and equally clear that they tended strongly towards an individualistic perspective in its deployment. The organism/environment paradigm of the first wave stands on biological foundations whereby awareness is brought to the manner in which the organism attends to its various biological needs (with particular emphasis given to the process of eating).

From a fourth wave perspective, the commonality of our biological nature – from our gross physical forms to the minutiae of our internal "wiring" – constitutes a primary existential dimension that unites us in relationship. Thus, we can move from holding the biology of personal being as the figure of our attention towards the notion that our shared biological inheritance is a profound transpersonal factor that underlies and shapes our relational possibilities. This is so obvious that it is easy to miss. Like culture and language, our biological constitutions become simply "how things are."[7]

Granted, the (so-called) animal kingdom presents countless examples of relational existence indicating that the biological dimension of our *human* relational ground is not exactly unique. It is only as we consider the increasing complexities brought about by the commingling of the biological with culture and language that the relational ground takes on uniquely human qualities.[8]

A repeated discovery of recent years has been the extent to which our human bodies have been "pre-wired" for relationship. "Relational" appears to be etched into the genetic code itself. The last decade has been witness to copious research results regarding the biological complexity with which we interact, co-regulate, empathise, attach and more (for a recent summary, see Goleman, 2006). Some effort will be required if these

---

[7] Try a quick thought experiment (credited to Merleau-Ponty, Moran 2000, pp, 418-419), try to glimpse how radically different life would be if we possessed eyes on the opposite sides of our heads. In the human relational arena, imagine the difference in the quality of the mutually held gaze with a loved one if you could still see what was happening "behind" you.

[8] It is worth re-emphasising that this linear presentation - *biological, then cultural, then language* - conceals the intricate, non-linear, mutually embedded interweaving through which these elements constitute the relational ground. In order to discuss them in turn, however, my inclination to order them in this way has been guided by complexity theory (cf. Layzer, 1990), in which the development of "life, the universe and everything" has been conceived in terms of *systems of increasing complexity* that have emerged in the following sequence: physical, biological, cultural, linguistic.

In other settings, the word culture is used to denote "culture, *including* language" (e.g., Staemmler 2005). Different again, Chomsky is famous for hypothesising language as an emergent function of biology. The merit or otherwise of the relational ground paradigm is not contingent on accepting the sequence or the particular category breakdown that I have presented here.

discoveries, mostly presented in reductionist terms, are to be usefully assimilated into Gestalt's holistic framework.

Culture

Culture is probably the most attended to, by Gestalt writers, of the relational ground's three elements. Though many definitions can be found gathered around the word "culture," all of them are relational. Indeed, a primary task of the fourth wave would be that we come to understand our biological constitutions and language as being relational in an entirely comparable sense.

Like language, culture has been a matter of emergence and invention. Before a child is conceived, culture and language are waiting in the wings, focusing, defining and limiting the possibilities within which being can emerge. In the context of this discussion, the term "culture" is intended to convey something about the collective contact styles by which different groups, large and small, organise the ways in which they relate, both among themselves and with other groups. Culture operates as a complex system of introjects, frequently out of awareness, providing the fuzzy limits that inform which actions are experienced, or determined, "acceptable," and which are disallowed or even punished.

By analogy, culture operates like the rules of a game in at least one revealing sense; even if all the players of a game are substituted, *the game itself will remain entirely recognisable.* Similarly, culture holds its different players in very particular, easily recognisable, relational systems. It is these recognisable features that constitute the character we discern in different groups.

Language

Language is the least explored of the relational ground's three primary elements. The fourth wave tests the possibilities of language more than any other wave, and this is particularly the case with language itself. As with culture, it proves extremely difficult to stand back and see the full play of language and grasp the manner in which it shapes unfolding experience because we live *in* it, we are *of* its field. Language (like culture and our biological constitutions), shapes us in the very moments that we seek to uncover the processes of shaping. To further confound our investigations, as we move toward describing the nature of language we find ourselves describing it *within its own terms*. It is like trying to describe the "nature of music" with a careful selection of musical notes.

A frequently cited entry point into this arena is provided by the work of Edward Sapir and Benjamin Whorf. Together, they developed the Sapir-Whorf Hypothesis (a.k.a., "linguistic relativism," or "linguistic determinism"), which proposes that the content and structure of a given language determines what its users can think and experience. Said another way, the content and structure of a given language brings its users together within rich and complex networks of shared meaning. The way that a language operates directly affects the potential for meaning that it can be used to convey. Consider the uphill battle faced by Gestalt's process thinking when we seek to express it in languages for which key words such as "self" and "being" are thoroughly familiar as nouns and rarely understood as verbs.

Whorf (1936/1956) studied the language of the Hopi American Indians which, unlike English, privileges verbs over nouns. "Wave," in the sense we have been using it here (as opposed to a hand "wave"), would be a verb in Hopi, not a noun. Hopi also makes no direct reference to what we would describe as time in terms of past, present or future: which is not to say that they lack temporal awareness, more that it remains embedded within a language of spatiality. One more example, Hopi makes no formal distinction between the completion and incompletion of actions. Such points do seem to furnish an argument that living with different languages implies living in different experiential worlds (Stawman, 2006).

While few agree with the Sapir-Whorf Hypothesis when stated in its most extreme form – *that one's reality is constructed by one's language* – many have been drawn to more modest renditions. One such individual was Paul Goodman who preferred to think that, "[p]eople use language, they are not determined by it; but when they do use it — and by the language they choose — they focus their experience and define and limit their thoughts" (1971, p. 171).

These then – our biological constitutions, culture and language – are the three elements that interweave to constitute the relational ground against which our sense of individuality stands figural. The relational ground is essentially a reevaluation and extension of the first wave's organism/environment field paradigm, one that seeks to tease out the detail in PHG's caution that it is pointless "to attempt to deal with any psychological behaviour out of its sociocultural, biological, and physical context" (PHG, p. 231).

This chapter is intended to contribute to an expansion of the relational perspective, to contribute to the pendulum swing back from the enduring theme of individuality that has dominated Western culture and language. This highlights the fact that the relational ground is not necessarily infused with a relational sensibility. There are other cultures and linguistic traditions (other relational grounds), in which our lively Western figure of individuality appears counter-intuitive and problematic. Count Korzybski instigated Gestalt's early insistence on the reflective pronoun "I." There is a growing urgency that we embrace "We."

The relational ground offers a complementary relational position to that encapsulated in Buber's I-Thou. The fact that each of us is one among more than six billion of our species, all compellingly shaped and related, or *contextualised*, by the bodies, cultures and languages into which we are born, acts as a fine counterpoint to the qualities of uniqueness and recognition we experience in moments of I-Thou.[9] It asks of our theory and practice a different class of questions from those that arise from the first three waves. Far from being fluent in the answers, we are still coming to understand the nature of the questions.

Final Comments

. . . a bare subject without a world never 'is.'

Heidegger, 1927/1962, p. 152

In this chapter, an attempt has been made to bring together in one place the various meanings that can be brought to the term "relational" in Gestalt discourse. Extending this exploration to what can be meant by "relational Gestalt *practice*" would exceed the reach of this chapter.

This discussion has been built around four postulated "waves" which have been described according to a necessarily

---

[9] Buber does make related points when, for example, he counterpoints I-Thou with being "a dot in the world grid of space and time" (1923/1970, p. 59).

imperfect, linear reading of the historical sequence in which they emerged. The waves do not exist. Rather, they are a device that has been used to structure this review of Gestalt's relational themes in which I have raised a few questions and, in the case of the fourth wave, allowed myself a degree of speculation. If there is any conclusion to be drawn, it is that Gestalt resonates through and through with the sense that to *be* is to *be with*.[10]

A relational focus does not eclipse the experience of individuality. Rather, we can view personal being through lenses of individuality *and* through lenses of relationality. These two perspectives afford different purchases on truth and it is tautological to note that emphasis on one viewpoint can, at least momentarily, de-emphasise the other. This human tendency, towards contrasting perspectives, has received vivid demonstration in the realms of physics where it seems we can view matter as comprising either particles *or* waves. This chapter has focussed on the waves.

References

Beisser, A. (1970). The Paradoxical Theory of Change. In J. Fagan & I. L. Shepherd (Eds.), *Gestalt Therapy Now* (pp. 77-80). U K: Penguin.

Buber, M. (1923/1970). *I and Thou.* (W. Kaufman, Trans.). New York: Simon & Schuster.

Farber, L. H. (1968). *The Ways of the Will.* New York: Harper Colophon.

Friedman, M. (1985). *The Healing Dialogue in Psychotherapy.* North Vale, NJ: Jason Aronson.

---

[10] "To be is to be with" is attributed at different times to either of two phenomenological philosophers, Martin Heidegger and Gabriel Marcel. Buber, a student of Heidegger, writes "The person becomes conscious of himself as participating in being, as being-with . . ." (1923/1970, p.113)

Goleman, D. (2006). *Social Intelligence: The New Science of Human Relationships*. New York: Bantam Books.

Goodman, P. (1971). *Speaking and Language: Defence of Poetry*. New York: Random House.

Heidegger, M. (1927/1962). *Being and Time*. (J. Macquarrie & E. Robinson, Trans.). New York: Harper & Row.

Hycner, R. & Jacobs, L. (1995). *The Healing Relationship in Gestalt Therapy: A Dialogic/Self Psychology Approach*. Highland, NY: Gestalt Journal Press.

Jacobs, L. (2003). Ethics of context and field: The practices of care, inclusion and openness to dialogue. *British Gestalt Journal, 12*(2)

Kohut, H. (1977). *The Restoration of the Self*. Madison, CT: International Universities Press.

Kohut, H. (1984). *How Does Analysis Cur.e* Chicago: University of Chicago Press.

Korzybski, A. (1933). *Science and Sanity*. Lakeville, CT: Institute of General Semantics.

Layzer, D. (1990). *Cosmogenesis: The Growth of Order in the Universe* Oxford: Oxford University Press.

Lewin, K. (1951). *Field Theory in Social Science; Selected Theoretical Papers*. (D. Cartwright, Ed.). New York: Harper.

McConville, M. (2001). Let the straw man speak: Husserl's phenomenology in context. *Gestalt Review 5*(3), 195-204.

Moran, D. (2000). *Introduction to Phenomenology* London: Routledge.

Merleau-Ponty, M. (1992). *Sense and Non-Sense*. (L. Dreyfus & A. P. Dreyfus, Trans.). Evanston: Northwestern University Press.

Merleau-Ponty, M. (1969). *The Visible and the Invisible*. (A. Lingis Trans.). Evanston: Northwestern University Press.

Parlett, M. (1991). Reflections on Field Theory. *British Gestalt Journal, 1*(2)

Perls, F., Hefferline, F. R., & Goodman, P. (1951/1984). *Gestalt Therapy: Excitement and Growth in the Human Personality*. London: Souvenir Press.

Sapriel, L. (1998). Intersubjectivity, Self-Psychology, and Gestalt. *British Gestalt Journal 7*(1), 33-44.

Staemmler, F.-M. (2004). Dialogue and interpretation in Gestalt therapy: Making sense together. *International Gestalt Journal, 27*(2), 33-57.

Staemmler, F.-M. (2005). Cultural field conditions: A hermeneutic study of consistency. *British Gestalt Journal, 14*(1), 34-43.

Staemmler, F.-M. (2006). A Babylonian confusion?: On the uses and meanings of the term "field." [Festschrift for Malcolm Parlett]. *British Gestalt Journal, 15*(2), 64-83.

Stawman, S. (2006). Preliminary thoughts on the interaction between language and experience. *Gestalt Journal of Australia and New Zealand, 1*(2), 7-19.

Stern, D. (1985). *The Interpersonal World of the Infant.* New York: Basic Books.

Stolorow, R., Brandchaft, B., & Atwood, G. (1987). *Psychoanalytic Treatment: An Intersubjective Approach.* Hillsdale, NJ: The Analytic Press.

Theunnisen, M. (1984). *The Other; Studies in the Social Ontology of Husserl, Heidegger, Sartre, and Buber.* (C. Macann, Trans.). Cambridge, MA: MIT Press.

Van De Riet, V. (2001). Gestalt therapy and the phenomenological method. *Gestalt Review 5*(3), 184-194.

Wheeler, G. (2000). *Beyond Individualism: Toward an Understanding of Self, Relationship, & Experience,* Hillsdale, NJ: The Analytic Press.

Wheeler, G. (1998). Towards a Gestalt developmental model. *British Gestalt Journal, 7*(2), 115-125.

Whorf, B. L. (1936/1956). The punctual and segmentive aspects of verbs in Hopi. In J. B. Carroll (Ed.), *Language, Thought and Reality: Selected Writings* (pp. 51-56). Cambridge, MA: MIT Press.

The Relational Attitude in Gestalt Therapy & Practice

•••••••••••••••••••••••••••••

Gary Yontef

G estalt therapy is systematically relational in its underlying theory and methodology. A relational perspective is so central to the theory of Gestalt therapy that without it there is no coherent core of Gestalt therapy theory or practice. Recently much has been written about a relational approach to psycho- therapy both in the Gestalt therapy and the general psycho- therapy literature. In the general professional literature this has been a discovery of a relational perspective (Aron, 1996; Mitchell, 1988; Mitchell & Aron, 1999; Stolorow et al., 1987). In Gestalt therapy, "relational Gestalt therapy" has been revisiting the relational perspective built-in to Gestalt therapy theory (Hycner, 1988; Hycner & Jacobs, 1995; Jacobs, 1989, 1992, 1998; Staemmler, 1993; Yontef, 1993, 1998, 1999).

The function of the current discourse on relational Gestalt therapy is to differentiate among significant variations in how Gestalt therapy theory is talked about and even more significant variations in how Gestalt therapy is practiced. Some common ways of talking about and practicing Gestalt therapy are not fully consistent with the basic relational theory of Gestalt therapy. Moreover, there are relational implications implied in the foundational theory that are not consistently, or sufficiently explicated.

In this article I will review each of three fundamental and indispensable philosophic principles of Gestalt therapy, i.e., existential phenomenology, field theory, and dialogic existentialism, and then discuss the variations of talk and practice that warrant taking a fresh look at the relational implications of each of them. I will then discuss shame as it relates to a relational perspective, and a concluding section on what relational Gestalt therapy is and what it is not.

Existential Phenomenology[1]

Gestalt therapy is based on the philosophy and method of phenomenology (Yontef, 1993). In Gestalt psychology the phenomenological method refers to "as naïve and full a description of direct experience as possible" (Koffka, 1935, p. 73). The phenomenological method is a discipline to identify and enhance direct, immediate experience and to reduce the distortion of bias and prior learning. An important aspect of phenomenological discipline is methodically refining awareness, reducing bias as much as possible, especially bias about what is valid data, bias of what is real. Edmund Husserl (1922) refers to this as putting it into "brackets." There is a kindred attitude in contemporary psychoanalysis: "holding one's interpretations lightly."

---

[1] For the discussion in this paper I use the terms existential phenomenology and psychological phenomenology as synonymous and the terms transcendental phenomenology and philosophic phenomenology as synonymous.

One special feature of Gestalt therapy phenomenology, as in Gestalt psychology, is that phenomenological study includes phenomenological experimentation.

Phenomenological theories are relational theories. In phenomenological thought, reality and perception are inter-actional co-constructions; they are a relationship be-tween the perceiver and the perceived. Thus all perception and statements of reality are interpreted (Spinelli, 1989). This basic phenom-enological attitude rejects the Cartesian subject-object split. There is no subjective experience that is not related to some object (intentionality); there is no experienced object except through some particular interpretive vantage point. This phenomenological position is different than a radical construc-tivist position.

The phenomenological method is central to all phenome-nological systems, including both existential/psychological and transcendental/philosophic phenomenology and also the phe-nomenology of Gestalt psychology.

In psychological phenomenology, including Gestalt therapy phenomenology, the study is of the experience of the subjects and is never finished, objective, or absolute. In the transcend-dental or philosophic phenomenology of later Husserl, the study is of the objects of perception. In this phase, Husserl claimed a bracketing complete enough to discover universals. Gestalt therapy is not based on transcendental phenomenology (Yontef, 1999). In Gestalt therapy it is not believed that one reaches objective truth by bracketing.

Discussion

In phenomenological theory there are multiple valid "realities." Insofar as it is phenomenologically derived, no perception can be validly dismissed as not real. Therefore: *The therapist's reality is not more valid or objective or true than the patient's.* This is especially true since psychotherapy is centered on the patient, it is the patient's existence that is the reason for the therapy, and it is the patient that has the primary data. The patient's sense of self is as phenomenologically real and valid as the therapist's sense of the patient. Conversely, the patient's sense of the therapist in the therapist-patient interaction is as valid a phenomenological reality as the therapist's self-concept. This attitude is crucial for a truly relational therapy.

Some Gestalt therapists talk and/or act as if the trainer/ therapist's reality is privileged in that it is more real or accurate than the patient's or trainee's.[2] When the term "obvious" (ostensibly referring to what phenomenologists call "the given") is used, it seems to indicate that all bias could be bracketed and an objective truth established. This often out of awareness attitude and its consequences is a key reason for this discussion of the relational attitude in Gestalt therapy.

The philosophy of Gestalt therapy explicitly promotes respect and appreciation of differences. Practicing this philosophy requires humility. Bracketing and personal therapy for the therapist and trainer support this practice. Unfortunately, even Gestalt therapists and trainers who know the philosophy sometimes treat viewpoints different from their own as subjective and interpretive but act as if their own points of view are true and objective.

This is especially important when the difference of perspective is between therapist and patient and when the difference is the patient's perception of something the therapist does that is out of the therapist's awareness. A fully phenome-

---

[2] When therapy is referred to in this article, it is meant to apply to both psychotherapy and psychotherapy training.

nological stance would be for the therapist to assume that there are two realities, both with some validity. The hubris of the attitude by the therapist that his or her view of self, the patient, and any interaction between them is correct and the patient's different perception is wrong is not consistent with the phenomenological attitude. Such an attitude indicates insufficient bracketing and personal therapy (Yontef, 1999).

Here is an illustrative example. I overheard a trainer at lunch at a training workshop talk with derision of an event that happened in the session of that morning. A trainee had said that he experienced a remark of the trainer as hostile. The trainer continued his derisive storytelling by elaborating that a large part of the group agreed with the trainee. However, the trainer insisted that it was ridiculous that anyone could say he was hostile when he did not experience himself as hostile. This attitude is not only incompatible with the values of Gestalt therapy phenomenology, but also incompatible with other main principles of Gestalt therapy, dialogical existentialism and field theory. This attitude can be a potent shame trigger (see discussion below).

Field Theory

Field theory looks at all events as a function of the relationship of multiple interacting forces. Interacting forces form a field in which every part of the field effects the whole and the whole effects all parts of the field. No event occurs in isolation. The whole field determines all events in the field, with some forces being in figural awareness and some operating in the background. In the example above, both the trainer and the trainees are responsible for the co-creation of the event of the experienced hostility and how it was processed.

It is inherent in field viewpoint that people are interdependent and not self-sufficient. The person and the field are not separate entities that are brought together. People are not "in a field," but "of a field." There is no field without the forces and no forces without the field.

There are different kinds of fields. In Gestalt therapy the field is a phenomenological field (Lewin, 1952; Yontef, 1993). Human events are perceived to be a function of an organismic environmental field. The individual and the environment are all "of the field." There is no "I" without a field – which includes an environmental context. There is also no environment except as a part of a field. We only know "environment" in relation to some observer, only when some observer defines it. The determination of the relevant environment is co-determined by what is out there and the observer.

Problems are problems of a field and the solutions are solutions of that field. Any process, problem, creative advancement, solution to a problem is a function of the relationship between the people "of the field" and the field as a whole. There is a fascinating discussion of this in Max Wertheimer's *Productive Thinking* (Wertheimer, 1945).

There are no human events that are not of an organismic-environment field. People are always of a field and are interdependent. The people of this field are all part of the force that determines what occurs, hence responsible. All events in the human field are a function of all of the participants and the interactions between them. The rugged individualism ideal, the ideal of self-sufficiency, is not consistent with a field way of thinking.

Living systems grow by contact with that which is outside the system and assimilating needed novelty. This is true both of individuals and of larger systems. A field, person or larger system, can only be defined in relation to its parts and the larger field of which it is part.

Discussion

There is an attitude in some Gestalt therapy circles, stemming from the confrontive tenor of Gestalt therapy in the 1960's, that need is a weakness, a flaw[3]: the patient/trainee is needy; the therapist/trainer is self-sufficient, and the therapist's job is to frustrate the manipulation of the needy patient. Sometimes the concept of "self-sufficient" hides under the term "self-supportive." Properly used, the concept of self-support refers to self-regulation as part of the field, referring to defining the needs of self and others, and does not refer to self-sufficiency. We are all "dependent," or, more accurately "interdependent."

The view of need and dependency as a weakness, and the creating of an icon of the self-sufficient hero, so prevalent in American rugged individualism, is fertile grounds for creating shame (Wheeler, 1996; see discussion in shame section below). If a therapist does not know or admit his or her dependency and other vulnerabilities, it helps trigger or create shame in vulnerable patients.

The discussion of the relational essence of Gestalt therapy is needed to correct the shame-creating attitude that was present in cliché level talks in the 1960's and that can still be seen in a more subtle form in some current practice and training. When the patient is expressing or showing a need or desire that could be confronted as needy or manipulative, it is usually more

---

[3] In this paper I use the term confront and confrontation in the sense of being negative, judgmental, non-respectful, and not consistent with the paradoxical theory of change. The terms can also be used to refer to anything that presents a point of view different than that which is already in the patient's awareness. In this latter sense psychotherapy properly confronts patients.

effective and consistent with Gestalt therapy principles to meet and understand patients' experience rather than confront or frustrate them. Support, healthy confluence, compassion, kindness, accepting the validity of the patient's wishes, are all part of a good therapeutic attitude, an attitude that is consistent with field theory (See discussion in section on dialogic existentialism, below).

Implications of a field perspective are also relevant to the issue of responsibility. The therapist and the patient are "of the field" and responsible for what happens. When there is a break in the therapeutic relationship, minute or huge, the therapist is part of that disruption; it is not accurate from a field perspective to say that the problem is the patient's interruption and hold the therapist, such a significant part of the field, free of responsibility (McNamee and Gergen, 1999).

Interdependence and the need to take in from others is as true at a system level as it is at an individual level. One of the issues generating this discussion is that some talk as if Gestalt therapy is a self-sufficient system and that knowledge of other systems is unnecessary. Perls would sometimes claim that Gestalt therapy is unique in that it is self-sufficient, unlike other existential therapies. The view of Gestalt therapy self-sufficiency is often expressed together with a regret or disappointment that some Gestalt therapists deem it necessary to take from other systems rather than creating anything necessary from within the Gestalt therapy theory. Those Gestalt therapists who take in from other systems are then sometimes characterized as inadequately prepared, weak and flawed, not knowledgeable enough about the basic theory of Gestalt therapy, not seeing the full potential of Gestalt therapy theory to be self-sufficient, or just having fallen into unfortunate error.

Relational Gestalt therapy has advocated exchanging perspective and experience with practitioners from other systems, e.g., modern systems of psychoanalysis. Many Gestalt therapists have expressed strong appreciation for relational Gestalt therapy for legitimizing the assimilation they have done in their own practice and also have appreciated the enrichment of Gestalt therapy by the integration accomplished by relational Gestalt therapists. Yet, when I have lectured or written about personality patterns in a manner that includes insight from sources other than Gestalt therapy (Yontef, 1993; Yontef, 2001), which trainees and trained Gestalt therapists have found very useful, I have sometimes received that reaction of disapproval discussed in the previous paragraph from some Gestalt therapists who think that Gestalt therapy should be self-sufficient.

Often critics of exchanges with other systems forget the difference between introjecting information or ideas from other systems and deconstructing, assimilating, and integrating that which is useful in Gestalt therapy. A more field theoretical view would include acknowledging the need to learn from other systems – to assimilate that which is useful. If the information is just added on, as in "Gestalt and ...," then the inherently integrative nature of a field is replaced by an introjective process of just adding new information or techniques on top of the existing system without the transformation of assimilation.

Another implication of field theory is the need to pay attention to the conditions of the field. I believe that we often pay *insufficient attention to the conditions in the field.* One of the main concerns of relational Gestalt therapy is what happens between therapist and patient, i.e., the field of therapist and patient and between patients in therapy groups. Increasingly relationally oriented Gestalt therapists have focused on the exact conditions in the field of patient and therapist as it develops moment to moment.

This field perspective is needed in understanding the processes in all groups and systems. It is important to understand the regulation processes that occur in the communities in which we live, e.g., the power relations in organizations, agencies, and in the larger community. This includes processes such as competition for power, ostracizing, sub-grouping, marginalizing. These processes happen in individual, group, couple, or family therapy. These are often ignored in both therapy and task groups in the Gestalt therapy community. One exception is Miller's discussion of these processes in couples (Miller, 1995).

Dialogic Existentialism

The phenomenological focus on the awareness of the patient is sometimes practiced as a one-person process, i.e., looking primarily at the awareness continuum of the patient without consideration of the relational matrix, including what is happening between patient and therapist. In Gestalt therapy, especially in "relational Gestalt therapy," clinical phenomenology is a two-person practice. Not only is the awareness continuum of the patient figural, and the phenomenological method expanded by the creation of phenomenological experiments by the cooperative efforts of both therapist and the patient, but the phenomenological method is also expanded into a two-person approach by the emphasis on dialogue. Dialogue can be seen as shared phenomenology.

Every intervention, every moment of therapy, is not only a technical event but also a moment of interpersonal contact. "We speak of the organism contacting the environment, but it is the contact that is the simplest and first reality. (Perls, Hefferline, and Goodman, 1951/1994, p. 3). " In the therapeutic methodology, the awareness work is done by the relational interaction of patient and therapist. But, what kind of contact is needed for effective psychotherapy?

Gestalt therapy made important modification of the classical psychoanalytic stance of neutrality and abstinence, the stance of the analyst showing nothing personal so that the patient can be induced into a pure transference neurosis. Gestalt therapy made a tremendous advance in its orientation around active personal involvement of the therapist, working primarily with what the patient is aware of rather than restricting practice to interpreting the unconsciousness, and adding phenomenological experimentation to the methodology.

Relational Gestalt therapy has been carefully examining what kind of contact is therapeutic. This started in earnest with discussion of "dialogue" in the early 1980's. This has been expanded into relational Gestalt therapy because of a growing realization of how dialogue was a part of a more fundamental and pervasive relational perspective and because of realization of the conditions of dialogue being violated by many talking the language of contact and dialogue. In short, relational Gestalt therapy has been concerned not only with "talking the talk" but also "walking the walk."

The kind of contact most consistent with Gestalt therapy principles is marked by the principles of dialogue.

Principles of Dialogue

Inclusion and confirmation.   Inclusion is putting oneself into the experience of the patient as much as possible, feeling it as if in one's own body – without losing a separate sense of self. This confirms the patient's existence and potential.

By imagining the experience of the patient, in a sense the therapist makes the experience real. Crucial to this approach is the paradoxical theory of change (Beisser, 1970). By contacting the patient in this way and not aiming to move the patient, by meeting the patient and not aiming to make the patient different, the patient is supported in growing by identification with his or her own experience .

The patient is the final authority on the accuracy of these reflections. In relational Gestalt therapy we tend to believe that if the patient says "you don't understand," you don't understand. I must also note that while it has a great deal of heuristic value to emphasize that the patient must be respected when he or she says that the therapist does not understand, and the patient has personal and direct access to his or her own self that is different than the therapist's access to that patient's reality, from a theoretical position it cannot be validly claimed that one party to the dialogue has the exclusive power of definition of what is true.

Presence. Dialogue, both in and out of therapy, requires not only practicing inclusion, but also a certain kind of presence. The required presence is not just lively, powerful or charismatic as was the highly visible Gestalt therapy styles of the 1960's. It requires a presence with authenticity, transparency, and humility.

Dialogue means being present as a person meeting the person of the other. Dialogue in therapy means that the therapist works on the therapeutic task by contacting the patient as the patient is, the whole person that the patient is, with the whole person of the therapist him or herself. A whole person includes being flawed and allowing that flaw to be a recognized part of one's existence, even in the therapeutic setting with patients.

Relational Gestalt therapy emphasizes the importance in therapy of compassion, kindness, wisdom, equanimity, and humility. It is my opinion that these qualities are not given as much emphasis in talk about Gestalt therapy as is warranted by their impact.

Commitment and surrender to the between. An indispensable core aspect of the relational approach in general and the dialogic approach in particular is the commitment to dialogue, the surrender to what emerges between the participants in the dialogue when the therapist and the patient contact each other – without the therapist aiming. The paradoxical theory of change predicts that identification with ones actual state, experience, and existence is ground that supports personal growth (Beisser, 1970). When the therapist practices inclusion with authentic presence and commits to what emerges in the contact, conditions maximum for growth and healing are created. This requires that the therapist is not committed to any predetermined outcome and can support "cultivation of uncertainty" (Staemmler, 1997). This also requires faith in the awareness and contact process.

In this approach, the therapist also changes. The therapist is touched, feels pain, gets satisfaction from the contact with the patient, learns from the contact in which the patient's perception is respected. The advantage to the therapist of accepting that the patient's perception of him or her might be accurate and point to a blind spot in therapist self-awareness, is that the therapist also grows. This is especially true when the patient criticizes the therapist. For the patient this can be an experience in which his or her experience, opinion, and feelings are respected. Also there is the experience that the therapist in which the patient has invested time, money, and respect is also an ordinary human being.

Discussion

Some Gestalt therapists do not practice inclusion in their work with patients. They share observations, make interpretations, set up experiments. When symptoms arise, they try to move the patients, to save or rescue the patient, rather than elucidate the patient's experience. Insight into cognition, body process, interruptions to awareness and contact can go hand-in-hand with inclusion and phenomenological focusing – or can be a form of behavior modification, i.e., the therapist being a change agent trying to cure the patient. I do not consider the latter good Gestalt therapy or consistent with basic Gestalt therapy principles.

Another practice that is inconsistent with the relational principles discussed here is the presence of the therapist in a manner that encourages charismatic or narcissistic elevation at the expense of the patient. The therapist or trainer in this pattern solicits or encourages his or her idealization, and the patient or trainee projects competence, wisdom, and goodness on the therapist with a concomitant diminishment of self.[4] The patient or trainee then can bask in the light of the therapist's magnificence. The form or style of the therapist or trainer doing this varies. It can be confrontive, seductive, rescuing, empathic, creative, and so forth. The problem is the nature of the relationship, the nature of the role the therapist plays in relation to the patient.

Probably the problematic pattern that is hardest to be aware of is the therapist or trainer that appears to practice inclusion,

---

[4] I do not advocate that patient idealization be immediately and actively confronted. I am advocating the therapist be aware of his or her role in actively eliciting it. Some patients do idealize the therapist and need to do so in one phase of therapy. Ironically, aggressive confrontation of idealization can itself elicit idealization of the therapist.

seems to be present in a dialogic way, but when the phenome-nological experience of the patient/trainee and the phenome-nological experience of the therapist/trainer meet, the therapist does not really take in and let him or herself be effected by the experience. In this pattern the therapist does not change, the self-concept of the therapist does not change, the therapist does not surrender to the between, does not surrender to what emerges between the patient and themselves if it involves error, pain or change on the therapist's part. This sometimes appears to give the message: "You are you, and I am I, and I am not going to budge an inch" – there is the "you" and the "I," but the between, the flow back and forth and emergence into dialectical synthesis, is stymied.

Shame

Relational Gestalt therapy partially arose out of an increasing sensitivity to and sophistication about shame (Lee & Wheeler, 1996; Yontef, 1993, 1997a, 1997b). Sensitivity to shame has shaped the sensitivity to the relational aspects of psychotherapy.

Noticing the field conditions in the practice of therapy has led to awareness of the interruptions in the contact and much of that interruption occurs when shame is triggered in the relationship. Some approaches to Gestalt therapy have triggered shame in the patient and defended the therapist from experiencing his or her own shame that might be felt with realization of limitations, errors, biases, countertransference, and so forth.

In relational Gestalt therapy we believe it is essential to good psychotherapy to be sensitive to the conditions leading to shame and to minimize iatrogenic shame in psychotherapy practice and training .

Patients are vulnerable to feeling shame just by coming to therapy. This is more intense in some patients than in others. Patients come to therapy because of some sense of being inadequate in finding satisfaction and solving the problems of their existence. They mostly start therapy with a sense of not being OK. This is not avoidable. But unnecessarily triggering shame in therapy and training can be avoided.

Insufficient awareness of and inept or defensive response to shame is an important relational issue. Shame can be triggered or increased by being ignored or treated inadequately.

There are many therapist activities that can trigger shame in the patient. Some of the triggers are obvious: Sarcastic humor, attack, condescension, and abandonment. Some triggers are less obvious. For example, one-person interpretations are frequent shame triggers. When the interpretation indicates that the source of difficulty is a process only of the patient, no matter how benignly intended, this increases the shame. An interpretation from a field perspective would take into account the contributions of all the participants in the field, including those of the therapist. A negative example: A trainee tells a trainer that he/she feels shamed by the trainer. The trainer responds: "I will show you how you shame yourself." The trainer is blameless, all difficulty is attributed only to the trainee.

Another shame trigger is an attitude that the therapist knows best. If the therapist is endowed by the patient with the aura of infinite wisdom, the patient assumes the status of "less than." If the therapist fosters this, does not maintain an awareness of his or her limitations and deficits, the patient is reinforced in his or her sense of self as not being competent, worthy, or lovable.

A relational approach requires careful and consistent observation of all the data in the field. Particularly relevant for our present discussion are subtext and metatheory. Shame can be triggered by therapist attitudes that are manifest in subtext or unacknowledged metatheory. For example, the attitude that self-sufficiency is better than dependence is a fertile ground for shame (Wheeler, 1996). This is not just a bias, but it is a theoretical stance that is not explicit in the official theory. Another example is a bias about the right level of emotionality. Unless the patient's level of emotionality is consistent with the particular level of emotionality that is valued, the patient is likely to have shame triggered. Relational Gestalt therapy brings sensitivity to issues of subtext and metatheory.

Subtext. Text refers to what is said; subtext refers to how things are said, e.g., tone of voice, body language, gestures, and so forth. A message that sounds innocent in its text can have a very critical, shaming, condescending, contemptuous edge to it. And, of course, what may appear harsh in the text may give a different message altogether when the whole subtext is taken into account. When the shame triggering communication is delivered through the subtext, it is more difficult for the other person to cope with and it can be easily denied by the person – "I did not say that."

Metatheory. "A metatheory has for its subject-matter the inquiry into, or theory of, a certain subject-matter; it is a second-order inquiry or theory." (Mautner, p. 353). "Meta" is a prefix from a Greek word-element meaning beyond or above. It refers to the implications of a theory that is a level above the theory itself. It is parallel to a metanarrative in which there is a narrative that justifies or gives context to a belief.

What we do and what we say as Gestalt therapists has implications broader, beyond the specific words or techniques. There are broad implications in terms of values and philosophy of living of what we say and do. I think we should pay more attention to these implications of what we do and say and not restrict ourselves only to the immediate words and objects we are addressing at the moment. I refer to this as metatheory. Metatheory refers to broad theoretical implications of a theory or act that are not explicitly dealt with in the text of the theory or talked about in the focus on action.

For example, we might be working with a mother who wants to go back to work[5]. For the sake of illustration, assume that the family has very young children and the family finances do not require her to go back to work. There are important values and implications to be considered. The mother's sense of well-being and development may be enhanced by going back to work. It may even be necessary for her mental health. The children's' sense of well being and development may be enhanced by the mother staying home with them. There may be societal implications for our children and for providing facilities to care for the children of working mothers. Such issues are never simple. At the level of metatheory, there are real value questions with real consequences for the whole organism/environment/ societal field.

My concern here is not the solution to the issue of the individual needs versus the needs of the children or society. I am focused here on the issue of being aware and attentive to the fact that we are dealing with important value issues, issues that go beyond the immediate affect of the patient. It is easy to focus on one value or another without awareness that other important values are involved. I am advocating some reflection on the issue of the broader implications, e.g., values such as individualism versus the needs of the community. I do not think that there is one right answer to those questions. But it is important

---

[5] Of course, the at home parent wanting to go back to work could be the father.

to pay attention to the fact that we are dealing with values and that therapists can be guiding awareness and action along a path without awareness of the larger implications. They may influence a course of action without the awareness, bracketing and other methodological principles of an extensive phenomenological exploration.

Metatheoretical issues include, but are not limited to:

- Attitudes about the person (patient or significant others).
- Philosophy of living, values.
- How growth happens and psychotherapy works.

Discussion: Relational Gestalt Therapy

In its present state of development, relational Gestalt therapy has focused on metatheoretical messages that are about the nature of the person, especially the patient, and how these influence the safety and self-esteem of the patients. This has especially been discussed around the issues of shame and the values concerned in confrontive approaches to Gestalt therapy, issues of the value of, for example, dependence, self-sufficiency, and interdependence. The patient, or significant others, can be characterized in ways that relegate them to the status of unlovable or not worthy.

Relational Gestalt therapy has also been concerned with metatheoretical messages about how therapy is done. An example of this area is the set of messages that has been promulgated in the name of Gestalt therapy that leads patients to think that therapy is just expressing emotions. Larger issues of value have not yet been fully addressed.

An example of the messages about how therapy is done can be illustrated with my experience with a patient who had a long history in psychoanalysis before seeing me in Gestalt therapy.

He had learned that the only acceptable data for him to present in therapy were his associations. This provided the material for the analytic interpretation by the analyst. Bringing in any other data was interpreted as resistance. When I suggested bringing in some material that illustrated a problem he was having, e.g., his emails at work, he objected that this was not legitimate data for therapy.

In the example (above) of the trainer who was told that his remark was hostile when he did not experience himself being hostile, a dialogic and phenomenologically open response might have been something like: "I wonder what it was in how I said what I did that gave you the impression that I was hostile. What did you observe and what did you think I was saying about you?" Then one might inquire: "What was triggered in you when I said what I did in the way that I said it? Did it trigger something about your sense of yourself?" I might also include something about how it affects me that my remarks were taken as hostile and had the effect that it did. For example, I might say, if I meant it, "I am really sorry that I was not more sensitive and that my remark hurt you." In the dialogue other feelings might emerge, e.g., my feelings about the patient or what was triggered in my sense of self in this situation. For example, if I was embarrassed or felt shame by triggering what I did in the patient, then I might say so.

What Relational Gestalt Therapy Is and Is Not

Relational therapy is an approach within Gestalt therapy that is strongly centered on existential phenomenology, dialogic existentialism, and cognitive grounding in field theory. It is not a whole, new system or approach. Rather it is steeped in what is central to Gestalt therapy and has sometimes gotten lost or neglected. It continues the Gestalt therapy tradition of assimilating new information into the system, e.g., from modern forms of psychoanalysis, cognitive behavior studies, mindfulness meditation, and so forth.

It is a form of Gestalt therapy that emphasizes respect, compassion, the fullest experience and respect by the therapist of patients' experience in accordance with the paradoxical theory of change and manifesting maximum trust in the process of contact with awareness and without aiming. This emphasis in Gestalt therapy has sometimes been mischaracterized as being restricted to empathic listening, being nice, and eliminating experimentation. This is not true. The relational emphasis is on honesty, which is more than being nice, but in a process that is attentive to shame-triggering. We are not interested in being empathic and/or sympathetic at the cost of honesty. Relational Gestalt therapy does not eliminate experimentation (active technology), but uses it in a relational manner.

Relational Gestalt therapy is centered around dialogue, contact that takes into account the person of the patient and the task of therapy. It is not a dialogue in which the therapist authentically expresses self without regard to the task of the therapy or the needs, strengths, and weaknesses of the patient.

Relational Gestalt therapy takes into account probable impact on the patient, patient vulnerability, and the impact of the therapy on others that will be affected.

In Gestalt therapy with this relational emphasis, careful attention is paid to contact moments and also to overall character organization and development. The quality of the connection of therapist and patient is a subject of central concern. Interruptions are carefully observed both for what it says about what is happening between therapist and patient and also for the here-and-now contact moments as manifestations of on-going characterological patterns that are a necessary focus in intensive psychotherapy. Each moment is seen as a hologram for the larger whole of the patient's life. This perspective gives guidance to diagnostic questions, and in turn is guided by diagnostic understanding or understanding of the particular characterological pattern of the patient.

References

Aron, L. (1996). *A Meeting of Minds: Mutuality in Psychoanalysis*. Hillsdale, NJ: The Analytic Press.

Beisser, A. (1970). The paradoxical theory of change. In J. Fagan & I. Shepherd (Eds.). *Gestalt Therapy Now*. NY: Harper. (pp. 77-80).

Husserl, E. (1922). Ideen zu einer reinen Phänomenologie und phänomenologischen Philosophie; Tübingen (Niemeyer).

Hycner, R. (1988). *Between Person and Person: Toward a Dialogical Psychotherapy*. Highland, NY: Gestalt Journal Press.

Hycner, R. & Jacobs, L. (1995). *The Healing Relationship in Gestalt Therapy: A Dialogic/Self Psychology Approach*. Highland, NY: Gestalt Journal Press.

Jacobs, L. (1989). Dialogue in Gestalt theory and therapy. *The Gestalt Journal*, *12*(1), 25-68.

Jacobs, L. (1992). Insights from psychoanalytic self-psychology and intersubjectivity theory for Gestalt therapists. *The Gestalt Journal*, *15*(2), 25-60.

Jacobs, L. (1998). Optimal responsiveness and subject-subject relating. In H. Bacal (Ed.), *Optimal Responsiveness: How Therapists Heal their Patients*. (pp. 191-212). NY: Jason Aronson.

Koffka, K. (1935). *Principles of Gestalt Psychology*. NY: Harcourt, Brace & World.

Lee, R. & Wheeler, G. (1996). *The Voice of Shame: Silence and Connection in Psychotherapy*. San Francisco: Jossey-Bass, Inc.

Lewin, K. (1952). *Field Theory in Social Science - Selected Theoretical Papers*, London: Tavistock Publications.

Mautner, T. (2000). *The Penguin Dictionary of Philosophy*. NY: Penguin Books.

McNamee, S. & Gergen, K. J. (Eds.) (1999). *Relational Responsibility - Resources for Sustainable Dialogue*. Thousand Oaks, CA: Sage.

Miller, M. (1995). *Intimate Terrorism: The Deterioration of Erotic Life*. NY: Norton & Co.

Mitchell, A. (1988). *Relational Concepts in Psychoanalysis*. Cambridge, Massachusetts: Harvard University Press.

Mitchell, A. & Aron, L. (1999). *Relational Psychoanalysis: The Emergence of a Tradition*. Hillsdale, NJ: The Analytic Press.

Perls, F., Hefferline, H., & Goodman, P. (1951\1994). *Gestalt Therapy: Excitement and Growth in the Human Personality*. Highland, NY: The Gestalt Journal Press.

Spinelli, E. (1989). *The Interpreted World*. Newbury Park, CA: Sage.

Staemmler, F.-M. (1993): *Therapeutische Beziehung und Diagnose - Gestalttherapeutische Antwort*. München (Pfeiffer).

Staemmler, F.-M. (1997). Cultivated Uncertainty - An Attitude for Gestalt Therapists; in: British Gestalt Journal, 6(1), 40-48.

Stolorow, R., Brandschaft, B. & Atwood, G. (1987). *Psychoanalytic Treatment: An Intersubjective Approach*. Hillsdale, NJ: The Analytic Press.

Wertheimer, M. (1945). *Productive Thinking*. NY: Harper and Brothers.

Wheeler, G. (1996). Self and shame: A new paradigm for psychotherapy. In R. Lee & G. Wheeler (Eds.). *The Voice of Shame: Silence and Connection in Psychotherapy* (pp. 23-60). San Francisco: Jossey-Bass Publishers.

Yontef, G. (1993). *Awareness, Dialogue and Process: Essays on Gestalt Therapy*. Highland, NY: The Gestalt Journal Press.

Yontef, G. (1997a). Supervision from a Gestalt therapy perspective. in C.E. Watkins (Ed.), *Handbook of Psychotherapy Supervision*. (pp 147-163). NY: John Wiley & Sons. Edited version: (1996). *British Gestalt Journal*, 2, 92-102.

Yontef, G. (1997b). Relationship & sense of self in Gestalt therapy training. *The Gestalt Journal*, 20(1),17-48.

Yontef, G. (1998). Dialogic Gestalt Therapy. in L. Greenberg, G. Lietaer, & J. Watson (Eds.), *Handbook of Experiential Psychotherapy*. NY: Guilford Publications.

Yontef, G. (1999). Preface to the German edition of Awareness, Dialogue & Process. *The Gestalt Journal*, 22(1), 9-20.

Yontef, G. (2001). Psychotherapy of schizoid process. *Transactional Analysis Journal*, 31(1), 7-23.

Section 2

••••••••••

The Crucible of the Consulting Room

Introduction

••••••••••••

$\mathbf{F}$rank-M. Staemmler's chapter cuts to the core of the relational endeavor: To be in relationship is to constantly reexamine my understanding of the other, and even of myself, and how we understand our mutual influences. We face the psychotherapeutic conundrum of how to respond, which always includes our interpretations, without doing an injustice to the meanings as presented by the client. In other words, how do we say anything with certainty, in the face of such uncertainty? The story of "misunderstanding" he uses at the beginning of his chapter provides a cautionary tale for every therapist. Our desire to explain can too easily lead to interpretive rigor mortis.

To help us, Staemmler invokes hermeneutics. He points out that, "you cannot not interpret." *All* understanding is ultimately interpretative: that is not fatal to understanding, rather it is the ground that needs to be acknowledged in order to approach understanding more accurately. Only in doing so is there the "chance to make more complete sense."

An appropriate subtitle for Margherita Spagnuolo Lobb's chapter, "Therapeutic Meeting as Improvisational Co-Creation" would be "The Therapist and Client at Risk." For Spagnuolo Lobb's focus on the improvisational nature of the therapeutic process means we can never know ahead of time how to respond to a client. This is the potential excitement and dread that shadows every moment of our work. After developing a strong theoretical rationale for improvisation and its cousins, co-creation and temporality, she further fleshes out this understanding by an example of risk-taking in her clinical work.

Lynne Jacobs' "Attunement and Optimal Responsiveness" argues "that the subjectivity of the therapist as an 'other'" is a fundamental dimension of the developmental process of the therapy, of the client, and of the therapist. Our unique otherness as a therapist is not some ancillary aspect of simply applying a set theoretical orientation, but rather is *essential* to eliciting the unique otherness of the client. With the wisdom of over thirty years of clinical experience, Jacobs helps us in this process by pointing concretely to affect attunement as one of the first steps in laying the basis for the exploration of this otherness. Lynne's clinical tale exemplifies what Spagnuolo Lobb's previous chapter highlighted about risk-taking in the therapeutic encounter.

Carol Swanson shows us how a "pull on a scarf" becomes the metaphor for exploring certain special moments. The scarf is also a concrete support for deepening the therapy. The visible scarf comes to symbolize the invisible relational therapeutic matrix. Swanson furthermore weaves a tale of therapeutic rupture and attempts at repair—"dropping," and "holding," a client. It is the paradoxical trust in uncertainty that leads us to creative leaps, and genuine healing.

With this chapter, we come full circle in this section of the book. We started this section with Staemmler's exploration of uncertainty as at the core of relational therapy, and we end with Swanson's profound acknowledgment that as therapists, we all live, and act, from a "wobbly pivot."

The Willingness to Be Uncertain:
Preliminary Thoughts About Interpretation and Understanding in Gestalt Therapy

• • • • • • • • • • • •

Frank-M. Staemmler

Modern hermeneutics emerged to an important degree from the phenomenological tradition; for instance, there is a train of thought that runs from Husserl to Heidegger to Gadamer. In this chapter I will follow this train. As Heidegger said, "from the very beginning our essence is to understand and to create comprehensibility." That means that we are all interpreting and creating meaning all the time — a fact that, in my view, has not been discussed thoroughly enough in the literature of Gestalt therapy. On the contrary, many Gestalt therapists still seem to be influenced by Perls's verdict, "Never, never interpret!" which from a phenomenological and hermeneutical point of view is just silly and impossible to comply with. The question has to be: how can we as Gestalt therapists interpret in ways that are compatible with our basic tenets? I will offer some preliminary statements and a clinical vignette, which may serve as a point of departure for further considerations.

> *Healing through dialogue is an eminently herme-*
> *neutical phenomenon indeed.*
>
> *Gadamer, 1974, p. 1072*

Although most philosophers and psychotherapists would agree ." ... that the central concept of a human psychology is *meaning* and the processes and transactions involved in the construction of meanings" (Bruner, 1990, p. 33 — original italics), there has not been very much written about the question of how meaning is constructed in Gestalt therapy, that is, what place understanding and interpretation should have and how they can be handled within the theoretical framework of the Gestalt approach (see Staemmler, 1999). This is somewhat surprising since already in the second sentence of the theoretical part of *Gestalt Therapy* the authors refer to that dimension: "... psychologically what is real are the 'whole' configurations ... some *meaning* being achieved" (Perls et al., 1951, p. 227 — my italics).

In this chapter I will try to offer some preliminary considerations, which I hope will be useful for future attempts to work out a theoretical framework that deals with this important issue.

A Short Story of a Long Misunderstanding

I would like to start with the summary of a short story that I recommend to anybody to read in full length because of its mental clarity and its literary quality. It was written by Nobel prize-winning Gabriel Garcia Márquez; the title of the story is "I Only Came to Use the Phone" (Márquez, 1994).[1]

The author describes what happens to a young woman, whose car breaks down on a country road in the pouring rain and who tries to get a lift to the next telephone. After a long time the driver of a van picks her up; in the van there is a group of sleeping passengers covered with blankets. As she is cold and wet, the woman sitting next to the driver gives a blanket to her also.

After a while the van stops. Together with the other passengers she gets out and enters a building. She meets a woman in uniform and tells her she wants to make a phone call. She is ordered to join the other women in the communal dormitory. Suddenly awake to the fact that she is in a psychiatric hospital, she tries to escape — to no avail. Her explanations, protests, and attempts to leave the building are unsuccessful; they are answered with force and sedation. The next day, she is introduced to the medical director of the hospital. He deals with her in a very friendly and patient manner. She tries to convince him that she has only come to make a phone call and repeatedly demands to be permitted to call her husband and inform him of her whereabouts. The doctor speaks to her in a fatherly voice saying "Everything in due course" — and finishes the conversation.

A few weeks later, she manages to send a message to her husband. The price is high; she has to give in to the sexual advances of a night nurse. The visit of her husband to the hospital from which she expects her liberation

---

[1] I have also used this story in an earlier paper (Staemmler, 1997).

begins with a conversation between him and the medical director. The latter explains to the former the mental disease of his wife. He talks of states of excitation, vehement outbursts of aggression and fixed ideas (especially the one to make phone calls); further treatments as well as the sympathetic cooperation of the husband for the sake of a positive course of the disease are strictly indicated.

After having been informed in this way, the husband sees his wife. He soothes her, encourages her, tells her that she will soon feel better, and promises to come to visit with her on a regular basis. At first she is perplexed; then she starts to rave and to scream like a maniac. On her husband's next visit, she refuses to see him. The doctor says to him calmly: "That is a typical reaction. It will pass."

This arresting story illustrates several ideas on which I would like to elaborate in this chapter. I guess that for most of you it is obvious that the hospital staff as well as, at a later point in time, the husband are all adhering to an interpretation of the woman's situation that to them is as unquestionable as it is false to the woman herself — and to us, the readers. From our vantage point it is easy to see that the staff mistreats the woman by diagnosing her as manic and psychotic, thereby, drives her crazy. Additionally, from our vantage point is it easy to be outraged at the apparent injustice that is done to the main character of the story.

The Question of Interpretations

However, let me say: It is easy, but it is a little too easy, for I think that this reading of the story only refers to one of many possible interpretations, which to me is not even the most interesting. I need to admit quickly, though, that it conveys an important message — a message that is in accordance with our phenomenological and dialogical heritage in Gestalt therapy: "Do not hold on to your prejudices about people, but listen carefully and seriously to what they have to tell you!"

As a consequence of this attitude some Gestalt therapists including Fritz and Laura Perls held that we ought to abstain from interpretations. For Laura Perls interpretation was "an intellectual shortcut. It promotes introjection rather than assimilation and integration, and this is a waste of time" (Perls, L. & Polster, M. 1992, p. 202). Fritz Perls simply demanded: "... *never, never interpret*" (Perls, 1969a, p. 121 — original italics).[2] Given his biography we can assume that the paradigm he had in mind when he imposed this ban was the classical psychoanalytic interpretation, that is an interpretation, which is derived from a certain kind of psychological theory and meta-theory. As an example for this sort of interpretation I give you one by Arlow, a psychoanalyst, who once wrote: "Certain patients have a difficulty in facing or dealing with reality, which is based on an unconscious equating of the female genital with reality" (Arlow, 1969, p. 962).

Those of you who are familiar with the person of Fritz Perls will know that his objection against such interpretations was not necessarily directed against their sexual content; usually he was quite interested in sexual issues (see Perls, 1969b). What he did not like was the certainty provided by a general theoretical bias

---

[2] At the time when Perls propagated this conviction he participated in a *zeitgeist* that not only affected psychotherapy but also other social realms such as art and literary criticism. A proponent of that realm, Susan Sontag, wrote in her 1964 essay "Against Interpretation": "To interpret is to impoverish, to deplete the world — in order to set up a shadow world of 'meanings'. It is to turn *the* world into *this* world. ... the world, our world, is depleted, impoverished enough. Away with all duplicates of it, until we again experience more immediately what we have" (in: 1967, p. 7 — original italics).

that understands all kinds of phenomena within the fixed framework of a certain prefabricated pattern of meanings and that makes it difficult for clients to find and/or invent their own understandings.

However, Perls's critique of psychoanalytic interpretations to a large extent blinded him to see clearly how he used to interpret himself. We all know, for instance, his dogma that any element in a dream was a representation of some disowned aspect of the dreamer's personality. If you read the transcripts of his workshops you frequently come across bold interpretations such as these: "If you avoid looking at another person, it means that you're not open.... By the way, this low voice is always a symptom of hidden cruelty" (Perls, 1973, p. 135).

The "Bracketing" of the "Natural Attitude"

One could call all of these interpretations *prejudices*. The hospital staff in the Márquez story, the classical analysts, and Perls as well as other Gestalt therapists who adopt his interpretive patterns — they all proceed on the basis of prejudices. But that is not as problematic as it may seem at first sight. The real problem is that they are *not aware* of the prejudiced character of their understandings of the situations they are in. This lack of awareness is what makes them too certain and thus unable to see things differently and to negotiate the possibility of different meanings at all. They are being neither phenomenological nor hermeneutical. They are obsessed by what Husserl (1922) called the "natural attitude" and guided by their respective beliefs and ideologies.

Husserl was not content to accept as true what appears to be first given. He wanted to overcome any preconceptualized way of looking at phenomena. His stated objective was to "eliminate traditional modes of thinking completely, to recognize and tear down the bounds of the mind..." and to establish "...an entirely new attitude which is opposed to the natural ways of experience and thinking" (Husserl, 1922, p. 3) through his method of the "phenomenological reduction." His primary method was to "bracket ... this entire natural world that is 'there for us'" (ibid., p. 56), a method he called "epoché." By means of the free variation of the objects of investigation and a second reduction, called the "eidetic reduction," he aimed to discover their "invariants" and, ultimately, their essence, which was to be free of any contingent (accidental) properties.

There has been considerable criticism of these ideas and, additionally even stronger criticism, of Husserl's notion of a "transcendental ego" which resulted from his third "reduction," the "transcendental" one. Philosophers (for instance Sartre and Merleau-Ponty, but, to a certain degree, even Husserl himself in his last years), historians, cultural sociologists, ethnologists, and others emphasized that it will never be possible to clean your mind of all pre-understandings and "... that certain aspects of an individual's horizon of understanding ineluctably are inaccessible to self-reflection" (Rennie, 2000, p. 486).[3]

I think the critics are right: "One can never know for sure that the phenomenological reduction has been successful" (Schmitz, 1980, p. 21). We as therapists (as well as most other human beings) are looking at our clients from a perspective that to a large extent is coined by the "natural attitude" and shaped by our historical and cultural biases. Even though we all try as much as possible to practice some kind of "bracketing," to

---

[3] In Gestalt therapy literature this was nicely addressed by Lolita Sapriel when she wrote: "The project of transcendental phenomenology seems to involve an implicit stepping outside the bounds of human subjectivity into a realm of presuppositionsless certainty..." (1998, p. 39).

become aware of such biases, and to be open to our clients, we have to confess that in our everyday work we remain quite far away from a radical "antiseptic" phenomenological stance most of the time. Our attempts at bracketing will always remain attempts, which may be successful to a certain degree — but: "The empirical individual in his 'social reality' cannot but bring back all these noxious interests, prejudices, traditions, cultural constraints and social pressures, which in Husserl's view stood in the way to truth and understanding" (Bauman, 1978, p. 129).

Interpreting and Understanding
Is Being Human

In my view this is no disaster, but a positive aspect of our being just as human as our clients. As far as I am concerned, as a therapist I do not find it desirable to be "not a human ego," which is the ultimate consequence of the transcendental epoché as Husserl (1962, p. 275[4]) himself admitted. And, what I say about myself also applies to my clients. One of my teachers at the university of Würzburg, phenomenologist Heinrich Rombach (1980, p. 81), pointed out that practicing a radical "eidetic reduction" means to sacrifice the individual person (i.e. the "empirical subject"). This may be appropriate for

---

[4] This formulation can be found in the third draft for his article for the Encyclopedia Britannica — a formulation to which Heidegger, who read Husserl's unpublished draft, added a critical remark. In the final fourth version Husserl wrote more carefully that "my transcendental ego is evidently 'different' from my natural ego ..." (1962, p. 294). — "It was Husserl as well who at the end of the road discovered, to his dismay, that 'the original problem remains: how can there be an identity between the solitary, unworldly Ego, and the intersubjective society of natural human beings in their cultural world?'" (Bauman, 1978, pp. 151f.)

philosophical purposes but it is definitely not what I am aiming for in my relationships with my clients.

Martin Heidegger, Husserl's most famous student and also one of his prominent critics, clearly demonstrated that even "any mere pre-predicative seeing of the ready-to-hand is, in itself, something which already understands and interprets" (Heidegger, 1962, p. 189). For him understanding and interpreting was not primarily a human *activity*, which you might as well not exercise; more than that it was a central trait of *being human*. He said: "From the very beginning our essence is to understand and to create comprehensibility" (Heidegger, 1983, p. 444). And Heidegger's most famous student, hermeneutic philosopher Hans-Georg Gadamer, assisted: "*Understanding is . . . the original form of the realization of Dasein* which is being-in-the-world" (Gadamer, 1989a, p. 259 — original italics).

In recent years modern developmental researchers have presented convincing evidence supporting the philosophers' assertions: Already

> by the end of the first year it is not events themselves, but what infants make out of them that determines emotional reactions and individual reactivity. Moreover, dramatic individual differences in the meaning of events and of emotional arousal itself have become established. (Sroufe, 1996, p. 131)

Even in perception we do interpret,[5] since we always see something *as* something. I see this thing here *as* a table, the other thing over there *as* a chair etc. (see Staemmler, 2002a, p. 26). Hence Heidegger (1962, p. 189) spoke of the hermeneutic "as-structure" of perception and understanding. And the Gestalt psychologists would not become tired of demonstrating, how human beings (as well as many animals, even bees and birds — see Hertz 1928a; 1928b; 1929; 1930; 1931; Köhler 1933, pp. 100ff.) organize our perception in meaningful wholes.

So the first basic statement I would like to make can be formulated following Watzlawick's (1967) famous sentence, "You cannot not communicate." Accordingly my statement is:

(1) You cannot not interpret.

The minute you perceive or understand something, you perceive or understand it *as* something; that is, you relate it to a category, you distinguish it from something else, you form a gestalt, you attach meaning to it etc. So in my view we can define interpretation simply as a necessary ". . . activity the aim of which consists in arriving at understanding" (Bleicher, 1980, p. 29).

Phenomenologists do not hesitate to admit that already a phenomenological *description* ". . . presupposes a framework of class names, and all it can do is to determine the location of the phenomenon with regard to an already developed system of

---

[5] The interpretive processes involved in perception may be regarded as *micro*-interpretations "as opposed to *macro*-interpretations," which build on the former. Both Perls's assertion that there is hidden cruelty behind low voices and Arlow's equating of the female genitals with reality are examples for macro-interpretations. What is important is the fact that both are interpretations and that, of course, there is no clear dividing line between micro- and macro-interpretations.

classes" (Spiegelberg, 1960, p. 673). In addition, a "... phenom-enological description ... can never be more than selective: it is impossible to exhaust all the properties, especially the relational properties, of any object or phenomenon" (ibid.). As a result, we cannot even assume, "... that different observers, who perform the phenomenological reduction with great conscientiousness and clarity, would necessarily arrive at identical results" (Schmitz, 1980, p. 22).

If we apply these insights to psychotherapy it becomes clear that

> ... to assert that a therapist ... can claim to engage in any form of dialogue with a client which is free of inter-pretative variables would not only be a false claim, but also an absurd one. In an important sense, from a mental standpoint we can do *nothing but* interpret. (Spinelli, 1996, p. 197 — original italics)

This may seem to be an unpleasant restriction for those who still hold the firm belief that they might be able to see things "as they really are" and have not yet understood that most likely things-as-they-really-are do not exist for us. But those who are willing to face some uncertainty will probably welcome the liberty that springs from the fact that we are not like automatons or like Skinner's rats.

> We become what we are and we are what we become, we do not have a meaning which could be determined once and for all, but a *continuously changing* meaning, and therefore our future is relatively uncertain, our behavior ... relatively unpredictable — we are free. (Lyotard, 1993, p. 135 — original italics)

We do not simply respond to stimuli. On the contrary, we are human beings who can take an intermediate step and choose which meanings to attribute to those stimuli and, therefore, have some freedom of decision about how we are willing to react.[6]

A Clinical Vignette

The following clinical vignette illustrates the ubiquity of interpretations in a therapeutic dialogue. I have inserted respective comments in the initial part as well as in the end of the vignette (in brackets, italicized). The reader is invited to also pay attention to the numerous interpretations that are made by both client and therapist in the intermediate parts of the vignette to which I have not added any comments.

The client is thirty-six years old and works as a masseur and physiotherapist in a cancer rehabilitation clinic where she works with patients who have undergone severe surgery.

This is the nineteenth session. The numbers indicate the time: "(00:50)" means that it is fifty seconds after the beginning of the session; this information is meant to enable you, the reader, to get an impression of the pace at which the session proceeds.

> Therapist: Last time we finished our session when we had just discovered that a certain kind of closeness is lacking between the two of us. (*The therapist speaks about his understanding of the previous session's ending.*)

---

[6] Miriam Polster mentioned another positive aspect; to her interpretation was "the attempt by one person to translate the unique experience of another person into significance extending beyond the raw event" (Perls, L. & Polster, M. 1992, p. 202).

Client: That's right. I also realized at home that I am either too compliant, for instance with my son [who is twelve years old], or too stern, for instance with my patients in the hospital . . . It seems like two poles: I am either too soft and too sloppy or I almost freak out when things don't go well. And somehow it is just like that with closeness and distance too. (*The client interprets some of her behaviors as representing two poles.*)

Th. (00:50): Yes, we have also found out between us that although you enter into contact with me some closeness is missing. — How do you experience that? Do you have a wish for that? (*The therapist says some more about his take on the last session and then asks the client for her interpretation of it.*)

Cl.: I am not sure if that has something to do with my wishes, certainly not only . . . It also has to do with getting involved with somebody else. I experience that with my patients too. Always a certain distance remains even with those I get on with well and with whom I feel a certain connection from the very beginning. (*The client tries to find contexts that can help her to make sense of her experience.*)

Th. (02:15): Yes, that matches my impression. I find that we are getting on well with each other, I like you, and I also have a sense that you like me too. You talk to me in a trusting manner and speak openly about the things that occupy or even oppress you. And yet I feel as if a nearness or some sort of a warm reverberation does not come about — or maybe some cordiality. (*The therapist conveys his understanding of an aspect of their relationship.*)

Cl.: That's true. To a certain degree it feels well rounded, but then there is a limit.

Th. (03:00): Maybe you can describe this limit in more detail?

Cl.: Yes, but it's strange... There is something... (Pause) Even with my son I draw this limit, although I frequently wish it were different. Sometimes I make it, but I easily fuse and am affected too much when he finds himself in situations that aren't pleasant for him. I don't want that... But I am not sure if that's a different problem again. If I think of you and me... There is something... (*The client is still looking for relevant contexts in order to make sense of herself.*)

Th. (04:30): I don't know if that would already be too close for you, but I would find it easier to look at what it is like between you and me. That's probably the most tangible, and we both have impressions, which we can share. (*The therapist suggests one context, which he thinks might be most useful for the creation of meaning.*)

Cl.: OK, fine.

Th. (05:00): Well, try and focus your attention on your awareness of the closeness between us: How do you experience that with me now?

Cl.: I don't feel completely good about it, not really flowing... A few minutes ago I was a little surprised when you said that I appeared trustful to you. I do not really feel that myself fully. I'm not really aware of that. (*The client refers to the therapist's previous interpretation of their relationship and points out that she has a different take on it.*)

Th. (06:00): You don't clearly *feel* trustful, although you *behave* that way... (*The therapist expresses his interpretation of her interpretation.*)

Cl.: Yes, right . . . But something is missing, something that would make me feel completely good so I could let go . . . Sometimes I have felt that more clearly, for instance when I have cried here. Then I have felt you more and differently, your attention, your favor . . .

Th. (07:00): Are you saying that when you are more involved emotionally you also have a clearer sense of me?

Cl.: Yes, then it is OK, then there is something well-rounded that does me good, that makes me feel wrapped up.

Th. (07:15): I am just thinking if we could try an experiment, which would require you to entrust yourself a little more . . .

Cl.: Oh!

Th. (07:30): . . . and that would make it easier for us to find out, what's possible for you and what isn't. — What is your reaction to this idea?

Cl.: Well, it is like I don't really dare to . . . Although I would like to try it out . . .

Th. (08:00): OK, let me make a suggestion. You do not have to accept it; we can also consider if there is another possibility that's better for you. — The idea I have is this: I could sit down on the floor cross-legged, then you could lie down in front of me on your back and place your head on my lap. Then I would place my hands underneath your head and move it gently to and fro. So you could get a sense of the degree to which you can give your head into my hands.

Cl.: (pauses, laughs, then:) Oh! . . . Trust! — I started feeling dizzy for a moment when you said that . . . But I'm going to do it anyway!

Th. (09:30): I find it important that you do not take the bull by the horns if that means for you to pass over something that's difficult for you rather than to attend to it and do it carefully so that you become exactly aware of what is going on in you. — This is not a feat to be performed, it is rather a discovery to be made.

Cl.: Yes. (pauses, remains motionless)

Th. (10:15): I know you're courageous. You don't have to prove that to me.

Cl.: (remains silent for a while, then slowly begins to cry softly)

Th. (11:30): What are you experiencing?

Cl.: I am touched by what you said, that you mentioned that intermediate step. I tend to forget that. It was important for me that you mentioned it... I felt myself being seen by you. I was ready to jump over it and to do quickly what you had suggested.

Th. (12:30): I guess you would have come to me outwardly, but not inwardly; inwardly you would have stayed in your chair.

Cl.: (laughs) Right! — And for a moment I thought: 'I don't want to.'

Th. (13:00): You don't want to come closer? — Can you hear your voice as you say, "I don't want to."?

Cl.: (begins to sob) I do not want to be forced! — I do not want to be forced to be close.

Th. (13:45): Of course...

Cl.: (blows her nose, then cries again)

Th. (14:20): This seems to move you a lot...

Cl.: But I'm not sure what it is... I don't know...

Th. (15:15): To me you look as if you are at a very delicate point right now. (Pause) I get the impression I need to be very careful with you now.

Cl.: (Pause) I don't know what's going on ... My head is pulsating.

Th. (16:15): You look very vulnerable to me, very sensitive.

Cl.: (Pause) I feel blank. I have no idea, no thought ...

Th. (18:00): It seems almost as if you were not there — no idea, no thought ... nothing ...

Cl.: (Pause)

Th. (18:45): Maybe a little lost too. As if you were in nowhere land now ...

Cl.: Hm ... (pauses, blows her nose) Yes, I have the feeling ... I feel empty. As if I was going out of my head here ... (points to a place at the back of her head)

Th. (20:00): Can you try to follow that? Where are you going?

Cl.: Away, backward, but there is still a connection, I only go that far (points to a place about two yards behind herself).

Th. (20:30): And in front there remains your empty body?

Cl.: Yes, I can see it.

Th. (20:45): And everything that I would get to feel, if I came closer to you, was this empty body. You wouldn't be there in your body. — I can understand that pretty well, if I recall that you said you did not want to be forced to be close. That seems like an efficient way to elude that force. If you cannot evade it outwardly, you can still evade it inwardly.

Cl.: Yes! (pauses, then begins to cry again)

Th. (22:30): Give way to that feeling.

Cl.: I'm thinking of the experiment you suggested ... I imagined you sitting there with my head in your hands ...

Th. (23:20): And then you start to cry?

Cl.: Hm.

Th. (23:30): Stay with that image for a while. You see me sitting there with your head in my hands.

Cl.: I really would like to be there ...

Th. (24:00): Do you long for it?

Cl.: Yes, but only briefly. And then I am going away again.

Th. (24:20): With the longing you were in your body briefly, and then you emptied yourself again?

Cl.: Yes, exactly. It's not possible with an empty body.

Th. (24:30): And you don't get anything out of it.

Cl.: Strange ... (pauses), to be this way, so empty ... (pauses). Now it occurs to me that in everyday life I'm also frequently leaving myself, daydreaming, not really being there ...

Th. (25:30): Yet there was also the longing ...

Cl.: But only very briefly! (laughs loudly) In the end I don't dare ...

Th. (26:20): Yes, if you do not pass over it you feel how shy you are and how hard it is to come close. Of course you would be able to pass over it and do it with your body emptied ...

Cl.: ... just functioning. — Now I realize what it is that I experience with my patients. I have to function no matter how they smell, how they look with their scars, I have to touch them, I have to do my work ...

Th. (27:20): Isn't that like being *forced* to be close in your work?

Cl.: Yes, it is. (begins to cry again) That's exactly what it is. (sobs vehemently) Oh, gee! Every time it is like being raped . . . I have to do it, and I know I can do it . . .

Th. (28:30): . . . if you empty yourself. If you don't, it's like being raped, if you stay in your body and feel it . . .

Cl.: Yeah, I couldn't bear it, if I would stay there . . . Many of my patients are mutilated. They have been raped by the operations and radiations. I couldn't bear it, if I would be there . . . I can only do it, if I don't feel it.

Th. (30:00): If you would let their bodies come close, these raped bodies, it would feel like you being raped yourself. (Pause). Then you would fuse and also feel what it means to be in a physical state like that?

Cl.: Yes. Sometimes I do it (sighs deeply) . . . A few weeks ago, for instance, I worked with a patient who had had an operation in her womb area. There was a huge edema at her pubic bone. It looks terrible and feels terrible. Then I thought to myself: Of course I, I can do it, I can cope with it, I can help her, I can do it all. — But it also made me angry: I have to do it. I cannot say, "I can't get it done." Then I thought, I wouldn't want to know what had been destroyed in her body, burnt by the radiation . . . She can forget her sex life, it is lost forever . . . (cries). There is also a part in me that likes to help and give some relief, but I hate to have to do it on orders. Then I function: I can do it . . . *(At this time the client's avoidance of closeness as observed by the therapist in the beginning of the session is understood in a new way, i.e. her attempt to resist to being forced to be close, her attempt to escape from her tendencies to become confluent with the suffering of her patients etc.) (The session continues for about fifteen more minutes.)*

Understanding Begins With Pre-Understanding

Since we all are human beings who attribute meanings, we need to be aware of the fact that in the very beginning of any encounter we are no better than the hospital staff in the Márquez story: Our cultural coinage, our personal history, our material conditions, our educational and professional backgrounds, our respective gender, our situational expectations etc., many of which we are not even conscious of and to a certain extent may never become conscious of — in short: our respective phenomenal fields determine the ways we first look at and understand things and events in our therapy sessions.

Heidegger said: "An interpretation is never a presuppositionless apprehending of something presented to us. ... one finds that what 'stands there' in the first instance is nothing other than the obvious undiscussed assumption of the person who does the interpreting" (1962, p. 191f.). Gadamer put it briefly: "The so-called 'given' cannot be detached from the interpretation" (1984, p. 33). If we as Gestalt therapists, who have been taught to work with the "obvious," accept this insight of hermeneutic phenomenology, then we have to become very careful not to confuse what is obvious to us — remember Husserl's "natural attitude"! — with what is 'real' in any objective sense of the word. Making this mistake is tantamount to leaving phenomenological ground behind and subscribing to naïve realism.

For Gadamer, "it is interpretation that performs the never fully complete mediation between man and world, and to this extent the fact that we understand something as something is the sole actual immediacy and givenness" (1989b, p. 30).

Although Perls was not very consistent in his thinking about this issue, he was apparently aware at times of the interpretive character of the given. Among the first sentences of his chapter on the "Philosophy of the Obvious" one can find the following: "We take the obvious for granted. But when we examine the obvious a bit closer, then we see that behind what we call obvious, is a lot of prejudice, distorted faith, beliefs and so on" (Perls, 1973, p. 177).

Let me sum up what I have just said in the form of a second statement:

(2) Our understanding of any situation necessarily begins with a prejudice or, to put it a little milder, with a pre-understanding[7],

as Gadamer (1989a) would never become tired to repeat: in the beginning of understanding is a kind of narrow-mindedness, a narrow "horizon." It is most important to be aware of this fact, because if we are not, we are in danger of feeling too certain, to be content with that pre-understanding, and not to inquire any further.

A person who believes he is free of prejudices, relying on the objectivity of his procedures and denying that he is himself conditioned by historical circumstances,

---

[7] In his critique of Gadamer's *Truth and Method* Hirsch (1967, pp. 245ff.) has argued for a clear distinction between "prejudice" and "pre-understanding" (ibid., pp. 258ff.). I will follow him in *this* regard. Notwithstanding this distinction Hirsch agrees with Gadamer about the necessity of that pre-understanding: "The preliminary grasp of a text that we must have before we can understand it is the hermeneutical version of the hypothesis we must have about data before we can make sense of them. . . . understanding is therefore partly dependent on pre-understanding" (ibid., p. 261).

experiences the power of the prejudices that unconsciously dominate him as a *vis a tergo*. (Gadamer, 1989a, p. 360)

Gadamer who, by the way, died recently at the age of 102 years (see Staemmler, 2002b) shows that since the age of enlightenment prejudices have acquired a very bad reputation, which became a new kind of prejudice — the prejudice against prejudices.[8] But in his view prejudices are necessary, for if we did not have them we did not have a point of departure for our attempts at understanding. Some prejudices may even be confirmed by subsequent scrutiny![9] "Having a particular point of view on the world is a condition of seeing it at all, so perspective in general is not a limit on knowledge but what makes it possible" (Cavell, 1999, p. 1231).

"Only through having a horizon at all, we can encounter something that widens our horizon" (Gadamer, in Dutt, 1993, p. 18). Hence Gadamer gave a second name to the prejudice, which does not have so much of a negative ring in our ears: He also called it a "draft,"[10] a first sketch that has to be handled

---

[8] As Horkheimer and Adorno put it: "The mystic terror feared by the Enlightenment accords with myth" (1972, p. 29).

[9] Gadamer found it important "... to distinguish the *true* prejudices, by which we *understand*, from the *false* ones, by which we *misunderstand*" (1989, p. 298f. — original italics). However, at the beginning of any hermeneutic process it is hard to tell the ones from the others.

[10] In his critique of Gadamer's use of the term "prejudice" Hirsch (1967) ignores this fact (see footnote 5). However, it has to be stated that Gadamer uses the term "prejudice" much more often than the term "draft." — Gadamer draws on Heidegger in many respects; so he does when he uses the word "Entwurf," which I translate with the English "draft." For readers of the English translations of *Being and Time* and *Truth and Method* it may be important to know that the German "Entwurf" is usually translated with "projection" or "fore-projection," which might lead to misunderstandings at least among psychotherapists who are likely to ascribe a different meaning to "projection."

with reservation and uncertainty and that is meant to be differentiated and, always only approximately, completed.

The Anticipation of Completion

Paradoxically, in order to widen our horizon, to revise the first draft and to gain a more developed understanding we even need to *rely* on a certain prejudice. We have to presuppose — and this is my third statement — in any situation or in any person we are trying to understand

(3) there is the potential to become more and differently meaningful and there is a chance to make more complete sense than we had conceived of in the first place.

Ultimately we even have to presuppose that she, he, or it will make *complete* sense, if we are to be motivated to search for new and more convincing meanings. In this context Gadamer speaks of what has been translated as the "fore-conception of completeness" (1989a, p. 293f.); I would rather translate it as the "anticipation of completion." We may never reach this completion, but we need to *assume* that it can be reached in principle.

The "anticipation of completion," however, is in no way tantamount to the idea that there is *one,* "right" or "last" or "perfect" or "final" interpretation. Gadamer underlined ". . . the fact that the meaning of a person's life is always uncertain and inconclusive at any time because the future is open ended and lacking closure" (Guignon, 1998, p. 572). Any interpretation is firmly tied to the perspective or the horizon of the under-standing person, which includes her or his "time perspective" (Frank, 1939; Lewin, 1951). In field theoretical terminology this term indicates the given point in time and history from which one's understanding originates. So the completion Gadamer advises us to presuppose is definitely not a perfection of our own interpretation! On the contrary, it is the possible completion we ought to attribute to the meaningfulness of the *other* person, the assumption that the behavior of the woman who says she only came to make a phone call may make complete sense to her.

However, I admit that Gadamer's "anticipation of completion" may be a misleading term, if one forgets that it is to be seen as a *heuristic principle* and not as a proposition describing facts. Davidson (1984) has proposed a similar assumption; he calls it the "principle of charity," which may be less in danger of misinterpretation. The "principle of charity" demands from the interpreter to prefer, if in doubt, interpretations that make it possible to understand the communications in question as *consistent* and *true* — at least for the time being, that is as long as there is no convincing contradictory evidence.

As the Márquez story clearly shows, this principle must also be applied to our professional diagnoses, no matter if they stem from psychoanalytical or ICD or DSM or other sources, of course including any Gestalt therapy approach to diagnosis. They may serve as useful points of departure in our pursuit of understanding our clients. But we need to be aware of the evidence proving that clinicians (as well as other humans) tend to hold on to their previously formed diagnostic judgments by only acknowledging or overrating confirming data — a fact known in social psychology as "spontaneous trait inference" or the "prior belief effect"[11], which leads to 'self-fulfilling

---

[11] See for instance Lord, Ross, & Lepper (1979), Nisbett & Ross (1980), Arkes (1981), Darley & Gross (1983), Turk & Salovey (1985); for a more recent overview see Darley, 1998.

diagnoses.' Moreover and on a more basic level, we have to recognize that "diagnoses . . ., if the hermeneutic approach is employed, cannot be viewed as disease entities and natural science 'facts,' but rather as temporary formations that change with changing times, historical eras, cultures, and prevailing prejudices and practices" (Chessick, 1990, p. 271).

The same applies in general to our experience both as private persons and professionals. Experience is apt to supply us with the comfortable certainty that goes along with the fact that you have seen similar things and events before; they do not come as a surprise anymore, and you can fall back on familiar ways of coping. As supportive as this may feel on the one hand, it can also turn into the laziness and denseness on the other hand that lead to being impervious to anything new (see Miller, 1990). Being experienced in a positive sense of the term must include the expectation that there is always the chance for some novelty. Therefore a person who has really learned from experience will be especially capable of making new experiences and to learn from them again.

> Thus experience is experience of human finitude. The truly experienced person is one who has taken this to heart, who knows that he is master neither of time nor the future. The experienced man knows that all foresight is limited and all plans uncertain. (Gadamer, 1989a, p. 357)

Asking Authentic Questions

The basis of such an attitude is open-mindedness or, to say it in the words of Socrates, the knowing that one does not know. The Socratic insight makes it possible to ask questions that aim at a fuller understanding of the person and the situation with which one is confronted. Of course I am thinking of *authentic* questions, not of pseudo-questions that already predestine their answers. "To ask a question means to bring into the open. The openness of what is in question consists in the fact that the answer is not settled" (Gadamer, 1989a, p. 363).

The main character in the Márquez story does not have a chance, because nobody, including her husband, is asking authentic questions. Nobody even ascribes to her the competence to give meaningful answers. But in any honest attempt at understanding we have to "... address others with a presumption that they are capable of responding meaningfully, responsibly, and, above all, *unexpectedly*" (Morson, 1986, p. IX — original italics).

This takes me to my fourth statement:

(4) Understanding is based on authentic questions,

that is questions — implicit or explicit — that do not lay down their corresponding answers in advance. This means that one needs to be prepared to listen[12] and to expose oneself to the uncertainty that goes along with the unpredictable impact of the other's utterance. In the same vein Martin Buber says, "genuine dialogue cannot be arranged beforehand" (1965, p. 87).

---

[12] There is a hermeneutic priority of *hearing*. Although you can also be impressed by perceptions of other sense modalities, hearing is of special importance since it is not only directed to *sounds* that can be percieved, but also to *language* that can be understood; thereby it allows access to another human universe.

Interpretation and the
Therapeutic Relationship

No later than at this point of this chapter it will have become apparent that hermeneutic philosophy overlaps with dialogism in some respects. There is a basic analogy: "Any true understanding is dialogic in nature. Understanding is to utterance as one line of dialogue is to the next" (Voloshinov, 1929/1986, p. 102).

Since among Gestalt therapists Buber's dialogical anthropology is known much better than other dialogic approaches,[13] I will briefly point out the parallel between hermeneutics and dialogism by referring to Buber's well known characterization of the "basic words," "I-Thou" and "I-It" (see Buber, 1958; Staemmler, 1993).

There are different kinds of understanding of a person, which can be assigned to either one of these basic word sets. A typical example of what one might call "I-It understanding" is the undertaking to find out what is characteristic of a certain person in order to predict and/or control her behavior. In this case understanding is part of a manipulative strategy. "It is the method of the social sciences, following the methodological ideas of the eighteenth century and their programmatic formulation by Hume, ideas that are a clichéd version of scientific method" (Gadamer, 1989a, p. 359).

Another widespread example for this I-It understanding can be found in the claim to understand the other better than she or he understands herself or himself. In the Márquez story, the medical director and the husband, after having been briefed by

---

[13] I am thinking for instance of Bakhtin (1986), Buytendijk (1951), Lévinas (1987; 1989; 1992), or Marcel (1992).

the director, display this kind of understanding very saliently. I think it is not by accident that the author uses exactly these characters with an attitude of arrogant possessiveness disguised as benevolence. In my reading of his story he tries to uncover a trait that can frequently be found in the helping professions. It springs from the dialectics of the relationship between the caring and the cared-for, which is akin to the dialectics of the relationship between the master and the slave. "The claim to understand the other person in advance functions to keep the other person's claim at a distance" (Gadamer, 1989a, p. 360).

In a recent publication Leanne O'Shea relates a personal experience which impressively illustrates a client's fear of being interpreted in an I-It-manner:

> Very early in beginning with a new therapist, I had a dream that was disturbingly erotic. It was not so much the sexual content that unsettled me, but that in my dream my longing and desire were directed towards my therapist explicitly and unambiguously. I felt stripped bare by the dream, and even though I understood it represented the work I needed to do, I recall arriving at therapy that day feeling vulnerable and ashamed. All I could manage to do was allude to the dream, and even though I felt myself to be in a safe place, I was unable to disclose its specific content. The reasons for this are of course quite complex, but in retrospect I have a sense that one of the things that in-hibited me was the fear that my dream would be inter-preted in a particular way, specifically that it would be understood as the expression of my unconscious sexual desire for my therapist. Whether or not this was true is, I think, irrelevant. It was more that somehow I felt that my capacity to make meaning of my experience would be lost

in the interpretation that I knew would be made. (O'Shea, 2003, p. 106f.)

By contrast, the kind of understanding that is compatible with Buber's I-Thou is based on the willingness to let the other person speak to me and to accept that she or he has something valid to tell me. It is based on a willingness to be uncertain, on an openness, which not only implies the possibility that I might learn something from the other, but also that I let something pass even against my own point of view. The kinship of this hermeneutic position with Buber's "between" is obvious, and sometimes Gadamer chooses words he may have adapted from Buber, with whose writings he was familiar, for instance when he states: "The dialogue has a transforming power. When a dialogue succeeds, something remains for us and in us, which has changed us" (Gadamer, 1993, p. 211).

Moreover, this kind of understanding is something, which connects humans to each other.[14] In order to make this clear Gadamer plays with German words: To listen to somebody (in German: *jemandem zuhören*) is linked with the experience of belonging to somebody (in German: *zu jemandem gehören*):

> In human relations the important thing is, as we have
> seen, to experience the Thou truly as a Thou — i.e., not to

---

[14] Although the cognitive aspect of understanding is more in the foreground in Gadamer's writings than the emotional aspect, it is easy to see at this point that his thinking is not restricted to the cognitive realm. However, for the purpose of a therapeutic theory of understanding it may be useful to supplement the emotional aspect more clearly. Stern's (1985, pp. 138ff.) notion of "affect attunement" may be helpful in this respect as he also underlines the interhuman bonding effect: "Tracking and attuning with vitality affects permit one human to 'be with' another in the sense of sharing likely inner experiences on an almost continuous basis. This is exactly our experience of feeling-connected, of being in attunement with another" (ibid., p. 157).

overlook his claim but to let him really say something to us. Here is where openness belongs. (...) Without such openness to one another there is no genuine human bond. Belonging together always also means being able to listen to one another (Gadamer, 1989a, p. 361).

Let me give you still another quote, which will both remind you of Buber's terms and which will help me to prepare my next statement. Gadamer says: "The true locus of hermeneutics is this *in-between*" (1989a, p. 295 — italics added). In other words, it takes a joint endeavor of the one who is trying to understand and the one who is to be understood, if understanding is to be achieved. The "between" in which that understanding takes place is a *whole*, which — in this instance as well as in others — is *more and different* from the sum of its parts. It is not just what the one person contributes plus what the other person contributes; it consists of what results from the mutual exchange within this encounter, and this result would never have been possible for each of the participants alone nor by means of what they brought into that encounter in the first place. It has an *emergent*[15] quality.

It would never have been possible, because each participant enters the dialogue as the person, who she or he is, that is to say: from the perspective of her or his phenomenal field including her or his *personal background*, which is both unique and *limited*. If we use the terms I have introduced before, we can equally say: each participant enters the dialogue

---

[15] I use the term "emergent" in a philosophical sense here. Emergent properties of a system arise with its increasing levels of complexity and cannot be directly derived from the properties of the system's parts on lower levels of complexity. For instance, the property "liquidity" of water cannot be directly derived from the properties of the individual H_2O-molecules (see Müller, 1988, p. 50).

with her or his own *set of pre-understandings* or with her or his respective *narrow horizon.* At the beginning of the dialogue, for each participant anything she or he thinks, says, feels, and does has its meaning in relation to her or his respective horizon.

The Integration of Horizons

Now let us assume that a dialogue would have taken place between the medical director and the woman who came to make a call — a dialogue, in which the doctor would have permitted himself to be uncertain and would have tried to understand the woman in a genuine way as described above. He would have started to ask authentic questions about her background, he would have listened, and he would have acknowledged her as a person who was able to tell him something meaningful that he had not known before.

In this case something important would have happened to him. His horizon would have become wider! He would have integrated at least parts of what the woman told him, and his background would not have been the same as before. It would have changed in the sense that his 'mental picture' of the woman would have become more detailed, more differentiated, and more complete. He might even have started to doubt the appropriateness of some of his own pre-understandings. The woman's horizon would have affected and extended his horizon. In other words, his horizon would have grown by the integration of the woman's horizon.

The integration of horizons is something different from putting oneself in the other's shoes as the idiom would have it. Doing so would mean to give up one's own horizon and to see the other as she or he saw herself or himself *before* and *without* any hermeneutic dialogue taking place. This would be a mere duplication of the other's perspective without any profit. There would even be a loss, since it would mean to deprive the other of the person who was going to understand her or him. "If the interpreter tries to see 'the other's point of view,' then he would be freezing both his object and himself into static patterns . . . The task consists, however, not in placing oneself in the latter, but in widening one's own horizon so that it can integrate the other; this is what occurs whenever understanding takes place" (Atari, 1991, p. 36).

According to Gadamer true understanding takes place through a "fusion of horizons" (1989a, p. 306). One might also say that understanding is a joint coordinating of meanings within relationships as a result of a dialogue that takes place within the frame of a certain cultural discourse (see Gergen, 2000). I suspect that the word "fusion" is likely to trigger some aversion in Gestalt therapists, who may associate it with "confluence." Although this would be an example for a misunderstanding on the basis of not genuinely asking Gadamer what he means by this word, I would rather sidestep this possible misunderstanding. Therefore, I put my fifth statement this way:

(5) Understanding goes along with an integration[16] of the other's background and, hence, a corresponding widening of one's own horizon.

---

[16] At first I was tempted to use the word "assimilation" instead of "integration" in order to make my formulation sound more 'Gestaltish.' I decided not to give in to this temptation. "Assimilation" is, at least in the context of this paper, in danger of being confused with pocketing the other's horizon (see below, section on "The Dangers and Limits of Understanding"). — Moreover, Sartre (1997) once spoke very critically of a "digestion" or "nutrition philosophy." Since it pervades gestalt

Sartre has said this much more saliently: "To understand means to change, to go beyond oneself" (1964, p. 18). I think it is legitimate to reverse this sentence and say that you did not understand, if you did not learn something new, if you did not change in some way. In other words, the answer to the question if you did change or not can help you to answer the question if you did understand or not.

Meaning is Continuously Changing

Here a potentially infinite progression has its beginning: if you change as you understand, you understand differently than before and you are not the one you have been before. So you have gained a new background, a new horizon, a new perspective from which to look at the person whom you are trying to understand. Sooner or later you will come up with a different interpretation. And the same applies to the other: the process that resulted from her or his wish to be understood has consequences for her or him too. It has brought the other in touch with your questions, your perspective, and your horizon, and in order to respond to these questions she or he had to understand you to a certain degree. The other had to widen her or his horizon too. So she or he has also changed in the course of this process. Nobody and nothing remained the same, neither you nor the other nor the subject matter that was to be understood. So "... the meanings that we give to the events, experiences, people, and things in our lives ... [are] communally constructed and inherently susceptible to trans-formation" (Anderson, 2000, p. 202).

---

therapy terminology and can lead to various implicit assumptions, which may not always be very useful, this metaphor would deserve a thorough discussion. Of course this discussion cannot take place in this paper.

In Gadamer's words — and this is my sixth statement —,

> (6) understanding a person is "... not merely a reproductive but always a productive activity as well" (1989a, p. 296 — italics added).

Although we can assume that in many cases there has been a more or less hidden meaning in the beginning of the hermeneutic process, this process never only consists of the mere "dis-covery" or finding of this pre-existing meaning. Meaning is not just there waiting to be uncovered or made conscious. Understanding is always also an innovative process in the course of which new meaning is *created*. We have to conclude that the process of

> ... *understanding contributes to what is to be understood*, or, phrased differently, that the fact *that* there occurs understanding is of importance for what is understood. ... understanding is in essence cooperative and ... this has important consequences for the content of what is understood. (de Gelder, 1981, p. 44 — original italics)

When different persons meet, when new horizons come into play, when other times impose their perspectives, new meanings and ways of understanding will emerge. Perls's dictum "there is no end to integration" (1969b, unpaginated), has often been paraphrased by Petzold (2001) as "there is no end to creation." This sentence can well be applied to understanding. If understanding is part of being human, it is part of our liveliness;

and what is the essence of liveliness, if not continuous pro-
creation and creativity?[17]

From this point of view, interpretation and understanding
are in accordance with our process-oriented thinking in Gestalt
therapy; they have to be seen as examples of the famous sentence of Heraclitus, "one cannot step twice into the same river"
(1979, p. 53). There is no such thing as 'the' interpretation,
which is true once and forever. This means that the process of
understanding will never be finished. Women and men are
historical beings who change continuously as time goes on; and
so do their environments. Therefore *"to be historically means
that knowledge of oneself* [as well as of others — F.-M. St.]
can never be complete" (Gadamer, 1989a, p. 302 — original
italics). No method, as sophisticated as it may be, will ever
assure us of the ultimate correctness of any understanding. As
Gadamer points out in *Truth and Method,* there is no secure
way from method to truth.[18]

> The whole of the hermeneutic enterprise and the
> conversation that it invites and provokes continues to
> emphasize the tentativeness of the process of relations and
> intersubjectivity; continues to remind us that ... the
> meanings that appear true at once can transform them-
> selves into something also seemingly true; that the truth
> lives in the relation of subjects during a particular time and
> according to a particular context. (Barclay, 1993, p. 99)

---

[17] In Whitehead's (1929) cosmology creativity is the primary
principle in the universe. If he was right, it is no surprise to come
across it in this context too.

[18] For a discussion of Gadamer's notion of truth, see
Grondin (1982).

The Dangers and Limits of Understanding Another Person

In the section on "Interpretation and the Therapeutic Relationship" I have already pointed at some dangers. Understanding can be abused for manipulative purposes and it can be misused in the service of an arrogant attitude, which claims to know the other better, in depth psychology "deeper," or fuller than she or he does herself or himself. These two dangers, if taken together and to their extremes, may lead to an "understanding" that tries to exert a kind of totalitarian control over the other person as it takes possession of her or him and assimilates her or his otherness to a degree, which is equivalent to negating or destroying it.[19] What happens to the woman in Márquez' story is a startling example. Theodor Reik, who is famous for his book *Hearing With the Third Ear* (1976) called this

> ... psychological cannibalism: the other is incorporated into the I and becomes, at least temporarily, a part of

---

[19] I have expressed my concern about the term "assimilation" before (see footnote 14). This concern may be more understandable now: "Assimilation" can be translated from Latin as "making similar." As gestalt therapists we have a tradition that has connected assimilation and destruction in a positive sense: "What is assimilated is not taken in as a whole, but is first destroyed (de-structured) completely and transformed — and absorbed *selectively* according to the need of the organism. ... If you can realize the necessity for an aggressive, destructive, and reconstructive attitude toward any experience that you are really to make your own, you can then appreciate the need mentioned previously to evaluate aggressions highly and not to dub them glibly 'anti-social'" (Perls et al., 1951, p. 190 — original italics). This positive connotation of assimilation and destruction (or aggression, respectively) may not be ethically defendable and appears in need of revision in the hermeneutic context (and maybe also in other contexts — see Petzold, 2001).

the I. By this process of psychological understanding the human lust for power asserts itself not only in its finest and most sublimated, but also unconsciously in its roughest ways. (Reik, 1935, pp. 189f.)[20]

By contrast, interpreting and understanding another person in the way, which I have called an "I-Thou-understanding," cannot be possessive or ignorant of the other's otherness. This kind of understanding is aware of its own limits. Moreover, it does not only accept these limits, but it *wants* them and *defends* them if they are threatened. I-Thou-understanding recognizes and acknowledges the paradoxical conditions on which it is based: the anticipation of completion (or the principle of charity — see respective section above) on the one hand and the engaged acceptance of its limits on the other hand.

What I have just described as "engaged acceptance" may also be called "voluntary self-restriction." I-Thou-understanding prefers to let go of grasping the presumed completeion of the other's meaning, if the integrity of her or his otherness is about to be jeopardized. It thoroughly knows that, although there are many similarities between human beings, the other will always remain a mystery, which has to be respected and left untouched for the sake of humanity (see Arnold, 1999, p. 43). Just like Gestalt therapy, hermeneutic philosophy cherishes differences.

One of the greatest moralists of our times, Emmanuel Lévinas (1987; 1989; 1992), has eloquently emphasized that any ignorance or disrespect of the other's otherness must be seen as

---

[20] What Reik says on an individual level can be called "colonialism" on an ethnic level: "Colonial power produces the colonized as a fixed reality which is at once an 'other' and yet entirely knowable and visible" (Bhabha, 1990 p. 76).

an inhumane act of violence or brutality.[21] His German trans-
lator summed up his position when he wrote that the
". . . seizing — not the ethically responding — understanding of
the other is violence towards him, since it just annihilates the
otherness of the other and subjugates it . . ." (Wenzler, in:
Lévinas, 1989, p. 71).

In a certain sense Gadamer anticipated the position of
Lévinas' when he wrote that ". . . we understand in a *different*
way, *if we understand at all*" (1989a, p. 297 — original
italics). However, Gadamer did so from a primarily *logical*
point of view, not so much from an *ethical* one as Lévinas.
Gadamer's reasoning went this way:

> Now certainly I would not want to say that the soli-
> darities that bind human beings together and make them
> partners in a dialogue always are sufficient to enable them
> to achieve understanding and total mutual agreement. Just
> between two people this would require a never-ending
> dialogue. And the same would apply with regard to the
> inner dialogue the soul has with itself. Of course we
> encounter limits again and again; we speak past each other
> and are even at cross-purposes with ourselves. But in my
> opinion we could not do this at all if we had not traveled a

---

[21] This danger may also be seen in Buber's version of dialogism.
Already in one of his first books Lévinas (1989) expressed two
objections against Buber, which Taureck sums up this way: "On the
one hand I-Thou-philosophy claims too much: since it begins with the
duality of I and Thou, the degree of separateness that exists between
subjects is underestimated ... On the other hand the I-Thou-
relationship claims too little: it remains an external relation of human
beings who are free for themselves and who remain free. The
relationship with the other has not become the basis itself" (Taureck,
2002, p. 37).

long way together, perhaps without even acknowledging it to ourselves. (Gadamer, 1989b, p. 57)

Conclusion:
The Potential Shortcomings of This Chapter

As I wrote in the beginning, my aim for this article was to offer some preliminary thoughts, which may serve as a point of departure for further considerations. Hermeneutic philosophy and its possible applications in psychotherapy are just too vast an area to be dealt with in such a relatively brief chapter.

So I expect that to everybody who has studied philosophy this chapter is obviously deficient since it only refers to a very small part of the hermeneutic tradition. This tradition can be traced back to the Ancient World, to the Middle Ages, and, in its modern form, to the 19th century. Well-informed readers will certainly miss the mention of names such as Schleiermacher (1996), Dilthey (1958), and Nietzsche (1964), as well as the names of important hermeneutic writers of the 20th century such as Betti (1967), Ricoeur (1974), Habermas (1982), Feyerabend (1995), Rorty (1979), Davidson (1984), Derrida (1976), and many others.

My preference of Gadamer springs from personal sources. He was one of the "grand old men" whom I met in my life and who deeply impressed me by the way they were as persons let alone by what they had to say. Even to him this chapter does not do justice. Too many important aspects of his philosophy have not been mentioned, — *horribile dictu*: — not even the famous "hermeneutic circle," which he had adapted from his teacher, Martin Heidegger.

Another serious shortcoming of this chapter has to do with the fact that many facets of the criticism of Gadamer's philosophy have been neglected. Except for Hirsch (and to him only in footnotes 7 and 10) I did not refer to any of Gadamer's critics, not even to his both famous and infamous discussion with Derrida at the Goethe-Institute in Paris, France, in April, 1981 (see Becker, 1981; Forget, 1984; Michelfelder & Palmer, 1989), which caused quite a stir. In addition, I have left out completely any discussion of the differences between understanding texts on the one hand (which is to what hermeneutic philosophy mostly refers) and understanding persons on the other hand. I have tried to avoid this discussion in that I have only tapped hermeneutic sources for ideas that I think can be transferred without theoretical problems to the understanding of persons.

Much remains to be done, if we want to draw on the hermeneutic literature and make use of it for our theory and practice of Gestalt therapy. However, I am sure that this philosophy can be very inspiring for us. I hope that this chapter has been able to offer the foretaste of a meal that promises to be delicious.

For me one of the most striking analogies between hermeneutic philosophy and Gestalt therapy theory can be found in the attitude that both of them favor: a well-cultivated uncertainty (see Staemmler, 1997; 2000). In this vein I would like to finish with a quote from Wittgenstein, who in his beautiful little book *On Certainty* warns us not to be impressed very much by the attitude of assurance. He wrote: "Certainty is *as it were* a tone of voice in which one declares how things are, but one does not infer from the tone of voice that one is justified" (1972, p. 6e — original italics).

References

Anderson, H. (2000). Reflections on and the appeals and challenges of postmodern psychologies, societal practice, and political life. In L. Holzman & J. Morss (Eds.), *Postmodern Psychologies, Societal Practice, and Political Life* (pp. 202-208). New York & London: Routledge.

Arkes, H. R. (1981). Impediments to accurate clinical judgment and possible ways to minimize their impact. *Journal of Consulting and Clinical Psychology 49*(3), 323-330.

Arlow, J. A. (1969). Motor behavior as nonverbal communication in analysis. *Journal of the American Psychoanalytic Association 17*, 960-963.

Arnold, W. (1999). The eclipse of reason: Is dialogue meeting dialectics a myth? – On Max Horkheimer, critical thinking, and some origins of Gestalt therapy. *The Gestalt Journal 22*(1), 37-44.

Atari, W. A. (1991). Gadamer's conception of hermeneutic understanding. *Dirasat, Series A, 18*(2), 25-50.

Bhabha, H. K. (1990). The other question: Difference, discrimination and the discourse of colonialism. In R. Ferguson, M. Gever, T. Minh-ha, & C. West (Eds.), *Out there: Marginalization and Contemporary Culture* (pp. 71-87). Cambridge, MA, & London: MIT Press.

Bakhtin, M. M. (1986). *Speech Genres and Other Late Essays - Edited by C. Emerson and M. Holquist.* Austin: University of Texas Press.

Barclay, M. W. (1993). The adequacy of hermeneutics in psycho-analysis and psychology. *Humanistic Psychologist 21*(1), 81-100.

Bauman, Z. (1978). *Hermeneutics and Social Science: Approaches to Understanding.* London: Hutchinson.

Becker, J. (1981). Begegnung: Gadamer und Lévinas – Der hermeneutische Zirkel und die Alteritas, ein ethisches Geschehen. Frankfurt/M. & Bern: Peter Lang.

Betti, E. (1967). *Allgemeine Auslegungslehre als Methodik der Geisteswissenschaften.* Tübingen: Mohr.

Bleicher, J. (1980). *Contemporary Hermeneutics: Hermeneutics as Method, Philosophy and Critique.* London et al.: Routledge & Kegan Paul.

Bruner, J. (1990). *Acts of Meaning.* Cambridge, MA & London: Harvard University Press.

Buber, M. (1958). *I and Thou.* New York: Scribner's Sons.

Buber, M. (1965). *The Knowledge of Man: A Philosophy of the Interhuman.* New York.: Harper Torchbooks.

Buytendijk, F. J. J. (1951). Zur Phänomenologie der Begegnung. *Eranos-Jahrbuch 19* (1950), 431-486.

Cavell, M. (1999). Knowledge, consensus and uncertainty. *International Journal of Psychoanalysis 80,* 1227-1235.

Chessick, R. D. (1990). Hermeneutics for psychotherapists. *American Journal of Psychotherapy 44*(2), 256-273.

Darley, J. M. (Ed.) (1998). *Attribution and Social Interaction: The legacy of Edward E. Jones.* Washington, DC: APA.

Darley, J. M., & Gross, P. H. (1983). A hypothesis-confirming bias in labelling effects. *Journal of Personality and Social Psychology 44,* 20-23.

Davidson, D. (1984). *Inquiries into Truth and Interpretation.* Oxford: Clarendon Press.

de Gelder, B. (1981). "I know what you mean, but if only I understood you . . ." In H. Parret & J. Bouveresse (Eds.), *Meaning and Understanding* (pp. 44-60). Berlin & New York: de Gruyter.

Derrida, J. (1976). *Die Schrift und die Differenz.* Frankfurt/M.: Suhrkamp.

Dilthey, W. (1958). *Gesammelte Schriften.* Stuttgart & Göttingen: Teubner; Vandenhoeck & Ruprecht.

Dutt, C. (Hg.) (1993). *Hans-Georg Gadamer im Gespräch.* Heidelberg: Winter.

Feyerabend, P. K. (1995). *Über Erkenntnis – Zwei Dialoge.* Frankfurt/M.: Fischer.

Forget, P. (1984). *Text und Interpretation – Deutsch-französische Debatte mit Beiträgen von J. Derrida, Ph. Forget, M. Frank, H.-G. Gadamer, J. Greisch und F. Laruelle.* München: Fink.

Frank, L. K. (1939). Time Perspectives. *Journal of Social Philosophy 4,* 293-312.

Gadamer, H.-G. (1974). Hermeneutik. In J. Ritter (Ed.), Historisches Wörterbuch der Philosophie (S. 1062-1074). Darmstadt: Wissenschaftliche Buchgesellschaft.

Gadamer, H.-G. (1984). Text und Interpretation. In P. Forget (Hg.), *Text und Interpretation — Deutsch-französische Debatte mit Beiträgen von J. Derrida, Ph. Forget, M. Frank, H.-G. Gadamer, J. Greisch und F. Laruelle* (pp. 24-55). München: Fink.

Gadamer, H.-G. (1989a). *Truth and Method — Second, Revised Edition.* New York: Crossroad.

Gadamer, H.-G. (1989b). Reply to Jacques Derrida. In D. P. Michelfelder & R. E. Palmer (Eds.), *Dialogue and deconstruction: The Gadamer-Derrida encounter* (pp. 55-57). Albany, NY: State University of New York Press.

Gadamer, H.-G. (1993). *Wahrheit und Methode — Ergänzungen, Register, Band II.* Tübingen: Mohr.

Gergen, K. J. (2000). From identity to relational politics. In L. Holzman & J. Morss (Eds.), *Postmodern Psychologies, Societal Practice, and Political Life* (pp. 130-150). New York & London: Routledge.

Grondin, J. (1982). *Hermeneutische Wahrheit? — Zum Wahrheitsbegriff Hans-Georg Gadamers.* Königstein: Hain.

Guignon, C. (1998). Narrative explanation in psychotherapy. *American Behavioral Scientist 41*(4), 558-577.

Habermas, J. (1982). *Zur Logik der Sozialwissenschaften — Fünfte, erweiterte Auflage.* Frankfurt/M.: Suhrkamp.

Heidegger, M. (1962). *Being and time.* San Francisco: Harper.

Heidegger, M. (1983). *Die Grundbegriffe der Metaphysik — Gesamtausgabe 29/30.* Frankfurt/M.: Klostermann.

Heraclitus (1979). *The Art and Thought of Heraclitus: An Edition of the Fragments with Translation and Commentary (C. H. Kahr, Ed.).* Cambridge: Cambridge University Press.

Hertz, M. (1928a). Wahrnehmungspsychologische Untersuchungen am Eichelhäher I. *Zeitschrift für vergleichende Physiologie 7*(1), 144-194.

Hertz, M. (1928b). Wahrnehmungspsychologische Untersuchungen am Eichelhäher II. *Zeitschrift für vergleichende Physiologie 7*(4), 617-656.

Hertz, M. (1929). Die Organisation des optischen Feldes bei der Biene I. *Zeitschrift für vergleichende Physiologie 8*(3-4), 693-748.

Hertz, M. (1930). Die Organisation des optischen Feldes bei der Biene II. *Zeitschrift für vergleichende Physiologie 11*(1), 107-145.

Hertz, M. (1931). Die Organisation des optischen Feldes bei der Biene III. *Zeitschrift für vergleichende Physiologie 14*(4), 629-674.

Hirsch, E. D. (1967). *Validity in interpretation.* New Haven & London: Yale University Press.

Horkheimer, M., & Adorno, T. W. (1972). *Dialectic of Enlightenment.* New York: Seabury Press.

Husserl, E. (1922). *Ideen zu einer reinen Phänomenologie und phänomenologischen Philosophie.* Tübingen: Niemeyer.

Husserl, E. (1962). *Phänomenologische Psychologie – Gesammelte Werke Bd. IX.* Den Haag: Nijhoff.

Köhler, W. (1933). Psychologische Probleme. Berlin: Julius Springer.

Lévinas, E. (1987). *Totalität und Unendlichkeit – Versuch über die Extoriorität.* Freiburg & München: Alber.

Lévinas, E. (1989). *Die Zeit und der Andere.* Hamburg: Meiner.

Lévinas, E. (1992). *Die Spur des Anderen – Untersuchungen zur Phänomenologie und Sozialphilosophie.* Freiburg & München: Alber.

Lewin, K. (1951). *Field Theory in Social Science: Selected Theoretical Papers* (D. Cartwright, Ed.). New York: Harper & Brothers.

Lord, C. G., Ross, L., & Lepper, M. R. (1979). Biased assimilation and attitude polarization: The effects of prior theories on subsequently considered evidence. *Journal of Personality and Social Psychology 37*, 2098-2109.

Lyotard, J.-F. (1993). *Die Phänomenologie.* Hamburg: Junius.

Marcel, G. (1992). *Metaphysisches Tagebuch 1915-1943 – Ausgewählt und herausgegeben von Siegfried Foelz.* Paderborn et al.: Schöningh.

Márquez, G. G. (1994). *Strange Pilgrims.* London & New York: Penguin.

Michelfelder, D. P., & Palmer, R. E. (Eds.) (1989). *Dialogue and Deconstruction: The Gadamer-Derrida Encounter.* Albany, NY: State University of New York Press.

Miller, M. V. (1990). Toward a psychology of the unknown. *The Gestalt Journal 13*(2), 23-41.

Morson, G. S. (Ed.) (1986). *Bakhtin: Essays and Dialogues on his Work.* Chicago & London: University of Chicago Press.

Müller, K. (1988). Gestalttheorie, Emergenztheorie und der Neofunktionalismus. *Gestalt Theory 10*(1), 46-56.

Nietzsche, F. (1964). *Sämtliche Werke in zwölf Bänden.* Stuttgart: Kröner.

Nisbett, R. E., & Ross, L. (1980). *Human Inference — Strategies and Shortcomings of Social Judgement.* Englewood Cliffs, NJ: Prentice Hall.

O'Shea, L. (2003). Reflection on Cornell: The erotic field. *British Gestalt Journal 12*(2), 105-110.

Perls, F. S. (1969a). *Gestalt Therapy Verbatim*. Moab, UT: Real People Press.

Perls, F. S. (1969b). *In and Out the Garbage Pail*. Lafayette, CA: Real People Press.

Perls, F. S. (1973). *The Gestalt Approach & Eye Witness to Therapy*. Palo Alto, CA: Science & Behavior Books.

Perls, F. S., Hefferline, H., & Goodman, P. (1951\1994). *Gestalt Therapy: Excitement and Growth in the Human Personality*. Highland, NY: The Gestalt Journal Press.

Perls, L., & Polster, M. (1992). Interpretation is . . . In E. W. L. Smith (Ed.), *Gestalt Voices* (p. 202). Norwood, NJ: Ablex..

Petzold, H. (2001). "Goodmansche" Gestalttherapie als "klinische Soziologie" konstruktiver Aggression? – Goodman, die Situation der Psychotherapeuten heute und eine Welt voller Aggression – Integrative und Gestalttherapeutische Aggressionstheorie angesichts von Terror, Gegenterror, Terrorismus (Teil 2*). Gestalt 42*, 35-58.

Reik, T. (1935). *Der überraschte Psychologe – Über Erraten und Verstehen unbewußter Vorgänge*. Leiden: Sijthoff's.

Reik, T. (1976). *Hören mit dem dritten Ohr – Die innere Erfahrung eines Psychoanalytikers*. Hamburg: Hoffmann & Campe.

Rennie, D. L. (2000). Grounded theory methodology as methodical hermeneutics. *Theory and Psychology 10*(4), 481-502.

Ricoeur, P. (1974). *Die Interpretation – Ein Versuch über Freud*. Frankfurt/M.: Suhrkamp.

Rombach, H. (1980). *Phänomenologie des gegenwärtigen Bewußtseins*. Freiburg & München: Alber.

Rorty, R. (1979). *Philosophy and the Mirror of Nature*. Princeton, NJ: Princeton University Press.

Sapriel, L. (1998). Can Gestalt therapy, self-psychology and intersubjectivity theory be integrated? *British Gestalt Journal 7*(1), 33-44.

Sartre, J.-P. (1964). *Marxismus und Existentialismus – Versuch einer Methodik*. Reinbek: Rowohlt.

Sartre, J.-P. (1997). *Die Transzendenz des Ego – Philosophische Essays 1931-1939*. Reinbek: Rowohlt.

Schleiermacher, F. (1996). *Schriften* – herausgegeben von A. Arndt. Frankfurt/M.: Deutscher Klassiker Verlag.

Schmitz, H. (1980). *Neue Phänomenologie*. Bonn: Bouvier.

Sontag, S. (1967). *Against Interpretation and Other Essays*. New York: Farrar, Straus & Giroux.

Spiegelberg, H. (1960). *The Phenomenological Movement – Vol. II*. Den Haag: Nijhoff.

Spinelli, E. (1996). *Demystifying Therapy*. London: Constable.

Sroufe, L. A. (1996). *Emotional Development: The Organization of Emotional Life in the Early Years*. Cambridge: Cambridge University Press.

Staemmler, F.-M. (1993). *Therapeutische Beziehung und Diagnose – Gestalttherapeutische Antworten*. München: Pfeiffer.

Staemmler, F.-M. (1997). Cultivated uncertainty: An attitude for Gestalt therapists. *British Gestalt Journal 6*(1), 40-48.

Staemmler, F.-M. (1999). Hermeneutische Ansätze in der klassischen Gestalttherapie. *Gestalt 36*, 43-60.

Staemmler, F.-M. (2000). Like a fish in water – Gestalt therapy in times of uncertainty. *Gestalt Review 4*(3), 205-218.

Staemmler, F.-M. (2002a). The here and now: A critical analysis. *British Gestalt Journal 11*(1), 21-32.

Staemmler, F.-M. (2002b). Hans-Georg Gadamer: An obituary. *International Gestalt Journal 25*(1), 129-131.

Stern, D. N. (1985). *The Interpersonal World of the Infant: A View from Psychoanalysis and Developmental Psychology*. New York: Basic Books.

Taureck, B. H. F. (2002). *Emmanuel Lévinas zur Einführung*. Hamburg: Junius.

Turk, D. C.; Salovey, P. (1985). Cognitive structures, cognitive processes, and cognitive behavior modification: Judgments and inferences of the clinician. *Cognitive Therapy and Research 9*(1), 19-33.

Voloshinov, V. N. (1929/1986). *Marxism and the Philosophy of Language*. (L. Matejka & I. R. Titunik, Trans.). Cambridge, MA: Harvard University Press.

Watzlawick, P. (1967). *Pragmatics of Human Communication: A Study of Interactional Patterns, Pathologies, and Paradoxes*. New York: Norton.

Whitehead, A. N. (1929). *Process and Reality: An Essay in Cosmology*. New York & London: Macmillan.

Wittgenstein, L. (1972). *On Certainty*. New York: Harper Torchbooks.

The Therapeutic Relationship in Gestalt Therapy

• • • • • • • • • • • •

Margherita Spagnuolo Lobb

Preliminary remarks on the setting:

Patient and therapist are seated in front of each other (with no table between them), the patient is free to adjust her/his distance and angle relative to the therapist. It is possible, especially in a group setting, to use cushions instead of chairs. Meetings normally take place once a week. The therapeutic contract provides, among other things, that the patient can leave therapy at any moment (after discussing this with the therapist): this is considered her/his right, despite the fact that it may be a choice not to face up to certain experiences. Particular attention is paid to the dreams the patient relates to the therapist, as well as to the movements, posture, and breathing, of both the therapist and the patient, since they define the implicit being-there, the *ground* of the relational situation. The therapist is defined not only as healer, but as fellow-voyager of the patient, in the sense that it is always the patient who guides how, and how much, to "plunge" into the therapeutic relationship. If the attention of the therapist is aimed at the *here-and-now* of the relationship, her/his treatment is centered on the *now-for-next*. The therapist's attention to the here-and-now is not intended in analytical terms: it's a way to consider the therapeutic relationship as a "real" relationship, which develops toward a therapeutic goal. The process of contact making and withdrawal that we observe is seen in itself, not for the sake of a past or external relationship that needs to be cured. The healing process is addressed to the actual contact between therapist and client. In order to support the spontaneity of contact making of the client, the therapist looks for the movement that has being repressed, therefore treatment is centered on the now-for-next.

Within the present phenomenological-relational trend, Gestalt therapy sees the therapeutic relationship as the occurring, the revealing of a co-creation between patient and therapist (Spagnuolo Lobb, 2006, 22; Robine, 2006). The value of the experience (*Erlebnis*) is set in opposition to the knowledge, the *creative adjustment* of the organism to sublimation as the only possibility of adjustment to the demands of the community, the self-regulation of the organism and holism to the necessity of control of the id over the ego.

This co-creation of the therapeutic experience is motivated – upheld and directed – by an intentionality, which for the Gestalt approach is always an intentionality of contact with the other. The term "contact" implies consideration of physiology in the experience: the previous interest of psychological sciences in mentalized experiences is firmly replaced by a phenomenological interest in the experience generated by the concrete nature of the senses. In this way, the experience is considered as a whole, rather than as a product of mind. In Gestalt therapy we speak of "excitement," referring to the energy perceived in the physiology of the experience of relationship (Frank, 2001; Kepner, 1997). This excitation upholds the organismic experience to go towards the other, but it may also block this movement, in the event that it is transformed into anxiety. Anxiety is in fact defined as excitation without the support of oxygen. Hence the concept of "intentionality of contact" has also to do with consideration of the unique and unitary nature of the experience. Gestalt therapy, which as is well known works on the process, mainly observes the implicit relational patterns with which the person enters into contact with the environment (the "how" of the therapeutic relationship rather than its content), starting from breathing and all the bodily processes of relationship, up to the relational meaning of the dreams related to the therapist.

In the current cultural trend, centered as it is on relationship, Gestalt therapy is rediscovering its original intuition of the experience that occurs at the contact boundary, in that "between" the I and the you. From the paradigm of self-regulating subjectivity of the 1950's, we have moved to a paradigm of reality considered as something which is never external to a happening, but arises from the relationship itself, which pertains indissolubly to its fabric. This perspective allows us to step outside the intrapsychic viewpoint which sees treatment as a process linked to the satisfaction (or sublimation) of needs, to enter fully into the post-modern perspective in which the power of truth has been replaced by the truth of the relationship.

Hence the therapeutic relationship is seen as a *real experience* which arises from, and has its own story, in the space subsisting between patient and therapist, not as the result of projections of transferal patterns from the patient's past. The relational dimension comes before the interior dimension, or at least *cannot be explained from the intrapsychic experience.*

Our phenomenological soul reminds us of the impossibility of stepping outside the field (or situation) in which we find ourselves, and gives us instruments which allow us to function while remaining within the limit imposed by the "situationed" experience. The founders of Gestalt therapy from the beginning proposed the "contextual" method (Perls et al., 1951), which long before Gadamer, proposed a hermeneutic circularity between the reader and their book: you cannot understand the book (or the other) without a Gestalt mentality, and you cannot have a Gestalt mentality without reading the book *à la* Gestalt (or being with the other *à la* Gestalt) (Sichera, 2001).

Thus we can say that the therapeutic relationship represents a way in which the patient implicitly gives the therapist (and her/himself) the opportunity to remake a relational history, restoring to certain intentionalities of contact which still withheld the possibility of a complete, spontaneous development. It is in fact, in the therapeutic relationship that the possibility occurs of bringing to completion intentionalities of contact that allow the patient to perceive her/himself and situations differently, to feel more free and able to make her/his own contribution to relationships and hence to the world in which s/he lives.

An example may clarify the concept. A female patient is moved speaking to me of positive things she has never said to her mother, and of how she feels closed since she moved to a different town. On the other hand she says she voluntarily chose a safe distance from her mother, one which would guarantee, that she would not have an overdose of emotions. As she tells me this, she lifts her feet from the floor. I point out to her that in removing that contact she is removing from herself the possibility of a bodily support for the emotions, and that in this way she is "taking her distance" from me, as she does from her mother. What emotions is she now avoiding *with me*? When she takes her distance removing the physiological support of the contact of her feet with the ground, she makes herself unable to contain her emotions. At my invitation she keeps her feet on the ground, looks at me, breathes and, feeling moved, manages to tell me how important I am for her. We have begun a new story at the boundary of our contact, which will change her relational patterns outside therapy too.

Hermeneutic Aspects of the Therapeutic Situation

Certain epistemological principles of Gestalt therapy seem to me to presently define the peculiar nature of the approach to the others. These are: the fundamental role given to the ability to deconstruct the environment; the unitary nature of the field and the demarcation of the contact boundary in the figure/background dynamic; and the choice of aesthetic values.

The role of aggression in the social context.

According to the Gestalt perspective, individual and social group are not separate entities, but parts of the same unit in mutual interaction, so that the tension which may exist between them is not to be considered the expression of an irresolvable conflict, but the necessary movement within a field which tends towards integration and growth. Fritz Perls' intuition on childhood development, which gives value to the ability to deconstruct as implicit in the development of the teeth (*dental aggression*, Perls, 1969), is based on a conception of human nature capable of self-regulation, certainly more positive than the mechanistic conception in force between the 19th and 20th centuries (a concept with which Freudian theory too was imbued). The child's ability to bite, supports and accompanies her ability to deconstruct reality. This spontaneous aggressive power, which is positive, has a function of survival, and allows the individual to arrive actively at what in the environment can satisfy her/his needs, deconstructing it according to her/his curiosity. The accent placed by Gestalt therapy on relationality thus has an anthropological worth in considering self-regulation (between deconstructing and rebuilding) of the organism/ environment relationship and a socio-political worth in considering creativity the "normal" outcome of the relationship between individual and society. *Creative adjustment* is the result of this spontaneous power of survival which allows the individual to differentiate her/himself from the social context, but also to be fully and significantly part of it. Human behavior, even when pathological, is considered a creative adjustment.

Here is a clinical example:

A member of an international training group comes to work with me during an experiential demonstration. She tells me she developed a sort of depression since she moved from one city to another in Russia. She even fainted once, and felt a great sense of loneliness. While she speaks, she seems depressed, rather than scared. She moved to this new town with good reasons, and she did it deliberately, in order to attend a university master's program which she likes. Her symptom seems inexplicable. I ask her to tell me something about how she lives, how come she has chosen to live alone, and things like that. She accepts and while she speaks she strongly scratches her forearm. She explains that she sometimes feels that itch, probably on account of an allergy. She continues to talk. I've been touched by the energy which accom-panied that gesture of scratching, so different from the depressed tone of her voice. Therefore I ask her to scratch my forearm, instead of hers. She starts to laugh, and seems very amused. She does it and this new gesture seems to give her a new strength. Then she continues to talk of herself, and the depressed tone is back. I ask her to scratch my forearm again and continue to talk of herself while doing it. Again, her tone changes completely: she looks amused, with much more energy. This time she connects this change with a relational process in her life. She understands that by scratching herself she adjusts creatively: thanks to it she can express her energy and prevent the others from receiving it at the same time. As a matter of fact she had to repress her energetic style of contact in order to adjust to the environment she grew up in. This auto-genic system isn't however acceptable any more: the symptom gives her the experience of discomfort and the connected need for change. By asking her to scratch my forearm instead of hers, I have supported her creative adjustment and the energy implicit in a symptom which allowed her in some way to keep her own energy, and at the same time I have given her the relational re-cognition she wanted ("You can scratch my forearm: I can bear your energy."). I gave her in this way the permission to identify with her own energy even in contact-making with others. The client ends this work affirming that now she knows what to do when she feels depressed: she can reach someone with her aggressive energy, she can scratch someone else, instead of herself!

Tension at contact and the formation of the contact boundary.

The therapist takes as background of her/his being in relationship a context of fundamental excitement to contact, rather than one of defense to be disrupted and hence of fulfillment of the "sense of reality." The *contact boundary* is the place where the self unfolds, that function of the human organism which expresses its capability/ability to come into contact with its own environment and to withdraw from it. Thus the self is conceived as a process, a "contact-function," and unfolds, "happens" in the place where organism and environment meet, where the senses are at work (Perls et al., 1951; Spagnuolo Lobb, 2001b). The self thus expresses both the contacting of, and its differentiating itself from, the environment. This procedural, holistic "protension" is constantly noted by the therapist who is focused on the *now-for-next*, on the support of the patient's movement "in gestation." The present emphasis on this epistemological aspect has led to a revision of the famous Gestalt technique of the empty chair which, as is well known, utilizes the externalization of an internal dialogue to increase the awareness of interior dynamics. Considering rather the central importance of the developing of the relationship between patient and therapist, the technique of the empty chair is replaced by saying *to the therapist* – instead of to the chair – what the patient would say to the person or to the part of her/himself placed on the chair (Müller, 1993). This change enables us to bring into the core of the situation, into the field of the present relationship, the relational block, the relational pattern which covers (prevents from feeling) the anxiety linked to the unexpressed unfocused excitation.

A psychotherapy based on esthetic values.

The concept of *awareness*, so different from that of conscious-ness (cf. Bloom, 2006), expresses the being present to the senses in the process of contacting the environment, identifying oneself spontaneously and harmoniously with the intentionality of contact. Awareness is a quality of contact and represents its "normality" (Spagnuolo Lobb, 2004). Neurosis, in contrast, is the maintenance of isolation (in the organism-environment field) by means of a heightening of the function of *conscious-ness* or of a decontextualized confluence.

This concept gives the therapist a mentality with which to be present at the contact boundary with the patient, and enables her/him to avoid facile diagnostic readings of the other. Only faith in the intrinsic ability of the human being to do the best thing possible at a given moment and in a given situation, together with an ongoing *dialogical diagnosis* that allows us to evaluate and respond to the patient's choice, can direct the Gestalt therapist towards being in the therapeutic relationship without depending on diagnostic patterns external to it. This is the kind of awareness that enables her/him to find a new therapeutic solution every time.

The *clinical consequence* of these three hermeneutic aspects of the therapeutic relationship is summarized in the attitude of the therapist who feels part of the situation, maintains the aggressiveness of differentiation, casts her/himself in the treatment role, stays at the contact boundary with the senses, rather than with mental categories. Furthermore, the therapist asks: "How do I contribute to the patient's experience at this moment?" For example: the patient tells the therapist of dreaming about an insurmountable wall the night before the session. The therapist wonders: "In what way was I or the situation an insurmountable wall for this patient during the previous session?"

This is not a matter of referring to the transferal logic of projection, but of the figure/background dynamic. I (therapist) ask myself why it should be that of all the many possible stimuli that the patient can gather from the background of my presence, s/he extrapolates certain stimuli and not others. The hypothesis I form is that that particular stimulus is attached to a relational need that the patient is motivated to solve. The "projection" (better called perception) of the patient always has a hook in the therapist, whose personal characteristics are considered necessary aspects for the co-creation of the relationship.

Here is an example: A patient says, "You don't give a damn about me. I'm never going to depend on you again," to the therapist who has not answered her/his insistent calls late the previous evening. The therapist's experiential background is still in the pleasure of closeness experienced during the last session with this patient, who had at last managed to experience warmth in the relationship. This situation (often generated by patients diagnosed with borderline disorder) triggers anger in the therapist: a sense of being manipulated by the patient's expectation that she will be listened to on the telephone late in the evening, and of frustration because the patient seems not to grasp or assimilate the positive experiences of the previous session. Rather than trust exclusively to the anger that such provocation arouses in the therapist, following the old humanistic mentality which stressed trust in the therapist's emotion (rebelling in his/her turn against the presumed neutrality claimed for psychoanalysis), the Gestalt therapist today asks her/himself questions referring to the field and the situation.

For example: "What is the background from which the expression of these words arises?" Certainly the patient expressed during the previous session the desire for closeness, and fear that such closeness experienced with a significant person would immediately be followed by coldness or withdrawal, a behavior that is in conflict with the spontaneous need that emerges in the person. The Gestalt therapist's faith in the intentionality of contact leads her/him to think and feel in the patient's words a request for contact, not just a need for separation. A good translation of the patient's words would therefore be: "Why didn't you answer the telephone last night? I thought you'd given me to understand that I can count on you. Where were you last night? You're just like everyone else, I'm afraid I can't trust you."

Faced with the patient's actual words, the therapist might therefore answer: "I'm touched by the dignity with which you say that." Understanding the words in terms of a challenge, and thus making the therapeutic choice to "train" the patient as to who makes the rules in the relationship (no late-night calls, no therapy outside the setting, etc.) would fail to grasp this patient's relational need, namely, to be confirmed as having the right to advance, and withdraw, to protect her/himself in the relationship.

The Relationship and
the Aim of Psychotherapy

The aim of treatment is that the patient recover spontaneity in contacting the environment. According to Gestalt therapy, what is being treated is not rational understanding and hence control of the disorder, but something that has to do with procedural and esthetic aspects. Treatment consists in helping the patient to live fully, respecting her/his innate ability to regulate her/himself in the relationship, and this not only on a verbal level, but above all at the level of spontaneous activation of the neuro-corporeal structures governing relational life. Spontaneity is the art of integrating the ability to choose deliberately (*ego-function*) with two kinds of experiential background: acquired bodily certainties (*id-function*) and social— or relational—definitions of the self (*personality-function*).[1] We are a long way from a concept of spontaneity that is confused with that of impulsivity (typical of Freudian anthropology), in that, differently than impulsivity, in spontaneity there is the ability to "see" the other. We are equally far from Rousseau's idea of childlike spontaneity: it is quite another thing than art – which is learned over the years – to integrate all experiences, including those which are painful, in a personal harmonious style, one that is fully present to the senses, which are the physiological means by which we enter into relationship.

An example of the child's spontaneous ability of contact may clarify in practical terms what I mean by "restoring spontaneity." That the newborn child knows how to suck is a general ability, a function indeed, whereas what it sucks is the content, and is variable. It is the ability to suck (like biting, later, or sitting up, etc.) that makes the child enter into contact with the world, which generates her/his spontaneity, or lack of spontaneity. In fact, if the child is in some way forbidden to suck, i.e., to spontaneously carry out the appropriate function, s/he must compensate by doing something else in order to enter into contact and resolve with a lack of spontaneity the need that generated the act of sucking. Certainly, the fact that the child sucks poor-quality milk will influence her/his experience. We

---

[1] These are procedural aspects of the self. For a study of the theory of the self in Gestalt therapy, cf. Spagnuolo Lobb, 2001.

Gestalt therapists are not interested in a judgment on the goodness of the milk, but rather in understanding how the child's organism reacted to the poor-quality milk, i.e., how s/he creatively adjusted her/his functioning to the poor-quality milk: in a word, what spontaneity s/he has lost. This enables us to focus on how the organism can be supported in order to retrieve the function of sucking with a certain spontaneity. What helps the child to retrieve spontaneity of sucking is not knowing that the milk was of poor quality, but having the experience of the possibility of returning to sucking different milk, of rediscovering her/his *functional spontaneity* of sucking with a new creative adjustment, a new organization of the experience of the organism/environment field (Spagnuolo Lobb, 2001a, 91 ff.).

Hence what changes in the Gestalt therapeutic process is the *perception of the contact boundary* between the patient and the therapist. It is a change which takes place not only in the patient, but also in the therapist; in effect it is a co-creation of a new contact boundary, a new experience reaching towards the future, not the reparative explication of past experiences.

The ultimate aim of the therapeutic relationship is that the patient feels interested in life, with permission to be creative in the social group to which s/he belongs (Spagnuolo Lobb-Amendt Lyon, 2003; Polster, 1987). This is applied not only to the individual setting, but to that of the couple, in which the partners experience feeling "at home" with each other, and thus accepted in their attempt to reach the other, whether a member of the family or of the group, in which the aim is that each person feel unique and at the same time an integral part of the group, that s/he feel recognized by the group and allowed to make her/his own creative contribution to the group.

The Development
of the Therapeutic Relationship:
Gestalt Therapy Praxis

It is certainly not the purpose of this section to summarize Gestalt praxis in a few lines. For a more systematic treatment, see Polster & Polster (1973), Yontef (1993), Spagnuolo Lobb (1992; 2003). Here I will simply provide what one might call an icon of Gestalt work.

This approach looks at process before content. This implies, on the one hand, consideration of phases, on the other the identification of a unit of time, which we call the episode of contact. Each episode is made up of a before, a during and an after. The phenomenology of the encounter for a Gestalt therapist develops following the phases of fore-contact, of contact/ orientation, of contact/manipulation, of full contact, and of post-contact (Perls et al., 1951). During these phases, the self of the patient and that of the therapist are mobilized at the contact boundary, working to acquire the novelty and integrate it. The relational block, experienced as a block in the spontaneity of making contact with the therapist, may be dissolved thanks to the support given by the therapist at the right moment, when the *ground* is ready for full contact, when the patient's awareness can provide the appropriate support to experience in a new, spontaneous manner the contact boundary with the therapist, to whom the patient entrusts the possibility of remaking a profound relational experience, and the awareness of the therapist can support the energy, the excitation of the patient directed to the fulfillment of the need for full contact with her/him. An example can be that of a therapeutic relationship with a psychotic patient, who is in the last stages of her therapy. She says to the therapist that she feels excited by their encounters, like a little girl, that she doesn't know whether she has to fear this excitement or not, that this excitement is a new feeling, which might become anxiety or a light, amusing experience. The therapist in this case – since s/he knows that the patient is much more aware now and can be supported by her id-function and personality-function – invites the patient to experience this excitement at their contact boundary, while at the beginning of the treatment it would have been inappropriate to fully experience this (anxious making) excitement.

This basic process of the development of the episode of contact can be applied – like a fractal – both to the therapeutic session and to the whole relationship. In the whole therapeutic relationship the being-with of the therapist and of the patient creates a field in which change is possible: supporting the development of the self at the contact boundary in order to obtain the spontaneous (non anxious) fulfillment of the intentionality of contact inherent in the patient's request for treatment.

The therapist's ability to create a context in which the patient can develop her/his own integrity is enacted by means of a dance between therapist and patient (Hycner & Jacobs, 1995). It is not the technique used by an expert on another person who is asking for help, but the co-creation of a contact boundary in which the values, the personalities, the personal ways of dealing with life play a fundamental part. They are two people who together find possibilities of fulfilling interrupted intentionalities. It is the dance that the therapist, with all her/his knowledge and humanity, and the patient, with all her/his pain and desire to get well, create in order to rebuild the *ground* on which the life of the relationship rests, the sense of safety in the territory and in the other, and hence letting go in intimacy.

What are the Challenges for the Development of the Therapeutic Relationship in Gestalt Therapy?

Our culture is undergoing rapid developments, and our patients too are changing rapidly. The patients of ten years ago are very different from those of today. The narcissistic society (Lasch, 1971) has given way to a technological society (Galimberti, 1999), which has by now developed into what has been called the "liquid society" (Bauman, 2000). The social feeling is becoming increasingly "liquid:" it may take on many forms and at the same time has neither containment nor structure. For example, children cannot stay still at school, they have to keep moving all the time (sometimes, with their enormous bodies, they look like rolling mountains), they are incapable of concentrating and breathing: their breath has no container, there is no experience of an entire body that contains the emotions. The function which a few decades ago was fulfilled by the recital of prayers at the beginning of the day could be fulfilled today by focusing on bodily sensations, on breathing and the emotions. This basic experience would enable children to stay in the classroom with a better contained sense of self.

Patients today are "liquid" too. They suffer from disturbances that have to do with the lack of the *ground* of acquired contacts and experiences (panic attacks, PTSD, eating disorders, serious psychopathies). Their experience is characterized by a lack of relational support and consequent lack of self-support. If some decades ago aggressiveness was linked to the self-affirmation of the individual and hence was seen as a function of independence from authoritarian figures, today aggressiveness is part of a certain "liquidity" of relationships, a rapidly "mutating" system. One may do anything in a moment of aggressiveness; one may even kill.

What is missing in our society is fore-contact: being in the relationship starting from the containment of chaos. What is missing is the taken-for-granted safety that represents the *ground* of our experiences. Without the sense of solidity of the *ground* there cannot be a defined figure. The therapeutic relationship must be capable of containing the chaos that characterizes the beginning of every experience, and must be based, as Stern et al. (2000) maintain, on the implicit relational knowledge, on procedural and esthetic aspects, capable of building the *ground* of taken-for-granted certainties from which the figure can emerge distinctly and powerfully, with that appeal that characterizes the harmony of opposites in the figure/background dynamic.

References

Bauman, Z. (2002). *Modernità liquida*. Roma-Bari: Laterza (or. ed. 2000).

Bloom, D. (2006). Awareness and Consciousness, unpublished manuscript.

Frank, R. (2001). *Body of Awareness*. Cambridge, MA: GestaltPress.

Galimberti, U. (1999). *Psiche e techné*. Milano: Feltrinelli.

Hycner, R. & Jacobs, L. (1995). *The Healing Relationship in Gestalt Therapy: A Dialogic-self Psychological Approach*. Highland, NY: Gestalt Journal Press.

Kepner, J. I. (1997), *Body Process*. Cambridge, MA: Gestalt Institute of Cleveland Press.

Lasch, C. (1981). *La Cultura del Narcisismo*. Milano: Bompiani (or. ed.1971).

Müller, B. (1993). Isadore From's Contribution to the Theory and Practice of Gestalt Therapy. *Studies in Gestalt Therapy* 2(1), 7-21.

Perls, F. S. (1942/1969). *Ego, Hunger and Aggression*. NY: Vintage Books.

Perls, F., Hefferline, R., & Goodman, P. (1951). *Gestalt Therapy: Excitement and Growth in the Human Personality.* NY: Julian Press.

Polster, E. (1987). *Every Person's Life is Worth a Novel.* NY: Norton.

Polster, E. & Polster, M. (1973). *Gestalt Therapy Integrated: Contours of Theory and Practice.* NY: Vintage Books.

Robine, J. M. (2006). *Il Rivelarsi del sé nel Contatto.* Milano: Angeli.

Spagnuolo Lobb, M. (1992). Specific Support in the Interruptions of Contact. *Studies in Gestalt Therapy* 1(1), 43-51.

Sichera, A. (2001). A confronto con Gadamer: Per una epistemologia ermeneutica della Gestalt. In M. Spagnuolo Lobb (Ed.). *Psicoterapia della Gestalt. Ermeneutica e Clinica* (pp.17-41). Milano: Angeli.

Spagnuolo Lobb, M. (Ed.) (2001a). *Psicoterapia della Gestalt. Ermeneutica e clinica.* Milano: Angeli (Spanish transl: Gedisa, 2002, French transl: L'Exprimerie, 2004).

Spagnuolo Lobb, M. (2001b). From the Epistemology of Self to Clinical Specificity of Gestalt Therapy. In J. M. Robine (Ed.). *Contact and Relationship in a Field Perspective* (pp. 49-65). Bordeaux: L'Exprimerie.

Spagnuolo Lobb, M. (2003). Therapeutic meeting as improvisational co-creation. In M. Spagnuolo Lobb & N. M. Amendt-Lyon (Eds.), *Creative License: The Art of Gestalt Therapy* (pp. 37-50). Vienna & New York:Springer.

Spagnuolo Lobb, M. (2004). L'awareness dans la pratique post-moderne de la Gestalt-therapie. *Gestalt* 27, 41-58 (in Spanish (2005): La consciencia inmediata en la pràctica post-moderna de la Terapia Gestalt. *Revista de Terapia Gestalt* 25, 24-33; tin Italian (2005): La consapevolezza nella prassi post-moderna della Gestalt Therapy. In P. L. Rigetti and M. Spagnuolo Lobb (Eds.). *Psicoterapia della Gestalt. Percorsi teorico-clinici* (pp. 59-71). Padova: Upsel Domeneghini Editore.

Spagnuolo Lobb, M. (Ed.) (2006). *L'implicito e L'esplicito in Psicoterapia. Atti del Secondo Congresso della Psicoterapia Italiana.* Milano: Angeli.

Spagnuolo Lobb, M., Amendt-Lyon, N. (Eds.) (2003). *Creative License: The Art of Gestalt Therapy.* Vienna & NY: Springer.

Stern, D., Bruschweiler-Stern, N., Harrison, A., Lyons-Ruth, K., Morgan, A., Nahum, J., Sander, L., Tronick, E. (2000). Lo sviluppo come metafora della relazione. *Quaderni di Gestalt* *30*(31), 6-21.

Yontef, G. M. (1993). *Awareness, Dialogue and Process. Essays on Gestalt Therapy*. Highland, NY: The Gestalt Journal Press.

Attunement and Optimal Responsiveness[1]

• • • • • • • • • • •

Lynne Jacobs

Background of this chapter

In January of 1995 I graduated from my therapeutic training program at the Institute of Contemporary Psychoanalysis in Los Angeles. I had spent three wonderful, intense years studying psychoanalysis with other eager, intelligent, creative classmates. During those three years (and the years since, during which I have taught a course called, "Emotional process and present-centered interactions") I have engaged in various projects aimed at cross-cultural sharing between contemporary psychoanalysis and Gestalt therapy. The theory section of this paper (with a

---

[1] Sections of this chapter were first published in: Bacal, ed. (1998) *Optimal Responsiveness: How Therapists Heal Their Patients, Jason Aronson.* Reprinted here with permission from Jason Aronson. The case study was first published in the International Gestalt Journal as, "The inevitable intersubjectivity of selfhood." (2005) International Gestalt Journal, 28:1, pp. 43-70.

different case example) was my graduation thesis. It will be obvious to you, the reader, that this chapter's original intended audience was psychoanalysts. I have decided to present it largely unchanged so that you can get a feel for the kinds of conversations that I, as a Gestalt therapist, have been having with my psychoanalytic colleagues. This paper also contains ideas that — while being presented in a somewhat dated manner of subject and object — are still being developed, refined and expanded in our current conversations about the relational perspective in Gestalt therapy.

For instance, the very notion of affect attunement is controversial, has undergone a more relationally-oriented reassessment, and the term itself should be changed to "emotional attunement" instead of "affect attunement." The term needs changing because "affect" refers primarily to biological arousal, whereas emotion refers to more complex meanings than the arousal itself.

The reassessment is that attunement was first described as something one did for another, and now it is being understood as an on-going, mutual, reciprocal process of being-with another. The patient helps the therapist while they work to make sense together, in that the patient is also endeavoring to understand the therapist's communication, often through an attunement process that operates in the background.

The controversy is that sometimes attunement is faulted as if it suggests that the therapist abandons her own world of experience and meaning in order to attune to the patient's world of meanings. I argue in my paper below for something quite different, in that I do not believe that I can be attuned to another without my own-full-bodied participation in listening. Attuned listening also needs to be differentiated from responsiveness, and I am arguing in this chapter that responsiveness that is emergent from attuned listening may well be different from responses that emerge from listening from outside the patient's frame of reference. This assertion in itself is probably not in dispute, but there may well be those who disagree with the degree to which I privilege listening from within the patient's frame of reference.

Introduction

Psychoanalytic theories that purport to embody the paradigm shift to a post-Cartesian perspective on development and treatment are exploring many dimensions of relatedness that may inhere in the consulting room. A generally neglected dimension is that of subject-subject relating. In subject-subject relating, the subjective worlds of *both* participants are considered meaningful to *each* participant. That is, each participant in an interaction is concerned with "otherness."

Intersubjective systems theorists[2] have not yet developed a theory of "otherness," despite having asserted strongly that all facets of development and living are inherently social – specifically "intersubjective" – processes. As with self-psychology theorists, they refer to the needed "other" only in terms of the self-regulating functions the other performs by listening and responding in an empathically attuned[3] manner. Such a

[2] Intersubjective systems theory has many contributors at this point, but is most widely known as originating with Robert Stolorow, George Atwood. A foundational concept of IST is that all experience is an emergent phenomenon of the human context in which we are embedded. Our experiential worlds are shaped continually by the interhuman world in which we live, whether or not we are aware of the shaping.

[3] Empathy is a listening perspective, one in which the therapist attempts to comprehend the patients world of meanings from within the patient's perspective. Attunement—resonance and sensitivity to the

description refers only to the meanings and functions of the other as an *object*. The meanings and functions of the other as a *subject* have not yet been elaborated. Intersubjective systems theory has much to contribute to understanding subject-subject relating by elaborating the developmental longings for, and meanings of, the "other." This paper is a beginning exploration.

Arguments abound from various sources that being able to contact another as a subject is a developmental necessity. From infant research (Stern, 1985; Lichtenberg, 1989) comes hypotheses about emotional sharing and other phenomena of what they refer to as "intersubjective relatedness"[4] as being central to the development of a sense of self. Intersubjective relatedness makes possible the experience of having a shareable emotional life, the development of a sense of belonging, and the development of the capacity to understand and relate empathically with others. From modern psychoanalysis, the voices of Hoffman (1992), and Aron (1991) have recently joined those of earlier advocates for the centrality of subject-subject relating, many of whom can trace their roots back to Ferenczi's influence. From the realm of philosophy, Martin Buber spoke eloquently of the necessity of "I-Thou" relating for the development of one's awareness of one's humanity.

In fact, Buber's philosophy, called the "philosophy of dialogue," provides a suitable philosophical underpinning for

---

patient's emergence emotional experience—is one of the processes through which empathic understanding develops.

[4] "Intersubjective relatedness" is different from the intersubjectivity of "intersubjective systems theory." Daniel Stern's concept of intersubjective relatedness refers to the developmental achievement of the capacity to recognize that others have their own subjectivity that may be different from yours. He uses the example of a baby suddenly showing a capacity to follow a mother's pointing finger instead of looking at the finger. This suggests that a baby understands intention, which is an aspect of subjectivity.

intersubjective systems theory. Atwood and Stolorow (1984) looked to existentialist philosophers for such an underpinning and found them lacking, largely because the existentialists were embedded in the isolated "monadic mind" perspective. But Atwood and Stolorow did not examine Buber's philosophy and Buber has some of the same criticisms of the other existentialists that Atwood and Stolorow raised.

Buber, in a quote almost forty years before there were intersubjective self psychologists, could be easily mistaken for one; 'He can know the *wholeness* of the person and through it the wholeness of *man* only when he does not leave his *subjectivity* out and does not remain an untouched observer [1965 p.124]'

....

In regard to the label 'existentialist,' it should be noted that though Buber's philosophy of dialogue was certainly within the broad thrust of existential thought, he did not view his philosophy as 'existentialist,' in the vein of Heidegger's or Sartre's outlooks. He criticized most of the existentialists because in their philosophies individual existence often was overemphasized at the expense of human interexistence – there was little room left for the possibility of genuine dialogue and relatedness between persons. Buber was primarily concerned with an inter-subjective existentialism, or what he preferred to call the 'interhuman' dimension of existence (Hycner & Jacobs, 1995, pp. 115/116).

There are some striking similarities between Buber's "philosophy of dialogue" and intersubjective systems theory. In both systems of thought, "self" and "other" are an indissoluble unit. Intersubjective systems theory posits that one's sense of self is an emergent phenomenon of intersubjective relatedness. In a very similar vein, Buber says one's selfhood emerges in what he calls "genuine relations" with others, often referred to as "I-Thou" meetings (1970). His entire philosophy is a radical affirmation of "self-in-relation" as the only meaningful characterization of human existence. For instance, in writing about psychological problems, he says, " sicknesses of the soul are sicknesses of relationship (1967, p. 150)." That is a poetic precursor to Stolorow, Brandchaft and Atwood's (1987) assertion that such pathological phenomena as borderline states are emergent phenomena of an intersubjective field rather than solely the property of the subject.

Another similarity between the philosophy of dialogue and intersubjective systems theory is that the epistemologies of both theories eschew efforts to describe "objective" knowledge. In Buber's thinking, I-It and I-Thou relationships are phenomenal events, having no "objective" reality that can be assessed by an outside observer. Those relationships can be understood only from within the perspective of the participants.

Another crucial similarity between the philosophy of dialogue and intersubjective systems theory is that Buber believed quite firmly that for a genuine dialogue to occur – and only genuine dialogue promotes the emergence of selfhood – the ground of the dialogue must be an immersion in the subjectivity of the other. He called this immersion "inclusion" (1965). Buber defined inclusion in therapy in this way: "The therapist must feel the other side, the patient's side of the relationship, as a bodily touch to know how the patient feels it" (1967. p.173). Inclusion means to enter into the world of the other as the other experiences it. He described in evocative language, the stance of empathic inquiry that has been explicated in self psychology and intersubjective systems theory. Buber claimed that inclusion is the basic scaffolding on which genuine dialogue in therapy stands. He accorded it the same central place that empathic inquiry holds in self psychology and intersubjective systems theory. However, Buber emphasizes an additional dimension of dialogue that he believes to be a necessary companion to inclusion; the presence of the therapist as an "other." I agree with this premise, that subject-subject relating is a necessary companion for empathic inquiry. It is the context within which the empathic inquiry unfolds.

In this paper I will argue that the subjectivity of the therapist as an "other" is an important dimension of the developmental process of therapy. Subject-subject relating is different from the usual psychoanalytic conception of selfobject relatedness. Our attention is drawn not just to the self-regulating, self-restorative or self-enhancing function that is being served, but also to the fact that such functions are being served by one who is a distinct other person. Thus the therapist does not only serve selfobject needs for the patient; she is also an "other" who can be met and known. Through meeting and knowing the "otherness" of the same therapist who serves selfobject functions, the patient develops a fuller apprehension of the world of human relatedness, and a fuller sense of his own selfhood.

While I have found Martin Buber's philosphy of dialogue to be a useful theoretical support for stretching intersubjective systems theory into the arena of "otherness," I have found Howard Bacal's clinical theory and method of "optimal responsiveness" to be a useful guidepost for understanding clinical interactions. For if the experience of subject-subject relating is necessary for self-development, the therapist who is open, in principle, to the patient's wish for engagement with the therapist-as-subject will have the potential to respond to the patient's developmental strivings in a facilitative manner. To be able to respond, the therapist needs an understanding of clinical interaction that can include the therapist's presence as an other. Optimal responsiveness, which has emerged from self psychology and intersubjective systems theory, provides the necessary framework.

The impetus for my interest in this topic derives in part from my own experiences as a patient, as well as from my experiences as a therapist. I kept encountering this simple experiential fact from my experiences as a patient; whatever deeply moving, facilitative selfobject experiences I had with my therapists and analysts, the transformative power of these interactive events resided – it seems to me – in the fact that they were offered voluntarily, by separate other people who willingly engaged their own subjectivity with mine, and used their subjectivity as a tool to serve my development. My awareness of this dimension – the otherness of the therapist – was crucial to rendering the selfobject experiences meaningful to me.

To date, the literature of intersubjective systems theory does not reflect my own experience as a clinician and as a patient. Intersubjective systems theory does not elaborate upon the developmental necessity of encountering the other as a subject. It is true that the literature is peppered with clear assertions that the consulting room is an intersubjective arena wherein reciprocal mutual influence shapes the experience of both participants. Stolorow et al. do not ignore the fact that the therapist is a subject as well as an object. They point out that the therapist, through her own subjectivity, is a co-constructor of the selfobject and repetitive transferences (1987). Nowhere, however, do they suggest that the patient may seek out, and *need* awareness of the therapist as a subject in her own right in order for his development to proceed. To date, with rare exceptions (Fosshage 1995, Shane and Shane, 1989), therapeutic references to the therapist's subjectivity address only the potential problems associated with the therapist's lack of ability to "decenter" from her own perspective. I believe that the therapist's subjectivity is also a positive ingredient in the patient's development.

An example of where intersubjective systems theory falls just short of appreciating how the therapist's "otherness" plays a positive role in the therapy process is in the area of affect attunement. I think the methodology of affect attunement has effects on two levels of communication with a patient, only one of which is explicitly addressed in the theory. On the one hand, it is the ground from which a sense of affect validity, articulation, and integration occurs. We have seen that such integration enhances and strengthens the patient's sense of self to a great degree. But the second level of communication may be even more crucial. Affect attunement serves also as a recognition of the wholeness of the patient. The therapist, in attempting to attune to the patient's affects and needs, and to understand them in the context of this patient's history and present life, is recognizing a unique and yet understandable person. The therapist is also first and foremost a human being, and can only attune to the patient from the depths of her own subjectivity. I think patients often apprehend – if mostly unconsciously – the significance of the fact that the therapist must process their communications through her own subjectivity, and her successes as well as her struggles to be as accurate as possible are affirming. We see signs of this awareness in our patients' struggles and hesitations as they endeavor to communicate their experiences to us, as well as their noticeable relief when we understand them deeply.

An example from my experience as a patient may be illustrative. It was my first session with a new therapist. I was in the process of interviewing analysts to find one with whom to work. I was already in tears, describing the recent death of one who was very dear to me. I felt shattered, lost, and I was struggling to regain my footing in the difficult aftermath of this person's death. At one moment the therapist sighed and said with great feeling, "What a nightmare!" I was surprised and warmed by the vehemence of his remark. The emotional tone was certainly attuned to my story and my state of mind. But more, he seemed to be expressing a spontaneous reaction of the impact of my story upon him. His remark did not seem to be aimed solely at communicating to me what he thought was my state of mind. Rather, he seemed to be balanced between being attuned to my state of mind, and expressing *his* state of mind as he was affected by being immersed in empathic listening. My reaction was an immediate, twofold sense of recognition. First, a bit of tormenting confusion lifted as I recognized that I *was* describing a nightmare. Second, I recognized that he was allowing my story to reverberate through his body strongly enough to be deeply affected. I felt affirmed, grateful, and knew that I wanted to work with him. In a sense, one could say that his tone of voice – in which he expressed *his* state of mind as well as trying to capture my own – was well attuned to a need (and doubt) of mine to know that I can have an emotional impact on another.

My point here is that the attunement was useful and affirming to me not *merely* in and of itself, but as much because of the metacommunication that such attunement was being proffered by a discernibly separate other who was available for engagement with me. My analyst's response could be considered optimally responsive because he seemed to find the right balance between communicating something of his own experience, and staying within my experience at that moment. Bacal's notion of specifity suggests that such a response was facilitative for me in that it was responsive to my longing to know that another can be moved by my experience. Such a longing is one among many which revolve around the "otherness" of the therapist.

I am not saying that *all* attuned responses to a patient must carry this metalevel message overtly in order to be usable. In fact, at other times, it has been very important in my own analysis for my analyst to stay very close to my experience, without "intruding" any hints of his own experience. Yet that first experience let me know that this analyst would have no objection to allowing his presence to be part of the therapeutic ambience, and I needed such a sign before I could begin. That first experience also enriched the meaning for me of those times when his own presence is kept further in the background. At those times I appreciate his commitment to his task, such that he is voluntarily holding more of his own presence in suspension, *for my sake.*

By "presence," I mean a therapist's willingness to be open to a kind of engagement in which the patient can touch the therapist's subjective experience, both directly and indirectly. Quite often the therapist's subjectivity is revealed indirectly, through tone of voice, choice of language, focus of interpretation, etc. But at crucial points in the therapy, for instance, in efforts to address serious disruptions in the therapy relationship, or at certain developmental thresholds, the patient may be intensely interested in, and require, access to the therapist's experiencing. From a perspective that asserts that all experience is embedded in a relational matrix, it seems almost self-evident that self-development proceeds not only through the experiences gained through sensitive attunement to the patient's experience, but through the experience of that attunement coming from a discernible, personal other.

In effect, in certain-sometimes subtle-ways, the therapist's presence is a continuous phenomenon, sometimes more in the foreground of the patient's experience, sometimes more in the background. For in the therapist's efforts at empathic inquiry, her presence is always, more or less subtly, coming forth. She does not simply parrot what the patient says, with the same inflection. She uses different words. She often articulates the feeling that is only implied by the patient. She changes inflection. In each of these slight (or perhaps not so slight) alterations of his original communication, the patient may find himself affected as much by the other's attempts to live in his shoes, as by the relative accuracy and depth of the attempt. This is the second level of meaning that is embedded in affect attunement; whether or not the therapist's attunement is accurate, she confirms the patient's existence as a live, feeling "other," merely by her attempts to understand him. In fact, an attuned response based on empathic inquiry is an enactment of the therapist's "otherness." Attuned responsiveness carries not only her understanding of the patient's communication, but her understanding and response to the emotional interplay between the patient and therapist. An obvious example of optimal responsiveness in the context of affect attunement is when the therapist adjusts her tone of voice toward gentle softness in response to the patient's expressions of hurt and shame.

All therapists are aware that a specter of "otherness" hovers as a constant presence in the consulting room. But we are used to thinking of the power of otherness and its influences on the patient in two negative ways. First, as I described above, is the therapist's "otherness" as a countertransference impediment when the therapist cannot decenter from her own perspective. Second, the patient is all too aware of the therapist's predilection towards having her own responses, and that awareness frightens and constricts the patient. In intersubjective systems theory, when "otherness" is feared, we might say the patient is in the repetitive dimension of the transference[5]. The patient tends to expect that the therapist's subjectivity will be perilously similar to the subjectivity of traumatizing caretakers in his life. But many patients also struggle towards an engagement with their therapist not just as a repetitive figure. They wish to meet, to find, the therapist as another human being. I think they strive for a more complex experience of the therapist in her subjectivity. I think the deep gratitude we so often hear from our patients is a sign of their recognition that we *are* a separate center of initiative, we have our own aims and needs and organizations of our subjective worlds, and yet we volunteer to suspend our aims and needs where possible to make room for them.

It is not uncommon for clinicians to talk of a developmental sequence in the therapeutic process, whereby the patient begins the therapy with little or no awareness of, or interest in, the "otherness" of the therapist. As the therapy proceeds, the patient moves from his "self-centered" original position to one with a greater appreciation of the mutuality of relatedness. As Bacal (Bacal & Newman, 1990 p. 233) has pointed out,

---

[5] Several contemporary psychoanalytic writers have described the therapeutic relationship as having two main dimensions: a developmental dimension and a repetitive dimension. Essentially they are referring to hope and dread as interweaving emotional experiences. Patients hope for experiences that can restore equilibrium and facilitate their development, and they dread a repeat of injurious and traumatogenic experiences with which they are all too familiar.

sometimes such apparent blindness to the otherness of the therapist may reflect the patient's lack of confidence that appropriate attuned responsiveness will be forthcoming. Patients may need to forcefully blot out the subjectivity of therapists in order to ensure that there is room for their own. For such patients, the discovery of a mutuality that is enriching to them – rather than leaving them bereft and depleted – while they explore the otherness of the therapist is often powerfully moving.

I have also encountered the opposite situation, where patients have needed to be able to contact me as a separate subject at the start of the therapy. For such patients, the lack of the therapist's accessible presence was akin to being lost in a terrible empty darkness. One such patient feared a repetition of rote caretaking activities similar to his experience with his distant parents. Another patient needed the reassurance that I would be able to think and respond from my own ideas and feelings if he became fragmented and chaotic. In these cases, it appears that an optimally attuned response was one wherein my reactivity as an "other" was apparent to them, along with my attempt to understand their particular longings for contact with my otherness in the context of their developmental strivings.

Sometimes the achievement for such a patient is *not* the discovery of otherness, but rather the discovery that the therapist's otherness can remain intact even if the patient does not keep his eye on it. These patients come to find an other in the therapist who can be used unselfconsciously, an other whose otherness does not disappear, but is sturdy enough to be left in the background for long periods of time, to be re-found at a later point, unharmed and available for engagement.

Presence and "Otherness"

Therapy is, in large part, a developmental process. At different points in the process, different qualities of otherness are sought and required for the patient's growth, or for the patient's healing. This is a view of interaction in therapy that goes beyond understanding and interpretation, and into the areas of affect attunement and optimal responsiveness. One of the arts for the therapist is to bring one's presence forward in a way that addresses the patient's current particular relational strivings. I believe that the impetus for various forms of engagement arises from the pushes and pulls one experiences when attempting to listen systematically from the patient's frame of reference and to be optimally attuned in one's responses. There often comes a time when the empathic inquiry into the patient's experience leads to an apprehension that the patient seeks to meet the therapist's "otherness." If the therapist does not recognize that her "otherness" is central to the therapeutic process (that is, a central factor in promoting the self-development of the patient), then she may miss the signals of the patient's interest in her subjectivity. She may also underestimate the place of her subjectivity in the process of exploration, preferring to think of exploring *only* when she believes her subjectivity is a hindrance to the patient's progress.

On the other hand, as Hoffman (1992) asserts so eloquently, we cannot always know when to reveal ourselves more fully and when to recede. So much of the therapeutic process is constructed by the seat of our (unconscious) pants, that it is only in retrospect that we can speak with *some* certainty of our motivations, assessments, reactions, technical judgments, etc. The case I describe below fits Hoffman's description well. I think the moments about which Hoffman speaks emerge from the overall discipline of sustained empathic inquiry as the primary listening perspective, and of course the events that occur are then examined from the stance of empathic inquiry.

In my opinion, presence and the listening perspective of empathic inquiry exist in a direct relation to each other. We can only understand the subjectivity of another by allowing our own subjectivity to come into a kind of free play with the other's subjectivity. Also, through empathic inquiry we arrive at an understanding of how our presence is being experienced by the patient. Finally, we come to understand what kind of "otherness" the patient seeks. We can adapt our presence to be optimally responsive to the patient's emergent developmental needs. The constant interplay between listening via empathic inquiry, attuned responsiveness (of which empathic inquiry may be one form), and the ever-shifting adaptations of one's presence are all played out in a therapeutic dialogue. I have tried in the extended case description below, to illustrate the intersubjectivity of the therapeutic process with a man who longed to be welcomed into a shared emotional world.

Case Example[6]

Pedro is a single, gay free-lance landscape architect in his thirties. We met three times weekly, for double sessions each time. He believed that our enterprise was his last chance to live without an empty hole at his center. He also believed that the means whereby his growth would occur was if he could "be himself," fully and unselfconsciously in my presence. The operative word about me in the prior sentence was, "presence." He was adamant that he

---

[6] The patient has read and approved of this paper for distribution

needed a therapist who was able and willing to be available as a subject who could be met, a therapist whose subjectivity could be engaged. He hoped to discover that I was resilient enough to weather the storms of affect that would be stirred in both of us, and still find a way to relate to him that was good for him as well as not destructive to me. This might confirm for him that it was possible to live in a world of "others" without having to deny his own sense of self.

Sessions with Pedro tended to be intense, and sharply focused. In the first few years of therapy, he often began sessions letting me know that the continuation of our treatment rested on whether or not I could "say the right things" in the current session. In fact, he put me on notice right away. Everything about him in our first meeting warned of sharp edges. Pedro was tall and thin, his hair was cropped very short, and his glasses were small and pointed on the sides. His mouth was thin and tightly held, with a grimace suggestive of having just tasted spoiled food. He moved carefully and authoritatively. He told me he was seeking therapy because he felt as though he had just jumped off a ledge and he needed a safety net. He had written his parents a long, anguished letter in which he detailed their abuse, neglect and ineptitude toward him, and he wanted no further contact with them until he could work his feelings out for himself.

Pedro had spoken with one other therapist. The therapist, a woman, had bathroom keys designated by color; blue for men, pink for women. Pedro was upset by this, but became even more upset that when he raised his concerns about the possible sexist attitudes the therapist might have, the therapist appeared unconcerned and uninterested in reflecting on whether she might be being sexist. I suggested that Pedro needed a therapist who would "take in" Pedro's experience, even when it was discrepant from the therapist's perspective, and that he needed the therapist to be able and willing to reflect upon herself and upon her impact on Pedro. If those conditions were not present then Pedro could not feel safe. Pedro concurred, and said he was afraid he would just be put in a box and diminished, and that "people expect too much of men, anyway."

Pedro went on to describe his anger, especially towards men who do not seem to respect his boundaries. He was constantly being injured by the insensitivities of others. He described several interpersonal experiences where it was patently obvious to him that the only conclusion to be drawn about each situation was that people were insensitive and selfish in their interactions with him.

By the end of that first session my body was rigid and tight. I was listening closely to every word he spoke. My comments had been careful and tightly reasoned, and I was tense and anxious about being able to be careful and finely honed in my interventions. This was the first of many uncomfortable reactions that were triggered by sitting with him. I was troubled by Pedro's close attention to the behaviors of others in a manner that allowed little room for ambiguity, or for the possibility of multiple meanings and interpretations of the same action. He decided for himself what particular behaviors "meant" about the character and motivations of the other person, and he acted on his conclusions in such a way that precluded the possibility of resolving misunderstandings with others (e.g., he might end the relationship with no further discussion).

I was tense for the first several months of our thrice-weekly therapy. Pedro described himself as having a "tiny bull's eye" inside him, and it was imperative that I be a good enough marksman to be able to hit it. Interestingly, we came to understand that "hitting it" meant responding with my most authentic truth as best I knew it, whether I thought my "truth" was what he wanted to hear or not. He commented several times that I "seemed to be saying the right thing" — that is, he could trust my integrity and judgment — when I was honestly searching out my reactions to his various requests of me (requests ranging from providing information about the treatment process, to phone contacts, to information about my subjective world).

Also very important was his awareness that I seemed to welcome the opportunity to expand our overt attention to my subjectivity as an integral and exciting aspect of our therapeutic relationship. In fact, as will become clearer below, my attitude of welcoming dialogue, even conversations that made me uncomfortable at times, served to affirm to Pedro that he was embedded in an on-going process of interrelatedness. Repeated experience of this particular dimension (my welcoming of our mutual exploration of my subjectivity, most especially my experience of the relationship with him), along with our exploration of such exchanges, enabled him to question deeply held beliefs that he was doomed to intractable isolation because he did not fit in among humans.

The first several months of our work together involved the gradual evolution of a sense of trust between us. Pedro needed to test and experiment and look for ways to assure himself that I was committed to assisting him in being able to live authentically, without devitalizing compromises. I needed to discover that there was room for me to be imperfectly attuned, and to disappoint his longings and desires, to have "messy" contact sometimes, without each misstep threatening to abort the therapy altogether.

We came to understand together that Pedro did not need me to be free of misattunements, even those that originated from my failures to sustain an I-Thou attitude when my personal vulnerabilities led to problematic reactions. Rather, he needed me to *have* them, to be responsible in my handling of them, and to use them to help him understand that he did have enough substance to affect other people. He also wanted to know *how* he affected me, so that he could get clues as to what his impact might be on others. Growing up an only child with parents who seemed totally unaware of his subjectivity, he found it difficult to sense his effect on others.

I was a bit leery of being used in this way at first. I feared that my reactions to him would be taken as some "objective truth," to which he would have to submit. But as I experimented with being open about my reactions to his impact on me, and to his ideas about others, he used my reactions in a variety of development-enhancing ways. He was extremely sensitive to my emotional process. Not only was he acutely aware of my mood changes, he also worried that each change was the beginning of a process of erosion of my willingness to engage with him. Once he felt relatively sure that our relationship would survive the exploration of whatever was transpiring between us, he frequently listened and responded sensitively to me when, in the course of the exploration, my own state of mind, or rigidly fixed Gestalten became apparent. His genuine interest — including a sense of fascination with how anyone's mind works — and his sensitivity to me and to himself, left me feeling both reassured that I was serving his developmental process, and gratified by his attunement to me. My gratification was, in turn, surprising and pleasing to him, as he struggled to understand why he believed he was too disgusting to allow anyone close. By my being open and not hidden, he felt reassured that he had not done permanent damage. He trusted that I was telling him my personal truths, and that these truths sometimes changed through our dialogue, so that his sense of efficacy grew as well.

One of the "fields of play" for our reciprocal discovery process was in the area of my limits and how we lived with them. Pedro lived in terror of accidentally tripping over my "invisible electric fence." An electric fence was a limit that could not be acknowledged and discussed. It had been Pedro's experience that when he tripped over another's electric fence they withdrew from him — usually abruptly and permanently — and he was left feeling alone, abandoned and cold. One of Pedro's deeply entrenched beliefs was that as he got closer to someone, eventually he would cross a boundary that would enrage the other person because they would feel violated, and then they would leave him, with no further discussion.

Limits that *could* be discussed were not a source of terror for Pedro. In fact although they may be disappointing and hurtful, they were also relieving to him because they reassured him that I had my own center of gravity. This meant I would not build up resentments toward him as he used me in the service of his healing and growth, because I would not make untoward sacrifices that would lead me to feel abused and then blame him for it.

Three examples stand out in my memory. These examples stand out to me, largely because they also represent a confusion that I often experienced in my work with Pedro. That confusion was the question of whether he was speaking metaphorically or concretely. Was he expecting a concrete action to address his current situation, or was he speaking metaphorically, in which case the urgency of his need would subside as its meanings were addressed between us? My confusion was significant because I saw him as looking for actions to assuage a particularly painful state of mind that was also, unfortunately, a *recurrent* state of mind. I became anxious about repetitive demands for action, and also about encroachments on my time and sense of freedom should I agree to participate in this way with Pedro.

Over time I came to understand that my reactions to Pedro's action *language* contributed to the exacerbation of his demands for action in the treatment. This confusion over whether he was speaking concretely or metaphorically paralleled confusion about whether I was being sought out as an object or as a subject. The misunderstandings and misattunements with Pedro that led to our most serious disruptions flowed from this confusion, and invariably I found with him that he had needed to reach me as a *subject,* even at times when I had little sense of myself as subject, or little confidence that an expression of subjectivity would do other than harm him!

I came to understand that I kept a certain distance from his feelings in order to spare myself anguished confusion over *what to do* to respond to his suffering. Pedro's demands for action often led me to question some of my most fundamental (and sometimes unexamined) "standard operating procedures." Standard procedures allow me to keep a relatively comfortable balance between the sometimes conflicting demands of my personal and professional life. Pedro's demands encapsulated his insistence that my treatment relationship with him be a *unique* balance between my personal needs and my professional commitment to him. His insistence reflected, I believe, an exquisite sensitivity to being treated as just "one of a crowd," and also an exquisite awareness of my tendency to rely on my standard operating procedures to an extent that occasionally blinded me to his uniqueness and the uniqueness of our relationship, thus leading me to objectify both of us to an extent intolerable to him.

Example One

The first example involved an unfortunate situation in which he faced a very difficult situation at a time when I was going to be out of town We would also have to miss a few sessions prior to that weekend. On a Monday session he appeared to be especially panicked, and insisted, urgently, that I reconsider my plans to be away. I was surprised by his vehemence, and in the course of attempting to understand the urgency of his request, I also said (defensively) that I would not reconsider taking my trip, and that I had decided long ago that I could not afford to change such plans based on what work events were transpiring. He shouted back angrily, "I am not asking you not to go! But if you don't even *consider* it, then you don't get it! You just don't understand how terrified I am!"

I was surprised again, this time by his emphasis, not on the action of leaving or staying, but on the subtler process of *thinking* about leaving or staying. I felt an immediate appreciation of his sensitivity to, and understanding of, the therapeutic process. I also recognized that I *had*, at one point, been so affected by the intensity of his suffering that I rued that I would be abandoning him at such a crucial time, but that I had quickly and defensively pushed that thought away, thereby muting the resonant sorrow, compassion and guilt which I had begun to feel towards him.

I responded to Pedro that I agreed with him, that I had not fully appreciated the depth of his terror. I also suggested that my misunderstanding the intensity of his terror might be what led him to insist on some change in my *behavior*. I suggested he must need some concrete sign from me that I was not taking his fears lightly. He agreed, and felt calmed by my attempts to set things on the right track again.

Upon my return, our explorations allowed us to develop more fully a theme from life with his mother, namely that his mother was generally passive and ineffectual, so Pedro had to insist on concrete behaviors in order to be taken care of at all, and yet when his mother did react she reacted hysterically. So although Pedro wanted to see more visible signs of concern coming from me, he also feared I might overreact and become panicky myself. This latter fear helped us clarify one reason why I had underplayed the severity of his distress earlier. He had presented himself as troubled but "able to cope," a familiar pattern from his childhood. And I, presumably like his mother, relieved that I could turn my attention elsewhere, was all too eager to take his presentation at face value.

Our crisis had passed, however I remained vaguely disquieted. I recognized that I had been reluctant to allow myself to be affected by his distress, and was unclear as to why. Ascertaining that he had balanced his distress by his posture of being "able to cope" was not completely satisfying. That accounted for a difficulty in recognizing his distress, but not for my *reluctance* to recognize it. My reluctance, which was a reaction to the anxiety and confusion I described above, had been a constant influence shaping our relationship, but it became more understandable to me only after several more months of working together.

Example Two

Meanwhile, a second incident revolved around whether or not I would carry his phone number with me at all times. One time he had left an incorrect phone number on my answering machine, so that when I checked my machine remotely I was unable to return his call. He asked me to carry his number with me. I reflected for a while and said I was reluctant to do so. I did not say so easily, as I worried that my refusal to take such a small concrete step to assuage his anxieties would plunge him into despair of being unable to affect me with the seriousness of his needs and anxieties. I told him I did not always carry my wallet with me, and having to think about putting his number on my person whenever I was away from home or the office felt too constraining of my freedom. I wondered aloud if the number represented his wish that I carry him in my thoughts and in my heart even when we were not together, and that when I had not returned the call to him, it might have felt to him as though he did not exist in my mind anymore. He confirmed my guess.

He also said this was a time when I had "said the right things." He needed to see me be thoughtful about the impact on him of my failure to return his call. He did not actually need me to carry his number with me, but had very much wanted to feel the freedom and sense of safety to be able to *make* the request, and let me deal with its impact on me. He had in fact been anxious that I might feel coerced into acceding to his request, and then become resentful of his forcefulness. He was gratified that I could turn down his request in a gentle manner that respected his need to make the request.

In this interaction, I gained more clarity regarding his use of action statements or demands as an effort to reach my emotions in a direct and immediate way. He seemed to hope to stir me up in a manner that would be difficult for me, but he sincerely hoped I could work with my difficult stirrings in a way that would be fruitful for him. He was especially reactive, and felt more urgently compelled to reach for my fresh feelings in this way, when he had experiences with me where he felt "objectified" by me.

Example Three

A third example occurred as a consequence of the Northridge earthquake of 1994, in Los Angeles. On the day of the earthquake I canceled my session with him, as my office was in shambles and needed to be set in order before I could see anyone (I was also in shambles and needed to be set in order again!). We had our next session by telephone. He asked me at the start of the session whether I thought I was recovered enough from the quake to have a session, and I said yes. It turns out, much to my chagrin that I was still distracted by the earthquake and its aftermath, was poorly attuned to him for much of the session, and neglected to warn him when there were only five minutes left in the session (a ritual we had negotiated several months previously).

When he arrived in person for his next session he began with the following angry question, "Well, don't you have something you want to say to me?" I looked at him quizzically, genuinely puzzled, and asked what he meant. He raised his voice, and with angry, panicked urgency lamented, "You just don't get it. This proves it. Why aren't you talking about having forgotten to warn me at the end of yesterday's session? You are not with it. You are not ready to work. And I have to take charge to protect myself, AGAIN!" We spent the remainder of the situation working with his disappointment and its various meanings.

The next day he came in with a plan, which he announced to me. He could not bear being "dropped" by me, and wanted to wait until I could hold him properly again, but he wanted me to return to my optimal level of functioning as soon as possible. To that end, he wanted to pay me for his sessions for the following week, but would not attend the sessions. He wanted me to use the sessions to do whatever I needed to do to "right" myself so that we could continue our work. I could use the time to go sit on the beach, read, talk with friends, anything other than work, that might help me to recover.

Attempts to explore with him his feelings and thoughts were to no avail. I noted, with some sadness, that he was being driven to resorting to a familiar childhood pattern of "managing" his parents in an effort to get some modicum of effective parenting from them. He agreed but did not want to explore further. He was insistent that I take his plan seriously. Among other things, he said that he did not expect an immediate answer from me, that I could think about it over the weekend and call him on Sunday. He said that he knew this was very unorthodox, and he implored me to be open to considering his plan, even though it meant stretching my definition of my professionalism. He asserted that he was not formulating this plan in order to take care of me, but in order to take care of himself. Although he was calmed somewhat by my attunement to the ravages that my poor attunement and poor self-assessment had wrought, he remained insistent that I at least *consider* his plan.

As the session drew near an end, I told him that although I could *barely* conceive of being able to take him up on his plan, I would do my best to consider it, and quite seriously. I said that with his permission, in fact, I would discuss the situation with two trusted colleagues. He was visibly relieved and appreciative. I told him I would call him Sunday afternoon. In the course of the two consultations over the weekend, I decided that I would not take him up on his plan, but rather wanted us to keep exploring the disruption in our relationship. I was confident that he could weather — with my help — my failures, and could perhaps learn something about the durability and resilience that existed in our relationship.

When I reached him on Sunday afternoon, he started the conversation by saying he had changed his mind himself. He recognized that these occurrences were "part of the process," and that he had felt so reassured by my willingness to *consider* his plan, that he did not need to carry out the plan.

In all of the above examples there had been an intriguing misunderstanding between us. Pedro had used concrete action language to describe what he needed from our therapeutic relationship. He insisted that I take his concrete ideas for various enactments (other examples have been: calling him every day for a set period of time, or helping him compose a letter to his father) at face value, even though he knew that his ideas were rich in symbolic meaning. Today, I understand his concrete ideas as an attempt to create an experience with me that could open doors to ever more intimate emotional experiences, and to broaden exploration of experiences that make him feel exceedingly vulnerable. However, his insistence on some form of action was usually initially unsettling to me. My consequent hesitation was then usually unsettling for Pedro. Sometimes, as we negotiated our way through articulating the various meanings — especially the meanings about what our relationship meant to him — of his concrete ideas, and he witnessed my struggle to respond in a meaningful way, the negotiation and struggle itself seemed to constitute the very experience he was seeking. Our shared negotiations and his participation in my struggle to understand and respond were a process of mutual emotional regulation and mutual shaping of each of our subjectivities.

In the examples above, he had presented a concrete demand to me, and I had reacted anxiously to the concreteness, rather than to the metaphoric dimension of the request. It turned out that Pedro was quite able to work with the request on a metaphoric level, *as long as he also experienced me as taking the concrete dimension seriously.* Also, it appears that Pedro's request "escalated" into a concrete demand for action as a reaction to his belief that he was not being well understood in the first place. Both of these misunderstandings were relevant in the occurrence of, and working through of, a suicidal crisis that occurred in our third year of working together.

Suicidal Crisis

In the weeks leading up to his revelation that he had decided to kill himself, we had many sessions that passed in almost total silence. He talked of feeling empty and like "nothing" inside. As he lay on the couch or sat with eyes closed, my thoughts would drift into a vague, suspended state. At the time I told myself that I was merely feeling my way into his experience of emptiness. My mind drifted aimlessly, to the point that my thoughts were not particularly drawn to attending to Pedro's experience. A crucial difference between us, however, was that I found the experience to be a pleasant break from the pressures and responsibilities of therapeutic work, whereas he found the experience (I found out later) to be an excruciating confirmation that he really was nothing inside. My silence meant to him that I agreed he was nothing, and he must now come to terms with that basic truth.

At any rate, on the Friday of his first announcement of his suicidal intentions, I had no idea what was happening. I knew nothing of what my silence had meant to him, little of what his silence meant to him, and I had not made an honest appraisal of my own flagging interest and its possible influence on his experiential world.

Our sparse discussions in between his bouts of prolonged silences had centered on three themes. One theme was his descent into depression and grief connected to his realization of how neglectful his parents were throughout his life. Another was his agony over feeling out of place in the world. Throughout our work together, we had often explored myriad and unrelenting prohibitions against his unique being-in-the-world. Lastly, he talked of needing to enter into the "nothing space" because any other existence felt false to him at this time.

Now he said he realized he did not fit in the world, but he no longer believed that he needed to try to fit anymore. He realized he was free to decide this world was not for him. He was free to leave it. He said that deciding that he was free to commit suicide was a rare experience of making an authentic choice. At first, I quietly affirmed the excitement and sense of vitality he felt at being free to determine the course of his own life. That seemed like a liberating breakthrough. He agreed, and was pleased that I was not "in a lather" about his decision to commit suicide.

At this point, I thought that his new found freedom and autonomy, although it was being expressed so negatively, might lead him to decide that if he could choose to die, he could also choose to live according to his own aims. In the past, he had often used action language and ideas to work out a symbolic issue. In the past I had taken his concrete action statements too literally. I thought that by creating a space between us in which he could contemplate suicide, he was using another action statement to begin to work out themes relating to authenticity, freedom and initiative — all crucial themes for Pedro.

Pedro went on to say that he was thinking of ways to disburse his belongings. He also said, seriously and with genuine concern for me, that he was concerned his father might sue me. In the course of this talk in the latter part of the session, I reiterated that I thought it was important to explore his thoughts and feelings regarding killing himself, and that while I was personally saddened by the serious-ness of his belief that killing himself was the resolution of lifelong feelings of alienation, I knew we had to follow his explorations, wherever they took us. He seemed sober but heartened, and grateful that I was not trying to talk him out of suicide. He talked a few times during the next sessions of his suicidal wishes, but mostly he spoke of example after example of the alienation he felt, and how nice it would be to be free of any struggle to fit in anymore.

By the Friday one week following his first mention of suicide, he was talking even more seriously of his intention to kill himself. I sensed he fully intended to follow through, and I began to ask more detailed questions. He had set a date (ten days away), and he only needed to wait that long in order to set his will in order. He said he had a plan for how to kill himself, but he did not want to tell me what it was, in case I had information about how messy such a plan might be. He did not want to be dissuaded, and he hoped his plan was a tidy one that would not "gross people out too badly." I asked him to retrace with me how he had come to this decision. He became angry as he recognized I was becoming unsettled and less aligned with his per-spective. He insisted he had been suicidal all of his life, and he really wanted me to accept his wishes.

Pedro spoke of how this choice seemed to him to be the logical culmination of our efforts to promote his sin-gular, authentic existence, and gave some examples of how our work together had encouraged his individuation.

He also insisted that making the decision had ended his agony of trying to fit into life. He felt so much better now, and calmer.

His relationship with me had taken on an odd quality; it was as if he had drawn a steel curtain around himself to wall me out. I told him I thought that more was going on here. I said I shared his excitement over his realization that he was free to choose his existence, but that if he killed himself he would no longer be able to exercise his exhilarating new freedom. I told him something did not feel quite right to me, and therefore I could not feel sanguine about his decision to kill himself. I needed us to explore further.

Pedro burst into tears of angry frustration and desperation. He practically shouted that he did not want to do any more exploring; "One explores when one has hope!" But the thin threads of hope that he had lived on were too agonizing, too risky, and there was so little return. He insisted forcefully that the only thing that could heal him was if I could be his mother, and I could not be his mother! Then, still full with emotion — mostly grief and despair — he told of a short story he had read over the weekend. The story involved a young boy and an insensitive and cruel mother. The crux of the story was how alone this boy was, without his mother to turn to at a time of crisis.

I said to Pedro that I thought the "nothing space" that had preceded his thoughts of suicide was perhaps the despair of being dead "inside" because there was no mother to be found, because I, too, had left him alone in his despair (his prolonged silent period had been preceded by deepening awareness of grief regarding his neglectful and exploitive mother). Pedro said the "nothing space" felt like it was him (in a very concrete sense), and that my silence had meant to him that it was OK with me that he was nothing. Thus, he was left with no hope, and he would rather be dead than suffer the agony of risking by wanting more, and yet have nothing come back to him.

Pedro ended the session in a fury that I was fighting for him to stay alive. He asserted he just wanted me to leave him alone and let him go. He insisted that my efforts to prevent him from acting on his wish to kill himself were for me and my interests, not for him and his needs. I said that I very much wanted him to stay alive for my own reasons, but also very much because I had hopes for him, as well. I was dismayed and quite concerned. I believed that Pedro might well commit suicide. He had no apparent conflict or ambivalence about his wish. He experienced my conflict as an intrusion on his peaceful state of mind.

I have worked with suicidal patients before, but never one who appeared so determined to be left alone to kill himself, and never one who had so walled himself off from contact with me. I was confronted with my own existential crisis. I tend to believe that people have the right to commit suicide. Pedro was firmly convinced of the rightness of his choice. He experienced my conflict as a painfully dis-appointing intrusion. I wondered if I was being blinded to his perspective by my personal anxieties about failing him, and about having any patient suicide. And yet, my instincts led me to fight against him killing himself. I was fairly certain that his suicidal feelings were, in part, a reaction to some disruption in our relationship. Our last session, in which he iterated that he had interpreted my silences as confirmation that he was nothing, reinforced that opinion. Also, I just had the sense that this was an important transitional experience for him and as such it was temporary, and his life would eventually feel rich with meaning for him.

Pedro called later in the day. He was enraged and desperately frustrated. He felt betrayed by me. He had thought I was on his side. Up until now he had given us one more week to work together. Now he was calling to cancel those sessions, because he saw no point in speaking further with me. I tried to talk further with him, but he refused. I told him I would not let it go at this, and that I would call him during the weekend. Now I was greatly alarmed.

I arranged a consultation with a trusted colleague. He was forceful in insisting that suicide was not in keeping with Pedro's developmental quest to be fully engaged in his relational world. He suggested I push relentlessly on the point that my agenda for Pedro was aligned with Pedro's agenda as well. He pointed out that Pedro was separating his agenda and mine because he could not imagine a relationship where his needs and my needs could be aligned.

My colleague pointed out that my own "maternal" needs to respond to him and to help Pedro grow could not be met if he did not stay alive. He said I could not collude with his belief that there was no symbolic "mothering" available from me. He may have experienced me as failing him when I was so passive with his silence, but that did not mean I was failing him in the same global way his parents did. He said that when Pedro rebuffed me again I should tell Pedro that I refuse to stand aside and let him die, and that I should ask him what a mother would do in such a situation.

I was heartened by the conversation, in two ways. First, my colleague was unambivalent about intruding on Pedro's peace of mind. Second, he pointed me in a new direction. When Pedro had wailed that only a mother could heal him and that I was not his mother, I had taken that as a sign that he felt dropped and abandoned by me, and I had merely attempted to attune to the horror of the experience of my failing him. I had not wanted to impose on his experience, even though my sense was that I was very much like a "good enough mother" for him. I had been afraid that I would violate his experience by doing so. Yet my colleague encouraged me to have confidence in how maternal my relationship with Pedro tended to be. In a sense, he encouraged me be more literal and concrete in responding to him!

I called Pedro. He started out guarded and angry, and again talked of how betrayed he felt by my efforts to keep him alive. But as we talked, and I used the perspective I had gained from the consultation, Pedro softened. He agreed to come back for a session on Monday, and asked me to explain my perspective to him more thoroughly. We spoke again one more time over the weekend, and he told me he felt better after our previous call, more like we were friends again.

When I saw him on Monday the crisis had passed, although Pedro was still in agony. He told me that he had put his decision on hold until he could form a better understanding of my perspective, and until he could better understand his own experiences of the past several weeks.

Together we began to try to unravel what had happened. I had mentioned over the phone to Pedro, when he was critical of himself for going to such extremes when he was upset, and wondering if he was manipulating me, that perhaps he had been driven to an extreme measure in order to get my attention when he was confronted with my passivity. Pedro explored this theme further in the next sessions. He talked of how hard it was to evoke a relevant response from either parent, and also of how once he got me to take notice of his agony, he would turn off the alarm too soon. We both noted, in fact, that he had turned off the alarm again in this very session, when he had told me at the outset that he would not kill himself for now. We explored a dialectic between us, where he feared if he did not turn off the alarm I would withdraw, but when he turned off the alarm he felt forgotten again as our normal routine resumed. We also noted that turning on the alarm did get my attention, while turning it off helped to create an exploratory ambience between us.

We began to speak of his dilemma in a familiar way between us — his "tidy self" and his "messy self." I told him it was true, his tidy self was so convincing that I often lost track of the pain and despair beneath it. That led him to say that he knew his messy self would fight me, hurt me, insult me, reject me, and that he needed me to hang in there and keep pursuing his messy self. When I said at one point that I thought he was talking of handing me his baby to hold, he wailed that it was more like a pig or warthog than a human baby, and that he was sure I would be repulsed.

We have since explored the many meanings of his "nothing space," of my reaching out to him, of times when I did not reach out, of his tidy self and how it almost got him killed but is a necessary protection when I am unreliable, and other themes that wove through this crucial period of time. For about a month after the crisis, I called him daily. We both saw this as a safety net for him, so that his tidy self would not lull me back to sleep, and as an enactment of my willingness to go the extra mile for him if need be.

Pedro's suicidal despair became part of a distant past as he became more directly his "messy self" with me. A special intimacy grew between us, a kind that only happens when people go to hell and back together. I am amazed at how strong our trust became. He trusted me enough to be really messy — overtly enraged, overtly depressed and despairing, thoroughly bitter, demanding, etc. And I trusted that no matter what happened, he would return for another session, even when he said he would not!

For my part, I learned to trust our discussions of his concrete wishes, my willingness to respond concretely to some of them, and my inability or refusal to meet others of them. He was able to make therapeutic use of our dialogue in these situations. The process of articulating, under-standing and welcoming the expression of the needs en-capsulated in his concrete wishes provided enough sup-port for further dialogue. He also drew support from my willingness to struggle visibly to establish an authentic and unique relationship with him and his wishes. Also, my willingness to offer alternative modes of connection be-tween us provided sufficient reassurance of my commit-ment to our work that he was able to tolerate the dis-appointment of his wishes. I also deeply trusted that my open revelation of my own subjectivity, in myriad ways from tone of voice to disclosure of problematic subjectivity, to playful shared moments of humor, all set him on a path toward inhabiting a shared human world.

When he first began therapy with me, Pedro said he wanted a place to be completely true to himself, and yet where the other person would not have to compromise himself in order to provide room for him. We seemed to find that place between us, and subsequent contacts with him suggest he continues to develop in the direction of graceful, full-bodied engagement with others that he yearned for at the start of our work together.

Conclusion

In the case described above, I endeavor to show that a patient seeks relatedness in differing ways, depending on past experiences and current developmental needs. Therapists can be guided by the developmental readiness of the patient in emphasizing or de-emphasizing their own otherness. The readiness of the patient is often discovered through systematic empathic immersion. The therapy process becomes a fluid interpenetrating mix of emotional attunement and presence. The guiding therapeutic methodological principle may be that of optimal responsiveness, and the understanding of what is optimal may be arrived at through a process of sustained empathic inquiry (which is also a response), as differing types of relatedness are sought by the patient at different stages in the therapy process.

References

Aron, L. (1991). The patient's experience of the therapist's subjectivity, *Psychoanalytic Dialogues 1*, 29-51.

Atwood, G., & Stolorow, R. (1984). *Structures of Subjectivity: Explorations in Psychoanalytic Phenomenology*. Hillsdale, NJ: Analytic Press.

Bacal & Newman (1990). *Theories of Object Relations: Bridges to Self Psychology*. NY: Columbia Univ. Press

Benjamin, J. Recognition and Destruction: An Outline of Intersubjectivity, in Skolnick and Warshaw, (Eds.).

Buber, M. (1965). *The Knowledge of Man* (pp. 43-60). New York: Macmillan.

Buber, M. (1970). *I and Thou*, (Kaufmann, trans.). NY: Scribner and Sons.

Fosshage, J. (1995, in press). Countertransference as the therapist's experience of the patient: The influence of listening perspectives, *Psychoanalytic Psychology 3*.

Hoffman, I.Z. (1992). Expressive participation and psychoanalytic discipline, *Contemporary Psychoanalysis*, *28*, 1-15.

Hycner, R. & Jacobs, L. (1995). *The Healing Relationship in Gestalt Therapy: A Dialogic - Self Psychological Approach*, Highland, New York: Gestalt Journal Press.

Lichtenberg, J. (1989). *Psychoanalysis and Motivation*. Hillsdale, NJ: Therapeutic Press.

Orange, D. (1995). *Emotional Understanding: Studies in Psychoanalytic Phenomenology*. New York, NY: Guilford Press.

Shane, E. And Shane, M. (1989) The struggles for otherhood: implications for development in adulthood, *Psychoanalytic Inquiry*, 9(3), 466-481.

Stern, D. (1985). *The Interpersonal World of the Infant*. New York: Basic Books.

Stolorow, R., Brandchaft, B., & Atwood, G., (1987) *Psychoanalvtic Treatment: an Intersubjective Approach*. Hillsdale, NJ: Therapeutic Press.

The Scarf that Binds:

A Clinical Case Navigating Between the Individualist Paradigm and the "Between" of a Relational Gestalt Approach

• • • • • • • • • • • • • • •

Carol Swanson

On Discouragement and Finding My Way

At a meeting with Gestalt trainers, the discussion focused on how a training curriculum would look different if the starting point of the training was from a post-Cartesian relational vantage point versus the more traditional curriculum of the usual foundational concepts in Gestalt therapy: awareness, contact boundary, contact functions, figure/ground and organismic self-regulation. In this meeting a colleague said the first text she read in beginning her study of Gestalt therapy was, *The Healing Relationship in Gestalt Therapy*. Her words knocked me back and I sank deeper into the soft sofa in our meeting space. What an admixture of feelings I experienced in that moment. "It's not fair," a voice screamed in my head. I've struggled for years undoing some of the study that focused on an individualistic model of self. "Fairness is something when you're in the Boy Scouts," I hear Isadore From's wry voice in my head. So what if my colleague had a different point of departure on her professional journey in studying Gestalt theory? Why make a big deal of it? My mood momentarily sinks, and I curl a large soft pillow in front of my body, as if a pillow could protect against this feeling of an empty loss. Our group discussion then moves towards how thoroughly embedded we are within the individualist paradigm. This discussion softens any self-criticism I feel about being a slow learner, and I realize one learns about a relational perspective by having a lived-in-the-world experience, in whatever ways one can, within a relational paradigm. The first text I read when beginning to study Gestalt theory was *Gestalt Therapy*, by Perls, Hefferline and Goodman. This book is the seminal text to any serious student of Gestalt therapy, and I studied this book with three other colleagues, reading out loud the entire text over the course of several years, discussing and struggling with the concepts. Though Gestalt theory is clearly embedded in a relational matrix of organism/ environment, the clinical emphasis in the 1980's was very much towards an individualistic model of self. In the 1990's the model of a more dialogically oriented Gestalt approach was written about and introduced into training programs, with a profound reverberation in the Gestalt community.

In the case I describe below, there is a blending of individualist assumptions and a reach towards a more relationally informed and lived world. Both the struggles of my client and my own in wrestling with individualist assumptions are revealed in the case. In addition, there is an emphasis on the quality of the relationship, the ongoing and unfolding process of the therapy, and moments of the "between" with the therapist and the client. The client has been in weekly therapy for two and a half years. The case example starts from the early phase of her treatment, and then continues two years into her work.

The Life of a Scarf

Joanne, a semi-retired middle-aged woman, came to therapy after being sick with the flu for several months. She became more and more depressed and was concerned if she would ever return to her "old" self. She complained of sleep difficulties, and as her insomnia grew worse, she became increasingly anxious and was suffering panic attacks.

Joanne was mortified and ashamed by her emotional, "needy and pathetic place." She had always been the person running the show. She was the person her kids, friends, colleagues would turn to for assistance and support. Now she was a total disregulated mess. She was disoriented and alarmed by her emotional state, and terrified she would not recover. She got through most days by taking anti-anxiety medication, and through nights with sleep medication. She tried several antidepressants for a period of time, with limited success. As her anxiety and panic continued she was in a state of perpetual dread that these intense feelings would overwhelm her. Some nights, she hunkered down and endured the pounding of these intense feelings, hoping it might look different in the morning. The next day would not ease her suffering, and she kept "circling the drain," and fearing her own annihilation. Her depression seemed to be seeping through her life, and more and more she felt like a "river overflowing its banks."

First Session:

Joanne sits on the sofa, cross-legged, her upper body erect, with her head tilted to one side. I can see the young girl in the middle-aged woman. I think to myself — a scared young girl/woman whose many longings have gone unfilled for years. I understand these longings from my own personal history. My client and I share a similar Mid-western, "we rejoice in our sufferings" kind of mentality. I understand the going-it-alone-thinking, the longing for a "listening ear," and the shame of feeling such a deep desire to be held and seen.

Joanne begins telling me she hasn't slept well for the last week. She has taken Ambien most nights to enable her to sleep. She says, "I remember how you told me it was a form of support, and that I can lean on it when I need to." This was a useful reframing for Joanne, since it enabled her to have the support of a sleep medication, rather than thinking of herself as "weak and inadequate." Again, my history would say something like, you haven't worked hard enough if you aren't able to sleep at night, and I justified my own prescription for Ambien by saying I used it for international travel to help me make adjustments to time zones. It was years before I could admit the occasional need for a sleep medication when I wasn't traveling. I don't tell this to Joanne, but I understand the shame she experiences when she describes herself as "pathetic and sick" for needing a sleep medication.

These beliefs are firmly rooted in an individualist perspective. Joanne looks down, with her black hair falling around her shoulders and partially covering her face like a curtain. She's turning in on herself, like a sea anemone that recoils into itself when touched. I feel the weight of my head resting on my hand, while my fingers gently massage my cheek. I wonder if my words penetrate her curtain of shame and self-loathing.

The physical space between us seems to be growing as if some invisible force is pulling us apart. This invisible force weights my body into the chair, and increases my feelings of helplessness. As my heavy body is nestled into the black leather chair, I'm holding onto a green scarf draped around my neck and rubbing the linen scarf with my thumb and fingers, a movement that soothes me. I shift my weight to the front of the chair, and leaning towards Joanne, offer her the other end of the scarf. She reaches for the end of the scarf, and pulls back into herself holding onto the scarf. I start pulling on my end, so she can feel a physical connection with me. Joanne begins sobbing, her body doubled over, the curtain of her hair enclosing her. I continue a gentle oscillation, pulses of slight pulls and releases on the scarf. It feels like I'm holding Joanne in my arms, rocking her gently. My body leans back into my chair, and for a second my eyes close and I feel only the pulsing movement of the scarf, and my deepened breathing. After several minutes Joanne looks up at me and says: "Hello," and mutual smiles of recognition and affection form on our faces. My hand relaxes holding my scarf end, and my fingers trace little circles on the scarf. The scarf drapes between us like a hammock and everything seems to be in a moment of quiet repose.

A few days after this session, I remember my own experience working as a client at the Pacific Gestalt Institute residential experience in Santa Barbara a few years ago. I was telling the group about my feelings of shame and guilt, and my vehemence that no one soften or lessen my burden. I didn't want anyone to talk me out of these feelings. A colleague said, "Ah yes, the gatekeeper emotion." Something in that moment connected and I begin physically sliding down my chair, and emotionally falling down a well with no bottom. The colleagues on each side of me draped a scarf across my lap. They held each end of the scarf, and I grabbed the middle. The concreteness of their offering of the scarf helped me find a floor of support to suffer this intense emotional experience.

As I remembered my own experience, after this powerful emotional session with my client, this full circle of experience delighted me. I also felt some awe as to some of the mystery in life.

The scarf became an important and visible embodiment of connection in the therapy. There have been repeated moments when I have reached towards Joanne offering her the scarf, and there are times when Joanne has asked to hold onto the scarf. At the moments that Joanne is spiraling downward, that she fears no one can meet her, that she'll tumble to darkness and there is no floor to catch her, she asks. The scarf has been a scaffolding of support, a place she can hang onto, or rest and be held, a supporting cord of connection she uses to pull herself onto more solid ground.

A memory unfolded for Joanne after several months into the therapy. She was a young woman preparing to leave for college. She was upstairs in her parents' house looking out the window and seeing her parents leaving the home to do an errand. She sees her mother collapsing beside the car and her body folded in on itself like a fan. Her father gets out of the car, picks his wife up, and helps her back into the car. Joanne knew that her mother's collapse was not because she was physically ill. She knew her mother was folding in on herself, because Joanne, the youngest of five children was leaving for college that day.

Her mother, now left to an unsatisfactory marriage with an alcoholic husband, was collapsing.

Joanne now feared that in her weakened state she was collapsing like her mother, who was "dependent and pathetic," and Joanne would need to be picked up as she became less functional in the world. This incident helped us understand some of her fears about collapsing, and her lack of any sense of resilience to recover from physical or emotional distress.

Session Two Months Later:

Joanne arrives a few minutes late, saying parking was difficult because of the Christmas shoppers. She starts: "I'm into it this year. We keep it contained who we buy for. Maybe it's the singing I'm doing, but I'm really into the holiday season."

Carol: "It sounds like you're enjoying the freedom of expression that comes with singing. The holidays often feel like a time of obligation and are draining and depleting for folks, and you're describing the opposite experience."

Joanne nods affirmatively and smiles in response to my comment.

Joanne: "How about you. How do you feel about Christmas?"

I pause for a moment, as if I have never been asked that question before. For a brief moment I have no idea how I feel about Christmas. I say to Joanne that's a good question, stalling until I have some intelligible response. I think Joanne's question is sincere in her inquiry about my reactions to the Christmas holiday, and that she is not merely shifting the focus to me as an avoidance strategy. I'm measured in my response. I say: "It's OK, We don't do anything overblown for Christmas. Our tradition is to go cross country skiing on Christmas day, which has always been fun." I think Joanne's need for me to be transparent comes from her genuine curiosity and desire to know me more fully as a person, at the same time respecting the boundaries of our relationship. A momentary cloud of self-doubt floats through my mind, a concern about using self-disclosure appropriately, and I notice the cloud disappear as quickly as it came. I was relieved though, that Joanne did not react to my tepid response about the holiday.

Joanne tells me about their New Year's Eve ritual of writing out things they want to let go of from the year. She laughed as she said: "I had two pages of things I wanted to let go of last year." She goes on to say: "This year I want us to celebrate things from the year, along with things to let go of."

Carol: "Yes. Celebrate. And what might you celebrate this year?" My lungs inhale fully, embodying this feeling of expansion and celebration.

Joanne: "My health. I would celebrate my health, and that there's little remaining of my 'symptomatic self.' I would celebrate my being present in every day." Joanne speaks this with fullness, with conviction. Her words reso-nate within our shared space.

Joanne then transitions back to a fan metaphor from last week. "I've thought more about my fan, and I think of the center of the fan as my core self, and the fan represents an integration of myself: All the parts of myself, from my overly controlling self, competent self, weakened self and my vulnerable self. This is how I experience being with my kids now. I don't feel caught in that terrible feeling of always being obligated. I feel my core, my center. I am living my fan."

My eyes open and close, in a resonant attunement to Joanne's metaphorical opening and closing fan. We sit in full empty silence for a few minutes. In a spontaneous moment I suggest: "Do you want to sing, we're almost at the end of our hour?" I'm surprised that I've allowed myself such a freedom to engage with Joanne this way. I secretly admonish myself and think no one would consider this a serious therapy, or me a serious therapist. I push aside all those beliefs about what it means to be a professional and allow myself to be in this creative lively moment with Joanne. Later I think, perhaps I wanted to join with Joanne in "living her fan," in having more permission myself to express joy in my life, something that I may hold as forbidden in my American Midwestern archaic way.

Joanne: "OK. Angels We Have Heard On High."

Carol: "I'll harmonize."

Joanne: "I need the scarf for this."

My wrist flicks the long red scarf draped around my neck to Joanne, and she catches her end with both hands. Now, linked by the scarf and our deepening bond, we start singing "Angels We Have Heard On High." We have a false start before we get the right key, and sing a verse of the song, and then the chorus. Joanne says she wants to attempt a soprano descant to the carol. She sings it beautifully and it is like a blessing on us. After Joanne stops singing she doubles over in laughter and I feel her joy and mine radiating throughout the room.

Session Two Weeks Later:

Joanne arrives, wearing black pants and her familiar red coat. In her ritual way, she unties her boots, takes her jacket off, and then rocks herself into a cross-legged sitting position on the sofa. I settle into my chair and flip my legs onto the ottoman. My hands absorb the heat from my coffee mug, and the warmth travels up my arms in a pleasurable sensation. Joanne looks younger today, softer, and her hair seems silky, like a shampoo ad. "I'm doing ok.

I don't have any pain with my hand since that fall, and it's clearly getting better. I've got a cold though, which has knocked me out. I'm having some of my stomach stuff though, and I haven't been sleeping well."

Carol: "It was clear when we talked on the phone last week, you needed to rest. I sensed how knocked-out you were feeling then."

I'm thinking I need to discuss with Joanne her cancellation of the previous appointment shortly before the scheduled hour. I need to address this, yet I feel ambivalent about bringing this up. A part of me wants to forget about this, and minimize it. It's no big deal. She's the ideal client, she pays full fee, never forgets her checkbook, and late cancellations have never been an issue. I know she was ill, or she would have made her appointment, as she had expressed her disappointment on the phone that she couldn't keep the appointment. I say to Joanne, holding my hands up by my face, obviously struggling with what I'm going to say: "I understand you were sick, and canceling was the best decision for you, but it was not within the usual 24 hour time period. I don't want to charge for the missed meeting, and I do want to speak to the fact this is an exception and unusual situation."

Joanne's eyes widen. My words hit her. "Do you want me to pay for the hour? The money is not the issue. I was sick. In the morning I thought I could come, but by mid-afternoon, I was in pretty bad shape. I can't believe you're saying this. If you 'got me,' understood me, you wouldn't be bringing this up." Joanne's voice and jaw tighten — a contrast to the silky smooth hair I noticed when she first sat down.

Carol: "It may have been better if I had spoken to my double bind." I say this, thinking there may be some seamless way through this rupture. "I do know you're responsible and you would have preferred to be here. I do get that about you, and yet if I don't speak to the last-minute cancellation, I feel unfinished about that."

Joanne: "I don't think that would have made a dif-ference, not to this feeling inside," as she holds her hand below her ribs. "I get the business end of this; that all makes sense to me, but the emotional side of me feels hurt and angered by this. I'm feeling incredibly vulnerable right now." Joanne says quickly, as if she could slide out of her feelings: "I need to evoke the image of me holding my little girl and you holding both of us."

Carol: "Right now, I don't think you feel like I'm holding you, more like I dropped you."

Joanne's eyes roll up slightly to look at me with her chin still pointed down. "Yeah, that's true," she says.

We sit in silence for a few minutes. I hesitantly grab my long scarf, and offer her one end. She takes one end, and looks at me. I pull on my end, so there's tension on the scarf and she can feel me on the other end. She starts crying, and doubles into herself for a few minutes. The visible, the scarf, provides support for Joanne and myself, as the invisible, our connection is tenuous. The scarf functions to compensate for how we cannot take for granted our connection. We resurrect this at times of rupture or fear of rupture. We sit for a few minutes, holding the scarf ends, alternately looking at each other not looking. I ask Joanne what she's experiencing now.

She says, in a quiet tone of voice, "I feel guarded."

"Yes," I say, "I understand. You felt dropped by me."

Joanne says again: "I understand intellectually why you said what you did, but inside, I still feel uncertain."

Carol: "And this is where you and I are living now, in this uncertain place." Breathing, glimpses of visual contact, all seem shorter and quicker in these last moments of the hour.

Next Session

Joanne has a visible energy in her body as she enters the room. Her routine of untying shoes, taking her jacket off, and writing her check, seem to happen in a blur and there's a bursting quality as she starts speaking. She was proud of herself for having two difficult conversations in the past week. One involved confronting a close friend who had promised to do some contract work on their country house. "I'd been feeling angry towards Doug. It's been over three months, and he still hasn't finished the sheet rocking in the bedroom. I want him to treat me not only as a friend, but also as a client, and I want the work done." The conversation was satisfying to Joanne, as she held her line with him. "He'd initially been defensive with me, and I didn't back down. Later in the day, Doug came back and spoke with me, about how he felt 'pretty yucky' about what was going on between us." She goes on to say: "I stewed about this for awhile after my conversation with Doug, fearing that the relationship might deteriorate, and not be the same as before."

I say: "like what happened between you and me last week. You want Doug to remember the business aspect of your relationship, like the position I held last week with you." Joanne nodded her head in agreement, along with a full body exhalation. I go on and speak of the difficulties when we don't have trust and confidence in the "ongoingness" of a relationship. We need to have some space to step on each other's toes, and trust the relationship will survive the inevitable ruptures that occur.

Joanne sits tall on the sofa and says again: "I'm proud of myself for taking on these difficult conversations." I metaphorically pat Joanne on the back, as I pat my own shoulder, feeling the vibrations as my fingers move on and off my shoulder.

Carol: "I'm curious, yesterday morning when you called, saying you might need to cancel, I said; 'we're getting smarter at this,' and you said, 'Yeah, but it was a little scary for me to call.' What was your scare about?"

Joanne: "I didn't want there to be another issue between us. If there was something else, things wouldn't be the same."

Carol: "Things wouldn't be the same and they could deteriorate and collapse?"

Joanne starts crying, tears of fear and relief. At this point, I hand her the scarf. She pulls on one end, and me on the other. Tears roll down her cheeks, and she reaches for a tissue on the table. Joanne wraps the scarf around her hand like a bandage and places her hand on her chest. After several minutes she looks up at me and says quietly: "You're there."

I reply: "Yes, I'm here."

Again, the scarf functions as a supportive visible connection for both of us, affirming the invisible connection of the relationship.

Next Session

Joanne calls from the waiting room, "I'm here," and moves effortlessly from the doorway to the sofa. She's light, and light-hearted. She sits on the sofa, unzips her red vest, and settles cross-legged on the sofa. She asks, "How are you?" I'm hungry, that's how I am, but I don't say this. I tell her I'm fine. Joanne's energy infuses me with a different kind of nourishment, and my hunger recedes for the moment. "I had an amazing day with Sandy (her daughter). We went to the Renaissance Book Store, and Sandy loved it. She'd never been there. We bought journals for each other. We spent most of the day together, had some difficult and honest discussions, and she was curious about me in a way she's never been before. I felt recognized by her. It was lovely." I respond to Joanne, affirming and recognizing what a long struggle she's had with her daughter, and how sweet and satisfying to have this mutually satisfying day with her. Joanne continues updating me about her week, the progress of her friend who had a recent surgery, and a mishap with her husband. There is a subtle shift from Joanne's expansive spontaneity to a reportorial quality as she is telling me this. I notice myself feeling flat and my hunger returning. She goes on to tell me about the potential new configuration of their household as she and her husband are forming an intentional community with several other couples. I am not getting an immediate sense of her concern and I suggest we write about it. I am surprised by my suggestion of the writing experiment, and think later I may have been responding to her earlier excitement in purchasing the journal books with her daughter.

"OK. I'm game, Joanne says, but I need the support of the scarf to do this." I toss the scarf towards Joanne. It lands at her feet and she picks it up, and rests it on her lap, while she gets out her pen. She suggests we write about the color red, her favorite color. We write for 10 minutes, and I ask Joanne if she's willing to read out loud what she's written. She clears her throat, and begins to read. She reads through her tears, and describes how red symbolizes her desire for dance, singing, and joy in her life. Her writing describes her Chinese red and black bedroom when she was an adolescent, and what a contrast this was to the rest of the family home. We discuss how the color red needs to be present symbolically in her new intentional community, and her fears that the new community could drain and deplete her, the way her mother did. Joanne asks me to read my writing, and I do, also through my tears. The flatness of her talking about her concerns has transformed to a contoured shape filled with color, feeling, vitality, and uncertainty. It's a beautiful shared fresh moment.

Eight Months Later:

Joanne continues in her therapy, though less frequently, as she and her husband spend more time in their country home. She has become increasingly resilient to the bumps and potholes of life. Recently her granddaughter had a weeklong psychiatric hospitalization. Joanne is able to hold both her deep concern for her granddaughter's health, along with the awareness of her own limitations, that she "can't fix this" for her granddaughter. Also, Joanne is living with some current disruptions in their intentional community and she's moving through this like her "living fan," aware of the many dimensions of her experience.

Reflections on the Writing

I have learned that the shift to thinking and working from a more embedded relational perspective is an ongoing process, not a place one arrives at. We know that we mutually influence each other all the time. Yet how do we reconcile our forward-leaning into the relational world, when much of our learning and life has been in the Cartesian world? I used to believe, as I read and studied more relationally informed work, that I could then "become a relational therapist," without any of the baggage of my Cartesian world beliefs. But these worlds clash. The Cartesian world tells me to be an expert, a professional who is knowing and certain, and the relational world tells me to be open to being mutually influenced, that the world is uncertain, and that we all live from a wobbly pivot. This is an ongoing struggle for me, as is evident in my process in writing this case. I take leaps with Joanne, questioning and doubting myself as I'm leaping. Yes, we need to "trust the process," the unfolding and ongoingness of relationships, but we also need support to jump and take these creative leaps.

Section 3

•••••••••••

A Wider Embrace: Groups and Organizations

Introduction

•••••••••••

There are Gestalt theorists who cut their teeth on relational thinking in larger settings than the crucible of the consulting room. Mark Fairfield and Leanne O'Shea are two such people. They have long been seeking ways to make practical use of the field theory sensibilities of gestalt therapy applied in various group settings. The "relational turn" has provided a pathway for developing a praxis for group therapy and training settings that is consistent with field theory. Other theorists cut their teeth in one-to-one therapy, but have expanded into other arenas and have taken their relational orientation with them. Such is the case for Sally Denham-Vaughan, who teamed up with organizational consultant Marie-Anne Chidiac to experiment with a Gestalt-based relational approach to organizational consulting. Judith Matson, primarily an individual therapist, was immersed in a group process in which all the members were experimenting with a relational Gestalt approach, and she has lived to tell the tale.

Fairfield's chapter challenges us to abandon the security of thinking of groups as having predictable, orderly stages of development. He cautions that we may shape what we expect to see, at the cost of suppressing the expression of minority viewpoints, or the loss of access to more subtle, easily disclaimed experiences. He also challenges us to resist what Hycner,

Staemmler and others have also warned against: premature closure. The inevitable press of many competing agendas and viewpoints in a group setting threatens a descent into chaos that may trigger defensive premature closure of emerging figures. Fairfield does not create a model that provides easy answers to these and other dilemmas that he raises, but he does expand our thinking to be more sensitive to the non-linearity and emergence that characterize relationally-based group process. He also argues for Gestalt practice as political as well as aesthetic and therapeutic, and that democratizing group process is part of the politics of a Gestalt worldview. Finally, Fairfield uses that scary word, "hermeneutics" in his title. By now, having read Staemmler's chapter in the previous section, hermeneutics has probably become user-friendly. We hope so. If not, Fairfield's clear explanation will lead you to think of hermeneutics as the best friend of dialogue. You will wonder how you ever lived without it!

O'Shea writes about reorienting the training of new Gestalt therapists in a way that reflects and draws upon the centrality of relationality in our work, and in the training of new therapists. However, she does not stop there. Her ideas about training *per se* are contribution enough, but her subtle theoretical contributions also expand relational thinking beyond the training setting. For instance, even if you do not train other therapists, you will learn something about envy and defensiveness. She takes a stand regarding current controversies and confusions about the term "field," and about how we think of repetitive patterns of experience and behavior. Her discussions may clarify the reader's thinking as well.

Denham-Vaughan and Chidiac take us to work with them, just as they say in their title. We get a chance to understand their passion for a relational approach to organizational consulting, some of which is motivated by particular — more communitarian — values that were not supported in their earlier understanding of more classical Gestalt therapy. We also witness their struggle to develop a model for a relational Gestalt approach. They have even included a set of distinctions that differentiate a relational Gestalt approach to organizational work from a relational Gestalt approach to individual therapy. To top it off, they take us straight into their consultation sessions with each other. We hear their concerns and vulnerabilities, both as coachee and as coach, because they provide running commentary of the experiences of both partners to the coaching conversation. Add to that, they punctuate their narrative with "asides" about the theory from which they are drawing in their consulting process. In their description of the details of the process, Denham-Vaughan and Chidiac have given us a sustained glimpse of what transpires in the coaching room in much the same way that Jacobs and Swanson took us into their consulting rooms in Section Two.

Lee, in the following chapter, looks at what he calls the hidden underlying regulators, shame and belonging, of any relational context. He does this through sharing with us his experience of learning about the phenomenon of scapegoating, from the inside out, early in his own training. This chapter illuminates a theme whose shadow is present in all the other chapters in this section, the value of looking for unarticulated anxieties when reception/connection is not sensed. It also provides an example of creative exploration that fosters greater confidence that reception is possible. This kind of knowledge (of elements that are often hidden and beyond awareness) is crucial in being able to navigate the "morass" (uncertainty, yearning, awkwardness, connection, disconnection, and so much more) that can occur when people attempt to meet each other.

We end the book as we began, with evocative experience. In the beginning, Hycner plunged us into the anxiety of being a therapist working from a relational perspective. Matson now plunges us into an intense, powerfully affecting experience of anguish, exploration and gradual recovery in an ongoing group process that was working from a consciously chosen relational perspective. Importantly, Matson's chapter does a careful exposition of the pressure for premature closure (that Fairfield discussed in his chapter) in the face of the intense anguish that all group members felt. The pressure was so great that members ignored the wisps of doubt that some of them felt. Only through the support for, and courageous commitment to ongoing dialogue, was the group able to unpack and repair the disrupttion caused by the premature closure, which finally allowed a more satisfying resolution of the original agonizing "mis-meeting." We appreciate this group's willingness, and especially the willingness of the two protagonists, to share their story.

Dialogue in Complex Systems:

The Hermeneutical Attitude

• • • • • • • • • • • • • • • •

Mark A. Fairfield

The purpose of this chapter is to deal with the question of how Gestalt therapy's concept of dialogue is applied to group systems. This question is explored with a focus on what kind of *attitude* may be associated with a dialogic stance in the context of group work. Dialogue will be compared to the tradition of *hermeneutics* with the intention of highlighting the ways these two strands of thought have shaped each other and continue to function as supports for the ongoing development of the Gestalt model. This chapter will argue for a more direct application of the hermeneutical attitude, along with a more explicit use of structure, both of which can support the group facilitator in managing the increased levels of complexity that will be shown to characterize work with larger systems. The chapter's conclusion will put forward some political implications of practicing dialogue at the group level – implications that emphasize Gestalt therapy's inherent relational sensibilities.

Concept of Dialogue

Gestalt therapy theory defines dialogue in terms of the cultivation of certain conditions (e.g., presence and inclusion) to ensure support for the kind of awareness we believe restores creativity and balance in the processes of self- and mutual-regulation. However, discussions of the conditions of dialogue are usually embedded in the situation of a dyad, and seldom reference larger systems as the context for understanding and applying the theory of dialogue. As such, there has been a gap in the application of dialogical principles to the more complex tasks associated with group work. In an attempt to address this, a number of Gestalt practitioners who work in groups have recommended a practical integration with group dynamics (Kepner, 1980) or group developmental stage models (Melnick, 1980; Zinker, 1980; Harman, 1984), an integration which has been shown to be potentially problematic (Fairfield, 2004).

Harvatis (2006) brought some attention to this issue, pointing out that discussions of dialogue to date have not adequately addressed group level encounters. I want to express agreement with this opinion; but not because I assume the theory of dialogue is in and of itself inadequate: Rather, it is my opinion that we have not adequately understood and applied the theory to more complex systems. Naturally we are limited by our terms — *I* and *Thou* — since in their most literal sense they say something very clear and specific about the dialogic stance in a two-person system while simultaneously anchoring the idea of dialogue in the dyadic context. Be that as it may, these terms do attempt to describe a particular stance taken in relation to "another," implying something that goes on between persons, though it might expand our understanding to say that it characterizes a way of orienting to the inevitable "otherness" we all encounter in each other. A meeting between *I* and *Thou* gives way to a deep-reaching appreciation for the unique wholeness, as well as the unavoidable connectedness of persons.

Appreciating a person's wholeness cannot happen without simultaneously appreciating that person's complexity. If we confront some part of the other which either does not seem to fit with our picture of that person or which confuses or even offends us, we may be tempted to avoid or reject that part. Wholeness implies a communion among the parts of the whole. Rejecting a part of the whole is tantamount to rejecting the wholeness of the whole: Wholeness is inseparable from complexity. If a person avoids or rejects some experiences of self, it is because the current situation most likely does not favor their integration (e.g., when a person's sexual orientation evokes disgust or anxiety in others and is therefore suppressed or disowned entirely). This temptation to resist our wholeness is itself a sign of the difficulty human beings seem to face when attempting to hold together what is experienced as complex with various and diverse dimensions. In the face of such a difficulty we need to be supported in our attempts to integrate the different parts of our experience and appreciate how they relate to each other. The *I/Thou* stance offers just such a support, not only because of its associated value for "otherness" but also precisely because such a value naturally invites contact with increasing levels of complexity.

To manage increased complexity, particularly when faced with the multidimensional situation of a group, we are faced with the tasks of holding together many differences of perspective and developing a capacity to tolerate discord. This way of working relies heavily on a certain prejudice: we must start with the assumption that divergent perspectives are *without question* valid and reasonable. Such a prejudice is not easily maintained in a culture bound by the concept of absolute truth, a concept with which Western tradition is always wrestling, particularly in its quest for so called scientific (i.e., scientistic) knowledge. We need help cultivating the opposite assumption, namely that points of view that do not match the one most reasonable "from our perspective" are nevertheless valid and consistent with some frame of reference or context not yet understood "by us." In fact, we need a whole approach to understanding experience that supports a discipline of inquiry steeped in this kind of attitude. We need *hermeneutics.*

Hermeneutics

Hermeneutics has been described as the development and study of theories of the interpretation and understanding of texts. The concept of "text" is meant to extend beyond the written word to any number of things subject to interpretation. In psychotherapy, we routinely take up complex human experience as the focus of our attention. A hermeneutic inquiry into human experience is an approach to understanding this focus of attention as though it were a dynamic and complex text subject to a variety of interpretations.

Essentially, hermeneutics cultivates an ability to understand things, experiences, and situations from somebody else's point of view, and to appreciate the cultural and social forces that may have influenced that outlook. In the last two centuries, the scope of hermeneutics has expanded to include the investigation and interpretation not only of textual and artistic works, but of human behavior generally, including language and patterns of speech, social institutions, and rituals. Hermeneutics interprets or inquires into the meaning and importance of these phenomena, through understanding the point of view of an insider or the first-person perspective of an engaged participant in these phenomena.[1]

The hermeneutic circle (Gadamer, 1989) is the process of understanding a text hermeneutically. It refers to the idea that our understanding of the text *as a whole* is established by reference to the individual parts and our understanding of *each individual part* by reference to the whole. Neither the whole text nor any individual part can be understood without reference to one another, and hence, it is a circle.

It is not difficult to see the resemblance between the assumptions of the hermeneutic circle and the presuppositions of Gestalt therapy theory, particularly in the above reference to the relationships among parts of a whole and between those parts and the whole itself.[2] This idea is almost a verbatim repetition of language Gestalt therapists have traditionally used to discuss figure/ground phenomena. In Gestalt therapy's attention to holism, the structure of experience, and contact, we can see a conspicuous similarity to hermeneutics, and this similarity is perhaps most evident in the Gestalt model of dialogue.[3]

---

[1] The origins of the hermeneutical tradition can be traced loosely to the middle ages and even earlier to ancient Greek philosophers; however, its most significant developments in contemporary philosophy are generally credited to the works of Friedrich Schleiermacher in the 18th century, Wilhelm Dilthey in the 19th century, and Martin Heidegger and his pupil Hans-Georg Gadamer in the 20th century.

[2] Framing the therapeutic process in terms of the hermeneutic circle is the direct contribution of the work of Frank Staemmler and Lynne Jacobs in their ongoing interest in examining the philosophical influences of Gestalt therapy, both historically and currently.

[3] This similarity is probably not accidental. We know, for example, that Laura Perls studied with Paul Tillich, and that Tillich was involved in the heady theological debates that followed the emergence of Bultmann's and Heidegger's thinking. Buber and Tillich also influenced each other and of course Laura was heavily influenced by Buber. It also seems probable that Lewin and Tillich had contact

Dialogue is our way of fine tuning contact in ways that support the client to appreciate how his or her experience is structured, to notice that this structure is comprised of a multitude of relationships, and to experience himself or herself as "part of" and "party to" that relational structure. Though it aims to "meet" rather than merely "understand" the other, dialogue nevertheless is a form of hermeneutical inquiry precisely because it assumes, and going even further, *confirms* the validity of the other's perspective. In fact, the dialogic stance guarantees interest in the "otherness" of the other, even when experiencing what is "other" becomes jarring, disorienting or confusing.

The *I/Thou* stance is Gestalt therapy's hermeneutical attitude: it orients us to embrace not only the "personhood" of the other, but also the "otherness" of the person. In dialogue, we start with the unquestioned assumption that other people are unique and coherent selves whose experience is meaningful and comprehensible no matter how fragmented or disharmonious it may appear to be. We assume others are whole persons and we hold their wholeness by virtue of a confirming attitude and a commitment to meeting them and also by bringing ourselves wholly to the encounter. The importance of this has been named and reiterated in Gestalt therapy theory in relation to dyadic work (Yontef, 1993; Hycner and Jacobs, 1995), but has not been explicated well in relation to group work. What I will demonstrate in the following sections is that by working out how the hermeneutical attitude can inform our understanding of group dynamics, we can better define a Gestalt approach to group work as well as generate some ideas about specific strategies for creating dialogic conditions at the group level.

---

during this period through their connections with the Berlin Group in the early 20th century.

The Economy of Experience

To begin understanding the hermeneutical attitude in group work, I think it is useful to look first at what would *not* be consistent with that approach. I have argued before that ignoring the phenomenological method and the attitudes and principles of field theory when practicing group work is a clear departure from the Gestalt model (Fairfield, 2004). In fact, another way of understanding this departure would be to think about the phenomenological method and field theory principles as measures of our competency in holding the hermeneutical attitude. It is by reframing dialogue in groups in terms of the "attitude" tied to the *I/Thou* stance that we will be able to see more clearly what complicates the practice of dialogue in larger systems.

The hermeneutical attitude carries with it an assumption, as mentioned in the previous section, that inconsistencies or dissonances encountered in contact with others, no matter how insignificant they may seem to be, are essential to the whole. In other words, what may seem a minor variance is not superfluous to the integrity of a whole, but rather has a critical role in helping us to understand how our whole experience is structured. An example of an allegedly minor inconsistency would be when a group is surveyed about what to focus on next and most (but not all) group members agree on one topic, while one or two only seem to go along with this decision but do not actually agree. Now it may still be wise to go with what most group members want, but an understanding of the whole group requires taking into account that some, perhaps only a few, seemed to want something different but did not make a strong case to have what they wanted.

The group facilitator's capacity to remember this point is linked to how well he or she appreciates and manages multiple perspectives among the members of the group. Group work requires an expanded capacity for complexity. However, complexity is often collapsed in groups, Gestalt groups included. Simplicity is routinely held up as a measure of efficiency and coherence, even at the risk of excluding minority perspectives. One version of this can be observed when a group leader intervenes with a list of points or issues meant to summarize the "essence" of a discussion in progress that nevertheless omits minor inconsistencies or subtle differences, as in the example cited above. Another version plays itself out when someone, often the facilitator, invokes the awareness of time constraints to pressure the group into prematurely acceding to the majority opinion.

I have come to regard this "collapse of complexity" — which is evident not only in group work but in much of our social discourse — as an indicator of our preference for finishing what is unfinished, or managing anxiety provoked by uncertainty and perceived limits on resources. When a discussion leaves too many questions open, I believe it triggers a need to clarify and condense ideas into their simplest form. This need is felt as an impulse to bring order to what is confusing, to draw associations between the novel and the taken-for-granted, all in the interest of restoring a condition of familiarity to our experiential world. In this phenomenon we can see a preference for "coming to terms" with novelty or difference *as quickly as possible.*

I have placed the phrase "coming to terms" in quotation marks as a reference to Kurt Goldstein's use of the phrase. Goldstein argued that the organism comes to terms with its surround in whatever ways are permissible within its specific context and consistent with its nature (1995). The Gestalt therapy value for being explicit, for *coming to the point* as economically and effectively as possible, seems to be an obvious link to Goldstein's idea. The suggestion is that, beyond mere cultural conditioning, the human organism is compelled by its very nature to confront its situation.

It is "natural" for human beings to simplify when doing so ensures the sustainability of life. This is a clear implication of Goldstein's point. When confronted by life-challenging circumstances we make rapid judgments that divide the world into quite primitive distinctions, e.g., safe/dangerous, pleasant/ aversive, friend/foe, etc. If we are under threat or in the presence of something extremely offensive or noxious, any thought of lingering to explore the situation in detail will be interrupted by a strong impulse to retreat. When we have the luxury of a second or even third glance, when other looming concerns diminish, we can of course appreciate the subtler aspects of our experience, the nuances that provide more complex information about the situation.

It is therefore critical to our survival that we support certain impulses particularly when they point us to immediate safety or soothing, even if they happen also to forestall a wider appreciation for the subtlety and nuance of the current situation. Conversely, if we agree that there is a need to build our capacity to be more discriminating in some situations, we will have to look beyond mere impulse as a guide for appreciating the complexity that comes with more finely discriminated experience.

Coming to terms with the environment takes place on many levels and in many time frames. There is the immediate confrontation that must be endured in the face of sudden changes. Such an urgent situation will certainly call upon the immediate energy of impulse. But there are encounters of a more complex nature, patterns of contacting the enduring features of an environment over long periods of time. The recognition of enduring patterns and themes provides something more than instinctual strivings or sudden reactions. Learning happens over time, through practice, by trial and error, with increasing wisdom, and upon deeper reflection. It is a coming to terms that happens by revisiting what seems to recur in familiar ways and by reevaluating what has eluded our attempts at making sense.

Somewhere between the immediate impulse to make things simple and the gradual inclination to examine them more closely, we find an effective range of permissible contact. By effective I mean that we are able to notice what is necessary to our survival and growth while simultaneously filtering out extraneous details that would otherwise delay or attenuate the sharpness and vividness of our experience. Gestalt therapy has traditionally relied upon a criterion of vividness as the measure of the quality of contact that favors optimal functioning (Perls, Hefferline, and Goodman, 1994/1951). This is not merely to foster a certain aesthetic — though I have often observed such an aesthetic being privileged for its own sake — but more importantly because vividness supports the best possibilities for coming to terms with our environment in a way that guarantees survival and enhances growth.

Here a dilemma begins to reveal itself: If it is true that awareness is supported by limiting the influence of variables extraneous to the development of the most compelling figure, it follows that dissonance, or excessive complexity, would bog down the awareness process. Certainly the possibilities to be contacted are numerous, but if the number of possibilities exceeds the threshold of what can be tolerated, nothing but the simplest task can be carried out. The nuances become a heap of clutter when salient organismic needs are persistently foiled. We need to understand the meaningfulness of dissonance if we want to stay engaged with it.

When working with groups, we tend to encounter dissonance in the form of those voices, often experienced as frustrating and annoying, that seem to confound the interests currently gathering momentum: Say that a juicy topic is on the table for discussion and the facilitator polls the group members to get a sense of how interested they are in spending group time on that topic. There seems to be a great deal of excitement and most members appear to agree that the topic is worthy of their time. However, there are some "grumblings." These are the barely detectable undercurrents of dissatisfaction that all group facilitators notice and sometimes are tempted to dismiss. The conclusion I sometimes draw goes something like this: "Let them speak up and take responsibility for what they want." This, however, neglects to take up the critical task of inquiring into what features of the group's various contexts may be ensuring that "grumbling" is the wisest way for these objections to be made. It will not be obvious at first, but these grumblings may be in part due to the effects of race, culture, gender, age and language differences among group members. Sometimes resorting to undermining what is widely accepted is the best way to draw attention to the way in which this wide acceptance has become oppressive to those who stand to lose something as a result of their own perspectives being ignored. Even a cursory investigation into these contextual influences will begin to yield some interesting data regarding the dynamics of oppression. Yet, it is just this kind of investigation that generally gets sacrificed in favor of the economy of experience provided through simplifying and condensing.

Dialogue with Complexity and Context

As I have just suggested, there is an inherent and ongoing tension between simplification for economy's sake and a commitment to creating the conditions of dialogue. In dialogue the practice of inclusion requires the therapist to turn respectfully toward "the other." If we take the example of dialogue with a whole group, "the other" is complex, consisting of many persons and therefore many perspectives. In order to hold the group as a whole, the therapist must find some way to take into account the multiple perspectives and various contexts that shape the way in which the group comes together. If the therapist notices contrast — e.g., different perspectives, no matter how subtle — then this difference is somehow critical to an understanding of the whole and not, as sometimes supposed, merely an indicator of the struggle for cohesiveness.

When working with an individual, the therapist is sometimes faced with a similar challenge of holding together disparate or polarized parts of the client's experience. It can be difficult to find integration especially when one part looms large, while others are only weakly expressed, or entirely disowned. Through dialogue, the therapist reaches toward the *integrity* of the other, holding together what is not yet experienced by the client as an integrated whole. It is the therapist's skill in managing the complexity that comes with appreciating the client's wholeness which contributes most profoundly to the client's own capacity to experience himself or herself as whole. Various experiments can be used to heighten that client's awareness of the splitting, or the overvaluation of one part in contrast with the others. These experiments reflect the orienting aim of Gestalt therapy: the heightening of awareness

of the structure of the whole situation and the relational interplay of its parts. We know that such awareness is cultivated
both through fostering dialogic conditions and by using the
phenomenological method.

The therapist also confirms an individual's wholeness by
acknowledging and valuing the many relationships, systems,
cultures, and conversations that function as background or
context to what emerges in the dialogue. Not doing so interferes
with a client's growth. To forget or ignore that an individual is
embedded in multiple contexts distracts that person from
noticing how his or her experience is relationally structured. I
will offer an example from the world of Gestalt therapy training.
Much of our training happens in the "context" of learning
communities, whether or not the communal aspects of such a
context are explicitly emphasized or even acknowledged.
Trainee A may have an unresolved issue with *Trainee B,* who
happens to be in a different training group. In such a case
where there is an obvious conflict in progress between two
members of a community but only one of the members to that
conflict is present, it is tempting — especially with our focus on
"here and now" vivid experience — to privilege the needs that
arise with regard to the suffering of the person nearest to us,
while letting other needs go "for the moment." Thus we may be
convinced that we are meeting *Trainee A* with compassion and
allowing him a free voice and necessary support to work on this
conflict. But by attempting to work with *Trainee A* when
Trainee B is not present, we are isolating them both from the
context most relevant to their shared suffering. We mostly do
this because it would seem cruel to interrupt what *Trainee A*
has to say because it risks silencing his suffering. But we forget
that suffering signals work to be done often in complex
situations that are difficult to resolve, thereby prolonging pain

and discomfort. To try to soothe anyone's discomfort by collapsing the complexity of the larger situation only creates more pain for all involved. Aired feelings often grow into rumors which in turn have the potential to harm those who were involved in the events described but were not present when the description was given. Conflicts are a special case of complexity, not just relational complexity but also personal complexity, and they point us to a very familiar, repetitive dilemma we constantly confront that challenges our capacity to structure our interactions in a more complex way than we are used to having to do.

Groups in particular are vulnerable to the tyranny of simplification, often compelled to manage the sheer volume of competing interests by overlooking what is viewed — mistakenly — as irrelevant or even superfluous to the needs of the moment. Simplicity is generally defined as that which lies within the parameters of whatever the majority of persons will tend to agree upon. Naturally, the simpler the issues are, the less tangled we get in the possibilities. Accepting the majority opinion or the most proximal vivid need as the threshold of sufficiency keeps the group "moving along." Yet ironically, this sharper, slicker contact has the potential to undermine the group members' capacities to appreciate the complex web of connections from which their group emerges and it consequently interferes with that same profound sense of wholeness that we would strive to support when working with an individual.

Now the tyranny of simplicity is not idiosyncratic to therapy groups. We can look to the larger socioeconomic situation and see a similar trend. For example, living as we do in the U.S. in a primarily market-based economy, we are pressured to "streamline" decision-making by marginalizing minority perspectives (i.e., taking our cues from what *most* customers want). A market operates on the assumption that consumers will pursue ownership of certain goods, the goods which are currently "in demand," literally *demanded* by those consumers who have the most currency to spend on acquiring those goods. This pursuit of exclusive property *is necessarily* a competition among consumers. The successful acquisition of that property puts the owner at an advantage over any others who may want to use that property at their own discretion. Private enterprise fosters exclusion by definition: having a greater advantage means having greater influence in shaping the conditions of the market. In this broader context, any form of grouping — bringing different people together to work on a common goal — at least potentially will evoke market dynamics. If people who are socialized to be "consumers" are brought together and told there is a limited amount of time (which is a resource) to be used by 7 to 10 people, this may cultivate the familiar pattern of competition for desired goods that leads to certain people soothing their concerns about being excluded by "hoarding" time as opposed to merely taking their fair share of time.[4] We can see these conditions operating in groups in various ways, for example the struggle to reserve time for our "own" needs, the race to get into the conversation, grabbing for attention or interrupting and overlapping others who are speaking, etc.

For those of us in democratic and market-driven societies, it is inevitable that exclusions, distortions and power disparities will pervade our customary practices of social discourse. Yet I believe that these conditions are actually critiqued by the

---

[4] In group work, fairness is usually defined according to the assessment of need, though the assessment is often loosely performed by the facilitator who then validates his or her assessment against the (majority of the) group.

hermeneutical attitude of dialogue precisely because that attitude holds open a space in our discourse for disagreement and contrast. It is not by parceling out bits of time in exactly equal amounts that we work against power disparities in larger systems. It would be impossible to put everyone at the same level of participation or influence in a group. Rather, we level the playing field by modeling a value for diversity and variety and by permitting unpopular and divergent perspectives a space in the life of a group.

We need to make a clear distinction between openness to difference and a demand for equality. Dialogue does not guarantee equality. More to the point, a demand for equal treatment can be just as oppressive as the tyranny of the dominant perspective if it does not allow us to admit differences in degrees of influence or power. In individual work we are not aiming to grant each part of the person equal time to speak or equal influence in taking action. In group work neither should we strive to redistribute the resources of time and attention merely to equalize the shares across all parties. A group develops over time; at any point in the group's development some perspectives may have greater influence than others. Making a moral imperative out of equal participation does not ultimately support a group's developmental needs. It is only when certain perspectives persistently overpower others that a problematic disparity exists. We need to be sensitive to context; the group's context evolves and influence evolves and is expressed through dynamics and patterns. The goal is to notice patterns — e.g., that someone has been very quiet for a long time or someone else has been very noisy during most group sessions — not to criticize or counteract what is noticed, but to bring attention to it and manage the complex experience it may evoke in the group.

Complexity and the Explicit

Having a flexible structure to support our navigation of complexity in groups is what will help us to maintain the same *I/Thou* stance in group work that we strive to hold in our work with individuals. Fortunately we can find this needed structural support by drawing from what we already know about dialogue in dyadic work. 1) We know that the therapist fosters dialogue through genuine presence. A factor that complicates the therapist's presence in a group is accessibility: how can the group leader be accessed by all the various group members in the same way that the individual therapist is available to the complex self-revelations of the individual client? 2) We know that dialogue is also cultivated by the inclusion of the client's whole experience. What makes inclusion tricky in a group context is the challenge of managing complexity; how does the group facilitator maximize the participation of all the group members in the same way that the individual therapist creates a space into which the individual client can bring himself or herself more fully?

One way I have attempted to deal with these questions is by thinking about dialogue with groups in terms of striving for high levels of transparency for myself and pushing for a high degree of explicit communication among group members. A group facilitator creates the conditions for dialogue in a group system by increasing access in all directions and by supporting the emergence of increased levels of complexity. It has been my experience that by striving for the greatest degree of transparency, I can ensure group members access to myself, thereby cultivating my genuine presence in the group. It is through encouraging group members to express their unique and different perspectives openly that I have been able to increase their access to each other, thereby fostering an inclusive group process. The terms are slightly different than the ones we are used to using when discussing dialogue, though the concepts are not all that dissimilar. To be present is both to reach and to be reachable, whether in the context of a dyad or a group. Inclusion works to give clients a voice in the relationship, whether the client is an individual or a whole group. However, there are elements of relating we simply take for granted in a dyadic encounter that must be made *more explicit* in a group encounter (e.g., which persons are being addressed and when, who has the floor and for how long, to whom a particular issue is important and to whom it is not, etc.). In fact, it is by being explicit about most things that the group facilitator gradually builds support for the emergence of diversity and creates a space for many perspectives, even the unpopular ones.

A highly participatory group process assures that the perspectives and needs of "all" members—not merely "most" members—are somehow taken into account. I will reiterate that by "taken into account" I do not mean every voice has *equal influence* in determining the outcomes of decision-making; as mentioned earlier this would actually work against efforts to safeguard diversity by potentially inhibiting the ascendance of certain perspectives which are more relevant to a particular decision than others. To take every voice into account is to consider every voice as *potentially* relevant to the issue at hand and to guard against prejudices that threaten to suppress any voice for unfair reasons. This is a link to both the field principle of *organization*[5] and the phenomenological practice of *horizontalization*[6].

Grouping always brings together multiple interests and needs that compete for attention and resources (e.g., time, space, energy). Even a Gestalt process group, with its focus on tracking emergent phenomena, must nevertheless be strategic in order to deal with the dilemma of sorting out issues as basic as how often to meet, at what time, or in what place and as complex as how to get started, whose issues to take up first, how much time to allot, how much emotionality to permit, or what kinds of experiments to attempt. All this demands structure; leaving these decisions to chance will merely reinstate the conditions that work against dialogue (i.e., the tyranny of simplifycation, the competition for attractive resources, the domination of the majority perspective, etc.).

Structuring group process is about making the choice points explicit. Gestalt therapy is concerned with choices, with people having the freedom and the awareness to make choices and notice what follows, then to make different choices and to notice what happens, and to continue experimenting with creative forms of coming to terms with the world. Without an explicit structure that encourages varied forms of participation over time, it is highly probable that some members of a group will miss opportunities to choose a different way of engaging with the others in the group. I am not suggesting that by missing opportunities to interact differently an individual will have less

---

[5] "Meaning derives from looking at the total situation, the totality of coexisting facts" (Parlett, p. 71, 1991)

[6] "Having stuck to an immediate experience which we seek to describe, this rule further urges us to avoid placing any initial hierarchies of significance or importance upon the terms of our descriptions, and instead to treat each initially as having equal value or significance" (Spinelli, 1989).

power to influence the group process; in fact, that would be the kind of influence that runs the risk of tyrannizing the group process just as much as the influence of the classic "group hog." The excluded minority can end up having a profound effect on what is possible for the majority. In individual work, a similar dynamic occurs when alienated parts of a patient's experience are "underrepresented" in his or her expression but ultimately "overdetermine" the patient's course of action. Were we simply to trust the dominant aspects to be those most important to the patient's individual work, then we would be excluding parts of the whole rather than holding them together and in contrast with each other. It is the *whole* person we are aiming to include in the dialogue.

I am proposing that we strive for no less in relation to a whole group. If we do not encourage diversity and contrast among group members, then we risk polarizing those parts of the whole that succeed in coming to the foreground against those features of the field that temporarily serve to frame what is figural. If we believe that perspectives held by the majority of group members can be trusted to represent adequately the interests of the whole group, we are essentially importing the political strategy of "majority rule" into the domain of group work. This strategy actually reinforces the very system whose conditions have disenfranchised minority perspectives in the first place.

Dialogue Addresses Power Disparities

Just as the privileging of the majority perspective risks a continued marginalization of minorities, so too does the imbalance of power inherent in the client/therapist relationship. The therapist has historically been granted comparatively more access to information than has the client. The therapist has access to the perspectives and experiences of the client, while the client is denied access to those of the therapist (or is denied the right to confirm the validity of his or her perceptions of the therapist). An imbalance of access equals an imbalance of power. The Gestalt tradition has sought to address this by encouraging the therapist to be transparent. Being *present* is not merely an opportunity for self-expression; it gives the other access to our own experiences, information, and perspectives. Being *inclusive* ensures that the other's experiences, information and perspectives can be considered, respected and valued. Dialogue encourages a greater balance of access in the therapeutic relationship; this inevitably adjusts the power differential even if it does not remove limitations that come with different roles and responsibilities (e.g., the therapist's time availability, office location, fee scale, level of technical skill, knowledge, education, etc.).

In dyadic work, this increase of access for both therapist and client is obvious. Both members of the dyad are encouraged to be present; both are included in the dialogue. The therapist is held responsible as a guardian of the dialogic conditions. She is vigilant to those moments when the client has been somehow barred from giving a voice to his own experience. She makes sure to bring her own perspective forward honestly in the dialogue whenever appropriate, allowing the client access to her process whenever it will not distract from the client's primary aim. The therapist is continually encouraging the client's participation simply by participating in the interaction. She makes space for both herself and the patient to have a voice without calling attention to that space. It is implicit in the conversation; there is little need to make explicit the *choice* to participate in the dyadic context.

Alternatively, the group facilitator must be far more explicit about choice points in the group process—choices about how much time can be used, which members are welcome to speak and about what, and when certain voices can be left out of a discussion. A group is like an organism with each part regulated by the interests of the whole. Creative adjustment is an exquisite mutual regulation that depends on continuous feedback and exchange of information. The bulk of what gets communicated among group members will happen implicitly and subtly but what is obvious and "goes without saying" for some may require more explicit clarification for others. To ensure that information is clear and readily available, group members must be encouraged to state explicitly what they are expecting and wanting from each other and from the group facilitator. However, this task must be balanced with a corresponding task of encouraging and deepening what is already being expressed. Achieving such a balance is challenging for the most skilled group leader.

Example

I want to give an example that serves to illustrate this challenge. During a session that occurred approximately six months into the life of a newly formed group, an individual in the group gave voice to her frustration that there were a number of people who didn't "say anything." Labeling them the "quiet ones," she continued her criticism by saying how angry she felt, and that they needed to get over whatever fear it was that was keeping them silent. A number of other group members joined in with what quickly came to feel like something of a moralistic tirade, which clearly privileged expressiveness over silence. Even if the group leader had been tempted to explore the issues raised among individuals in the group, the conversation had gathered the kind of momentum that would have made this difficult. The issues raised touched on concerns relevant for the whole group and required an intervention that somehow managed to frame the dilemma as a group issue, and one that invited exploration of judgments raised and an eliciting of the broader group experience. However this needed to be done in a way that was equitable and which avoided privileging those louder voices in the group by colluding with their need for the quieter ones to speak up.

Resorting to having a conversation among individuals would have resulted in a foreclosure on allowing the group to sit with the dilemma that the group leader was facing. As an alternative, the leader chose to make her dilemma explicit to the group and to invite group members to reflect on what function or purpose the qualities of expressiveness and quietness might have in the group.

The group then constructed an experiment, whereby someone was asked to split the group into those that were expressive or noisy, and those that were considered to be silent or quiet. Those nominated as quiet then formed a smaller group in the center of the room and carried on a conversation in which they explored how they understood silence in the group and what function it served in the life of the group. The rest of the group observed "in silence." Interestingly, the conversers concluded that the privileging of expressiveness over quietness risked the possibility that contact in the group might remain merely reactive and superficial, even if it simultaneously gave voice to the group's energetic life. The discussion was then broadened to include the observers in the conversation. What followed was a very rich exploration of the range of fears around the deepening of intimacy that might occur if a greater degree of reflective engagement could be supported in the group. Not surprisingly, it was a conversation in which many more group members were able to voice their perspectives.

This example illustrates how important it is for a group leader to hold the wholeness of the group by reframing what may appear to be characteristics of individuals or subgroups as necessary and diverse functions for the sustainable life of the group. The fact that certain group members tend to take on a particular function consistently, and even at times inflexibly, may say something about their characteristic ways of self-regulating, but this fact will also serve to point out how essential that frequently held function has become to the group's regulation, enough that certain individuals are willing to become tyrannized by the responsibility to hold it. Loosening tightly held positions is a fairly familiar Gestalt experiment and can often lead to a more flexible movement between attention to figure and attention to ground. In the above example, the outcome of offering this experiment was that a more complex development of diverse perspectives was supported and valued by the whole group.

Conclusion:
Gestalt Group Work as Activism

To assemble together a group of persons we must accept from square one that whatever resources become available as a result of that assembly will have to be divided in some fashion amongst all its members. The very act of bringing people to-gether necessarily introduces the need to negotiate time, space, attention, energy, priority, etc. The patterns that control how resources get distributed in the broader sociopolitical context are bound to influence how they will get distributed in the groups we facilitate. If we believe that those patterns are unjust or unfortunate, then perhaps we are in a position to disrupt those patterns in the way we facilitate groups.

Clearly I am advocating political activism in group work, whether small groups, large groups, organizations, communities, nations, etc. That activism is not unrelated to the political philosophies that so profoundly influenced the evolution of our theory. Perhaps this is easier to notice in the case of working with groups than in the case of working with individuals, since a grouping of many persons more dramatically resembles a political entity. Even so, it is no less the case in work with individuals that we are taking political action.

Holding one another responsible for, and also as competent at, determining the course of our own lives is a political act. It is a form of activism to insist on making space for another human being to "be" where he or she is and to be free to reach for what he or she needs. In an industry such as mental health which has been so profoundly influenced by paternalism, it is revolutionary for a professional service provider to form a true partnership with a client, a collaboration in which the client is held as an authority on the subject of his or her own experience. In a field dominated by behavior change approaches, it is truly visionary to understand that change flows paradoxically from the acceptance of what is. Dialogue is a political act, and not one restricted to the dyadic encounter. If it is revolutionary to form a true partnership with another individual, then it is all the more radical when the same kind of partnership is formed in a group. When applied to larger systems, we can see with profound clarity the possibilities dialogue can have both for individual growth and radical social change.

Gestalt therapy may well be at the cutting edge of consumer-driven services. If this is true, it is precisely because we have a theory that supports us in the effort to include the client's perspective. Incorporating the client's voice in service planning not only guarantees him or her the right to "consume" services at will, but also fosters the client's core sense of agency and creativity. Still, I believe we may be missing the opportunity to assume a dialogic stance in group work if we are not careful to oppose a "tyranny of the majority" in the groups we are leading. Our ethics of care encourage us to interrupt the "free market" and "democratic" sensibilities that can so easily creep into the Gestalt group encounter. In our hermeneutical attitude of dialogue, we have an alternative to the majority rule system.

My aim has been to demonstrate how the hermeneutical attitude supports openness to what is not yet understood, and curiosity to understand more. I have attempted to show how that attitude helps the group leader to structure the group process in ways that lead to the confirmation of the wholeness of the group, in the same way the individual therapist confirms the integrity and validity of the client in dyadic encounters. I have also attempted to demonstrate that by supporting the group's experience of increased complexity, the group leader has the opportunity to include and confirm increasingly more aspects of the group as a whole. I have suggested that it may be difficult to manage our feelings when confronted by increasing levels of complexity, but that we can benefit from developing the skills and resources to stay engaged with this challenge in the service of the dialogic stance. In short, I have argued that dialogue in any group intervention depends on the capacity to manage increased complexity in the process of identifying diverse and multiple perspectives and the commitment not to collapse that complexity prematurely. Our dialogic theory is not inherently inadequate to support us in this endeavor, but we must understand and consistently emphasize the hermeneutical attitude if we are to expand our competence in working with complex systems.

References

Fairfield, M. (2004). Gestalt groups revisited: A phenomenological approach. *Gestalt Review*, *8*(3), 336-357.

Gadamer, H.-G. (1989). *Truth and Method* (2nd rev. edition. trans. J. Weinsheimer and D.G.Marshall). New York: Crossroad.

Goldstein, K. (1995). *The Organism*. New York: Zone Books.

Harman, R. (1984). Recent developments in Gestalt group therapy. *International Journal of Group Psychotherapy*, *34*(3), 473-83.

Harvatis, A. (2006). Dialogue in groups. *British Gestalt Journal*, *15*(1), 29-39.

Hycner, R. & Jacobs, L. (1995). *The Healing Relationship in Gestal Therapy: A Dialogic-self Psychological Approach*. Gestalt Journal Press: Highland, NY.

Kepner, E. (1980). Gestalt group process. In B. Feder & R. Ronall (Eds.), *Beyond the Hot Seat: Gestalt Approaches to Group* (pp. 5-24). New York: Brunner/Mazel.

Melnick, J. (1980). Gestalt group process therapy. *The Gestalt Journal*, *3*(2), 86-96.

Parlett, M. (1991). Reflections on field theory. *The British Gestalt Journal*, *1*, 69-81.

Perls, F., Hefferline, R., & Goodman, P. (1994). *Gestalt Therapy: Excitement and Growth in the Human Personality*. Highland, NY: Gestalt Journal Press. (Original work published 1951)

Spinelli, E. (1989). *The Interpreted World: An Introduction to Phenomenological Psychology*. London: Sage Publications.

Staemmler, F.-M. (2005). Cultural field conditions: A hermeneutic study of consistency. *British Gestalt Journal*, *14*(1), 34-43.

Yontef, G. M. (1993). *Awareness, Dialogue & Process*. Highland, NY: The Gestalt Journal Press.

Zinker, J. C. (1980). The developmental process of a Gestalt Therapy group. In B. Feder and R. Ronall (Eds.), *Beyond the Hot Seat – Gestalt Approaches to Group* (pp. 55-77). New York: Brunner/Mazel.

Exploring the Field
of the Therapist

••••••••••••

Leanne O'Shea

T his chapter provides a reflective framework for therapists
wanting to develop their capacity to work from a relational
perspective.[1] It is written with beginning therapists in mind
and aims to support them by deepening their awareness of what
organizes their experience, or phenomenal field, as they meet
with clients. It is also written for therapists seeking to integrate
relational insights into their clinical work, and provides a
framework to support this process. The chapter could also be

---

[1] The terms 'dialogue' and 'relational' are often used inter-
changeably. This is both unfortunate and inaccurate, and contributes
to a lack of theoretical clarity. A relational approach can be defined as
"any post-modern theory whose epistemological assumptions are
constructivist and which understand human beings as evolving to
resolve complex situations... Gestalt therapy is a particular form of
relational theory, deriving its specific relational emphasis from its
scientific theory – field theory – as well as its technologies of phenomenological method and dialogue, all of which rely heavily on
contextualist assumptions. – i.e., that all human experience is
emergent of a perspective shaped by a specific context." (Fairfield &
O'Shea, 2007)

used as a resource for trainers and supervisors wanting to teach and supervise from this perspective.

Through the application of field theoretical principles this chapter invites reflection in four differing but related domains of experience, with the intention of increasing awareness of how these domains can shape the emerging therapeutic relationship. These are: 1) Stories of helping and being helped; 2) Theoretical allegiances; 3) Emotional resilience and the regulation of contact; and 4) Relational patterns.

The assumption underlying this chapter is that our work as therapists is supported and enriched by our capacity to deepen our awareness of the values, life experiences and varying contexts that shape our respective phenomenal fields and therefore our relational capacities. In some respects this awareness adds a layer of complexity that while exciting, can often feel daunting. This chapter is also written in the hope that a greater appreciation of these issues will provide support for managing this increased level of complexity.

Developing A Relational Sensibility

The work of training therapists is complex, and training therapists to work relationally even more so. In beginning to think about how to orient trainees to the most fundamental tasks associated with being a therapist, many issues compete for attention. Practical issues abound, for instance how to manage the time, the negotiation of fees, and even how far apart to place the chairs. Governance issues and matters relating to the disclosure of information and confidentiality need to be addressed, as do basic issues of ethical competency. Textbooks for counselors and therapists generally provide quite useful overviews of these more practical tasks, both in terms of seeing a client for the first time, and also in terms of outlining the tasks that require attention during an initial session.

Of course there are other concerns that occupy therapists beyond these basic issues of what to do and the skills required for these tasks. Therapists worry about their competency and whether or not they will be good enough for their clients. There are concerns that relate to being too much, or paradoxically, not enough. Beginning therapists often express uncertainty about just what it is they are doing anyway, and not uncommon is the fear of doing harm. These issues are often normalized as part of the developmental journey therapists must make, and reflect concerns relating to the development of clinical competency, as well as those which are more characterlogically based.

However, what is typically given less attention is how these feelings and concerns impact the way the therapist meets the client, and how the broader values and life experiences of the therapist inevitably shape the emerging relationship, constraining some things while making others more likely. The reasons for this lack of attention are complex, but at least in part relate to the individualistic assumptions that underlie much psychotherapeutic theory.

A relational perspective assumes that the therapist and all that he or she brings to the therapeutic task is part of what shapes and constructs the meeting between client and therapist. From an individualistic or Cartesian perspective, it is assumed that this can be put aside. This assumption underlies the traditional psychoanalytic notion of the "therapist as blank screen" and persists in more contemporary perspectives, though often more subtly. In the history of Gestalt practice this has its parallel in what I believe to be a misunderstanding of the concept of bracketing. Zinker (2001, p. 60) describes the therapist as "ground against which the figure of another self (or selves) can flourish, brighten, stand out fully and clearly." This risks implying a neutral ground, but the so-called ground of the therapist is hardly neutral, and this idea, although not without a certain aesthetic attraction, risks perpetuating the view that with the right quality of awareness the therapist can simply put aside all of her/his responses and reactions (and presumably history and context) in a way that doesn't influence or impact the emerging experience of the client.

This is fundamentally at odds with a relationally oriented understanding of Gestalt. If we hold that the space between client and therapist is co-constructed, or to say this somewhat differently, if we understand that what happens between the client and therapist emerges from the context of who they both are (as individuals and also together) and what they bring to the therapeutic process, then it is crucial to pay attention to the experiences, beliefs and assumptions the therapist brings into the room. It's not so much a matter of putting aside what we bring, but understanding that what we do bring (both what we are aware of, and what remains beyond our immediate awareness) shapes and organizes our experience. By deepening our awareness in this way, we increase our capacity to respond choicefully and with awareness, and decrease the likelihood of more reactive, unaware responses. As such, finding ways to support this reflective process is a crucial aspect of developing therapists that can work from this more complex, contextualist, field perspective.

This reflective process can be extended to include an exploration of core organizing issues or the enduring relational themes that shape the therapist's work. The task is not only to recognize these themes in clinical practice, but also to learn how to work with them, understanding what they make possible and what they limit in the therapeutic relationship. This often leads to an increased appreciation of the therapist's fallibility, in itself a necessary aspect of what it means to work relationally. Typically this is the work senior trainees engage in, and after all the hard work of learning skills and integrating theory it can be a difficult and demoralizing process. Sometimes I think we enter training with the hope that the theory will save us from ourselves, but in the end we find ourselves back with ourselves, appreciating our fallibility and finally knowing that our awareness, growth and healing is what forms the core of our capacity to be good-enough therapists.

Realistically, this deeper work of exploring relational patterns is often beyond what beginning therapist can usefully integrate. Nonetheless giving trainees and therapists a framework for engaging in this reflective practice is both useful and productive, and over time will support their capacity to think and work with increasing levels of sophistication and complexity, while also supporting a more consistently sustained relational perspective.

A Field Theoretical Perspective

Any therapeutic approach that describes itself as relational necessarily rests on certain constructivist assumptions[2]. Gestalt's particular relational emphasis draws substantially from the principles of field theory. However, what is meant by the term 'field' is neither as clear nor as straightforward as might be assumed. The resulting confusion can make the consistent application of field theoretical principles difficult if not impossible. Some clarification is therefore necessary.

---

[2] Constructivism can be described as a philosophical perspective that views knowledge as constructed from human perception and social experience, rather than something that has an objective or ontological reality.

Making an important contribution to this debate, Frank Staemmler (2006) has traced the usage and various meanings of the term 'field'. He points out that a number of writers have made significant contributions to defining and describing the place of field theory in Gestalt thinking. He notes the debate published in the Gestalt Journal between Latner (1983; 1984), Yontef (1984) and Wright (1984), and the contributions of Wheeler (1991) and Parlett (1991; 1993; 1997; 2005). Staemmler (2006) makes the point that these papers have been a success in so far as they have persuaded a whole generation of authors of the importance of field theory. However this proliferation of the term 'field' has not been without cost. Staemmler goes on to say that he does "not welcome the fashionable, sometimes inflationary, sometimes stereotyped, use of the term 'field' that is in danger of emptying it of any theoretical meaning" (Staemmler, 2006, p. 64).

The lack of theoretical clarity surrounding the use of the term 'field' is complex and probably attributable to several factors. Aside from differences of meaning in the common usage of the word, 'field' has a number of theoretical meanings and is used in both physics and psychology. Its use in psychological theory emerges from post-Cartesian philosophy and, if this wasn't enough to create confusion, its psychological usage is further complicated by the fact that there are a number of different 'field' theories (Staemmler, 2006). Writers do not always make clear which theoretical framework they are drawing on and sometimes move indiscriminately between different meanings, even within the same article. This points to what I think is the main difficulty. In current Gestalt writing and teaching there are a number of crucial differences in the way the term is understood and applied.

Gestalt's field theory is most usually attributed to Kurt Lewin. For him 'field' always refers to a phenomenal field, with no physical reality beyond the experience of the person whose field it is. He also uses 'field' synonymously with his term 'life space', by which he means 'the person and the psychological environment as it exists for him' (Lewin, 1997, p. 210). Part of what makes for confusion is Lewin's use of the term 'environment'. What he means is the *psychological* environment as it exists for the person, not the actual physical environment or social surrounds. Although he does refer to a 'multitude of processes in the physical and social world' (Lewin, 1997, p. 210), and their relationship to the life space of the individual, he never uses the term environment to refer to these processes or surrounds. This differs from the common meaning of the word 'environment', which is generally understood as referring to the physical environment. I suspect this slippage between terms contributes to what is essentially an inflation of the idea of 'field' beyond Lewin's phenomenal field to a 'field' that has an actual physical reality and an existence independent of the experiences of the individual.

Of course this idea of an actual or reified field can also be seen in Gestalt theory. Staemmler (2006), after a careful examination of the use of 'field' by Perls, draws the conclusion he was primarily influenced by the writing of Jan Smuts and the ideas associated with Holism. For Smuts, 'field' represents a monistic outlook, which seeks to describe the complex way in which all things are connected. The categorical differences between psychological and physiological, or phenomenal and transphenomenal are collapsed into a view of the organism/ environment field that is wholly undifferentiated; everything exists in a field, or is of a field.

I suspect this way of conceptualizing the field is compelling precisely because it challenges the idea of things as separate or linked only in more causal or linear ways. As a poetic metaphor it is appealing in that it affirms connectedness. However there is an implicit mysticism in this that works against more rigorous thinking, and this probably more than anything else has contributed to pseudo-theoretical formulations that tend to be vague and all encompassing. To give an example, I often hear people making reference to field theory as if it means that everything is connected to everything else, the "butterfly flaps it wings in China" argument. As compelling as this might be as an argument for the interconnectedness of all things, it is all but useless at a practical level.

Clearly this way of understanding field theory differs from Lewin's conceptualization, and it's not that this way of defining 'field' is wrong, or not able to be substantiated from the theory. The problem is the more general and less rigorous way this idea of the field tends to be applied. It is an oversimplification of the theory that potentially gets in the way of the very challenging task of exploring what it is that is relevant to the emergence of current experience.

In attempting to find a way forward to greater clarity, Lynne Jacobs (2003, p. 40), whilst acknowledging that different writers use the terms in different ways, asserts her preference for the 'Husserlian concept of field as descriptor of one's experiential world'. She refers to McConville's (2001) work, and agrees with his description of a phenomenal field, which is essentially the Lewinian view as described above. Jacobs agrees there are influences that exist beyond us which are part of the constitution of our experiential or phenomenal fields, but rather than describe this as being *part of a field* she prefers to describe this as embeddedness within a context.[3]

This emphasizes that our phenomenal fields are emergent from the contexts in which we are embedded, and that although we have the capacity to shape and influence these contexts, they do precede us, and have an existence that is not dependent on us. This rather neatly solves the problem of trying to use the one term, 'field' to talk about two different things. The idea of the phenomenal field is retained, while at the same time the ideas implied by a reified field are captured by the term context, itself complex, multidimensional and dynamic, from which all experience emerges.[4]

It is my intention to follow Jacobs's usage of the terms. I think 'phenomenal field' and 'context' make for a greater degree of clarity. And as far as meaning is concerned, essentially I am interested in how our subjective experience, or our phenomenal fields, are shaped and organized by this inseparable interplay of self-experience and context.[5]

---

[3] I believe this to be a crucially important point. Understanding that our experience is both emergent from, and dependent on contexts that precede us, is an important counterpoint to the more extreme edges of the constructivist argument, and remind us that there are limits and constraints in terms of what it is possible to create or construct. This is a necessary corrective to what is often an egocentric and anthropocentric worldview, and ought to be a humbling reminder of our not so significant place in the universe (Roberts, 2000)

[4] The term 'experience' could be used as an alternative to 'phenomenal field'. While more accessible, I think the multiplicity of ways we use the term 'experience' makes it harder to retain the sense of the word as referring to experience, as it is constructed. An alternative to 'context', sometimes used by Gestalt writers is 'ontological field'. However the term 'ontology' comes out of a whole tradition of religious and philosophical thought, and consequently I think this ends up creating more problems than it solves.

[5] I recognize I am using the term 'context' in a particular way, and one which differs from those definitions typically applied to the

This brings me back to the importance of a field theoretical perspective in training therapists with a relational orientation. Crucial to working relationally is an increased understanding of what shapes our experience (or phenomenal field). We can give time and attention to looking at the various contextual factors, be it the client, the setting or the various tasks and skills. But if we are to work from a relational perspective, then even more important is understanding how our experience is shaped in these complex and multi-dimensional ways.

In essence then, this article is an application of field theoretical principles. It seeks to deconstruct and explore some of what shapes and organizes the phenomenal field of the therapist, and therefore the emerging relational experience with clients. A framework that enables therapists to reflect on these aspects of their experience and the meaning that emerges is an invaluable support for working dialogically, and is essential to the development of an approach that is consistently relational.

Four Domains of Enquiry

It could be reasonably argued that everything, all present and past experience, contributes to the emerging experience between therapist and client. While this may be true it is a generalization, and as such is not particularly useful in supporting the therapist to reflect in a more specific or focused way. In addressing this concern, Parlett suggests that "what is most relevant and pressing is readily discoverable in the present" He goes on to say "it is important to differentiate the relevant

---

common usage of the word. Stawman (in this volume) addresses this with his development of the idea of context as 'relational ground.' In his important contribution, he explores more fully the meaning embedded in this complex term, and builds what is an important theoretical concept.

ground that goes with the figure of interest and to be specific without being exclusionary or fixed" (2005, p. 45). Essentially he is making the point that while there will always be things that exist beyond the horizon of our current awareness, what is most relevant to the current 'figure of interest' will, with adequate support, be accessible and within reach.[6]

Therefore, in terms of exploring aspects likely to be instrumental in organizing or shaping the phenomenal field of the therapist, there are some aspects more likely to be relevant, and therefore more usefully explored.

Any division is necessarily arbitrary, however I think it is useful to divide this exploration into a reflective framework of four differing but overlapping domains. 1) *Stories of Helping and Being Helped*: Exploring the experiences of helping or being helped that we bring as part of our histories, and the attitudes, assumptions and beliefs that are inevitably embedded in these experiences. 2) *Theoretical Allegiances:* Looking at the various theoretical allegiances we make, particularly in terms of the purpose and practice of therapy, as well as the theoretical assumptions about change and the process of change within therapy. 3) *Emotional Resilience and the Regulation of Contact:* This exploration is concerned with how our capacity for contactful engagement is shaped by both our emotional range and our capacity to tolerate emotional arousal,

---

[6] There are some cautionary remarks to make in relation to this point. Whilst Parlett argues that some things remain beyond the scope of our current awareness, the task of "bringing adequate support" to those things is not necessarily straightforward or even achievable with any certainty. In the case of trauma for instance, certain memories may remain inaccessible because there are not sufficient supports to enable them to emerge more fully into current awareness. We need to be able to recognize and hold that there are limits to what can be supported within a therapeutic relationship and how this can constrain the unfolding of awareness.

in both ourselves and with our clients. This is inextricably linked to the last area of exploration; 4) *Relational Patterns*: Here the invitation is to explore what we know about the patterns that typically shape our interactions with others. For instance, how we move towards the other, how and when we move away, and also our moving against. Put more broadly, it is a means for exploring how we habitually negotiate and manage the relational space.

1) Stories of Helping and Being Helped

I want to suggest that our experiences of being helped in periods of struggle or distress are foundational in forming us as therapists, particularly in terms of our values and attitudes, and our beliefs about what therapy should be. It may be that the impact of these stories and life experiences lessens as we continue in our training and development, adding layers of theory and therapeutic experience. However I believe they make for a useful starting place in terms of self-reflection.

I am using the term 'helping' quite deliberately. Whilst it would make sense to also discuss and reflect on experiences that relate more directly to therapy, quite a number of people come into training without any experience of being a client. The notion of 'helping' is broader in its reach and hopefully encourages reflection on a richer range of life experiences.

This reflective exercise on stories of helping is something I have done regularly in training groups, but could easily be done individually. Students are invited to locate and write down stories of times when they were struggling, or in difficulty, and needing help of some kind. They are encouraged to do this in a way that is descriptive, and essentially phenomenological. They are asked to locate what kind of help they needed, and more importantly, what kind of help actually made a difference. I also ask them to identify what *wasn't* helpful. From this, students construct a list of values or qualities they see as being important or even necessary to the therapeutic process.

As straightforward as this exercise might appear to be, the results are often quite surprising, with people able to recognize in their more immediate experience the impact of stories or experiences they had forgotten about, or thought of as being unimportant and unrelated to their values as a therapist. For instance, a student might realize how his/her absolute determination to provide a warm and supportive presence comes not from any clinical appraisal of what might be needed, but because in a moment of past anguish, warmth was what he/she longed for, received, and felt soothed by. Equally, the student may realize that they have a tendency to relieve their own anxiety by providing others with warmth and soothing. Someone else might register that an unyielding adherence to the practice of self-disclosure is located not in any judgment about what makes for good practice, but because in a key moment of distress, the needed other was experienced as closed off and withholding.

With regard to the examples I have given, I am not saying that warmth or self-disclosure are inappropriate, only that it is helpful to recognize that some of the values we hold as being important, or even essential, come not always from a place of theoretical or clinical thoughtfulness, but rather from the experience of either being helped, or not helped in critical moments.

I know for instance that much of what initially shaped me as a trainer were key educational and training experiences. I knew what had supported my own learning and growth, and wanted to make those aspects part of who I was as a trainer. I also knew what had gotten in the way for me, and held a very clear sense about things I wouldn't do. Recognizing that these values were attached to my own experience was crucial in being able to stretch my thinking about myself as a trainer beyond these constraints. Not everyone in my training groups needs what I needed, and the same can be said for my clients.

Recognizing how these preferences and patterns can be embedded in the way we make contact, particularly when the other is distressed and seeming to need something, is a crucial support for sharpening clinical judgment. Without this increased awareness, our perception of the other is potentially vulnerable to being shaped more by our own experiences and needs than by clearly discerning what the particular client needs in the here-and-now moment.

This exercise can also be helpful in identifying key attributes that at a more general level support clients to engage in the therapeutic process. For example out of a group of students listing what worked for them, it became clear that the attributes of personal warmth and presence were critical in establishing a therapeutic relationship. At the same time the process reinforced that different people need different things. For the therapist less inclined to start with information, it is helpful to realize that for some clients this is an absolutely essential support.

This reflective exercise gives people the opportunity to see how their own experiences shape what they offer, and highlights that this can happen quite subtly, without the therapist necessarily having attended to whether those things are needed or called for in the current situation. In essence it supports the therapist to be more discriminating about what is needed clinically and better able to see how their judgments can be shaped by what has been useful for them. Developing an enhanced awareness of this supports the therapist in attuning to the client and the current therapeutic situation.

A final word on this exercise: My intention is not for it to be applied in a way that assumes causal interpretive links between past events and current practices. I always try to encourage people to stay with those stories that in some way seem important (certainly those that most readily come to mind when asked to think about experiences of being helped), and to find the resonance between what was and what now is. The benefit of the exercise is in the awareness that we are vulnerable to recognizing certain needs and responding in particular ways, while not seeing and not responding to others. Appreciating this allows us to stretch the range of our responses and sharpens our discernment of what is actually needed.

2) Theoretical Allegiances

A next step is to explore the beliefs beginning therapists hold about therapy. Having asked students to identify what was both useful and not useful for them in times of being helped, it is valuable to encourage them to speculate about what makes for effective therapy. The range of questions may include the following: What is the purpose and function of therapy? Why does it work and what makes it effective? What are the key theoretical assumptions that inform how you work?

These questions uncover some of the beliefs and assumptions people hold with regard to what therapy should be, and are particularly useful in that they start to make clear the stances people habitually adopt as therapist. Unexamined, these beliefs can too easily develop into roles or ways of being that are fixed and inflexible: For instance, the therapist who needs to be warm and supportive, or the therapist who is always challenging and uncompromising, or the therapist who needs to be able to fix and solve problems. Through this process therapist can begin to explore how their assumptions inevitably shape both what they allow in the therapeutic relationship, and how they can be at risk of perceiving the needs of the client through the unexamined lens of their own beliefs. This exercise is not dissimilar to the previous one, and in a sense it seeks to uncover a similar set of unexamined assumptions. The primary difference is that in the first instance the reflective lens is that of helping experiences, in this instance, the self-examination occurs through the exploration of the various beliefs and theoretical stances the therapist as adopted.

For some people this exercise lays bare their uncertainty about the tasks and nature of therapy. A very helpful intervention at this point can be to encourage students or beginning therapists to read some of the literature on what makes for therapeutic effectiveness. Not only does it give them the chance to critically engage with the research, it also gives them an opportunity to test their thinking and beliefs against the ideas and experience of others.[7]

It is also valuable to encourage students or beginning therapists to give some thought to the theoretical maps and therapeutic modalities they have adopted. It is no accident that I became a Gestalt therapist. It is a theoretical framework and method of practice that continually pushes me beyond the habitual retroflective response that is my tendency, and at the same time has supported me to live closer to my experience than other life circumstances might have allowed. My longing and need for connection has been validated, and through this much healing has been possible. In short, it was the kind of therapeutic approach I needed for myself.

---

[7] Of particular value is a text by Hubble, Duncan & Miller (1999), *The Heart and Soul of Change: What Works in Therapy.*

The theoretical frameworks we choose will also have an impact on how we make a range of judgments necessary in practice. In part, how we manage boundary issues, questions about touch, and a range of other ethical decisions will be informed, either implicitly or explicitly, by our theoretical allegiances and the traditions they represent. Sometimes these theoretical frameworks will be in conflict with other belief systems or work contexts. For example a trained social worker, experimenting with Gestalt practices in a community welfare setting, might find herself caught in a confusing mix of differing beliefs and values. Untangling these differing frameworks, and understanding how each informs and shapes our practice can be an invaluable exercise.

3) Emotional Resilience and the Regulation of Contact

Nancy McWilliams (1999) makes the rather lovely point that however affect might be understood in the psychoanalytic literature, the therapist never really has the choice not to attend to it. Referring to clients, she says, they "fill our offices with their feelings; they touch us, inspire us, frustrate us, and surprise us. They weep and laugh and rage and tremble with anxiety. We learn from them about feelings we never knew we had" (p. 105).

Before exploring how reflection on emotional processes and our capacity to tolerate feeling can be a useful exercise for the beginning therapist, I want to say a little more about the place of affect theory in contemporary therapeutic literature and explore a connection to the Gestalt model of contact.

As Gestaltists we have tended to talk about contact, and contacting processes, rather than feelings, and yet as McWilliams suggests, we attend to and work with feelings all the time. This begs the question of what relationship might exist between contacting processes and emotion.

Some contemporary psychoanalytic thinkers have come to the view that affect provides a plausible alternative to not only the Freudian drive model, but also to more current theories that privilege cognition and behavior (McWilliams, 1999). McWilliams, goes on to quote Spezzano (1993), who argues that character can be seen as "the container and regulator of a person's affects" (p. 183). Character therefore becomes a means of defending against emotions that are unpleasant, unsettling or distressing; emotions such as shame, guilt, rage, envy, grief, fear, and even lust. Paying attention to emotional patterns necessarily becomes part of the process of understanding how a person is in the world. It is a small leap from here to the language of contacting processes.

In Gestalt theory, the idea of contact is used to describe the means by which we engage with, interact, and function in the world. As such, descriptions of contacting processes, particularly as they become more fixed and habitual, and less responsive to the needs of the individual, are a description of what elsewhere might be termed as character. However, is it emotion that is being regulated when we think about the regulation of contact?

This is an interesting question, and one not really addressed in the Gestalt literature. It is only in the last decade that there has been a shift from understanding the various contacting styles as resistances, to a more relationally consistent position that appreciates that contact is regulated in response to particular needs and situations. This shift in thinking, led by Wheeler in his ground-breaking book, *Gestalt Reconsidered* (1991), and supported by a number of writers, notably Mackewn (1997), has fundamentally changed the way contacting processes are both thought about, and worked with. However, these processes still tend to be talked about in reified ways that disembed them from the relational contexts from which they emerge. For instance, I will talk about my tendency to retro-flect, but do so in a way that fails to look at what it is that I am retroflecting or the contexts in which I am likely to make such a response. Often we do this for the sake of simplicity, and use the language in jargonistic ways that make for easy verbal shortcuts. However, in doing this we do ourselves a disservice and risk not giving sufficient attention to what gives rise to a particular response, and therefore what this might support and constrain. It is a way of thinking that invites a collapsing of the complexity, and leads therefore to overly simplistic formulations. As we think with more intentionality and consistency about what gives rise to a particular contacting style, what may become clearer are the ways in which the regulation of emotion sits beneath, or drives, the way our contact is regulated. To say this in a slightly different way, I am suggesting that emotion is a field dynamic that shapes our capacity for contact. While beginning therapists could quite usefully think about their contacting styles, I think it may be of more value to reflect on their emotional processes, and from this to think about how this might shape their contacting processes.

There are many ways this can be done. A simple starting place is to invite people to make a list of emotions. It's interest-ing to note what comes easily, and what is forgotten. For instance, grief, sadness, despair, rage, anger, guilt, shame, fear, love and longing form the currency of everyday exchange in therapy. Joy can be harder come by. Being thoughtful about how we experience or engage in these emotional states outside of the therapy room will also provide useful information. As much as we might like to think that taking up a professional persona will support us to be less reactive, it is likely that there will be clear points of similarity between how we are in our lives generally and how we are with clients, particularly when we find ourselves in less grounded or less solid places.

I recently conducted a workshop on envy, something given little attention in the humanistic tradition. What was interesting was the degree to which people resisted the strict definition of envy as longing filled with ill intent or malice, and looked for a positive spin. Without this more generous definition, locating envy in personal experience proved to be a difficult task. However, when we moved to thinking about stories in history and literature where envy is the central theme, it was no longer possible to resist its pervasive presence in human experience. It was a nice example of how the felt experience of envy was largely out of awareness, and apparently absent in the experience of many in the room. Not surprisingly, in the initial stages of the discussion, few felt that it had any relevance to their clinical work. However as people were able to recognize stories of envy outside of their own experience, they could begin to locate it within their own responses and reactions. As the discussion unfolded, a number of people were able to recognize how they defended themselves against the experience of envy, and how in particular instances, their contact with clients was shaped by this need.

Another exercise, though designed more for work in pairs, is to invite people to recall and describe personal stories that have a particular emotional quality. For instance, a story of a time of feeling overwhelming by a sense of despair, or the experience of being stricken by grief, or a moment of being filled with a profound sense of joy and well-being. In pairs, the task is to then tell one of these stories, with someone sitting in the role of listener or therapist. The point of the exercise is not for the therapist to make any particular kind of response to the story, but to notice the impact the story has on her/his capacity to remain present. For instance do they notice they tend to move away, or seek in some way to blunt or dull the emotion it evokes? Doing this, with a range of emotions, can be useful in beginning to establish a sense of which emotional states the therapist is able to tolerate, those they are more likely to struggle with, and how they habitually respond to heightened levels of arousal. What can be useful is to notice the point at which the capacity to be responsive and attuned shifts to either a reactive or defensive response, and how this in turn shapes the contacting process.

Elsewhere, I have written about how feelings of attraction toward the client can unsettle and disturb the therapist (O'Shea, 2000; 2003). If uncomfortable with these erotic feelings (either their own or those of the client), therapists are likely to respond in a number of unhelpful ways, ranging from desensitization and a disowning of the feelings, to 'projecting' them with the risk of shaming the client, or acting on them in some way. Being able to tolerate and stay with our feelings, gives us not only a greater capacity to stay near to the client's experience and to maintain a supportive therapeutic presence, but also allows us to explore what we are feeling and what it might be telling us about our own needs, as well as those of the client and what might be called for in the therapeutic process we are engaged in.

The ways in which we move towards clients, and move away from them can be subtle, and sometimes out of our awareness. Developing a greater sense of those emotional states we are less able to tolerate, and increasing our capacity to recognize the phenomena associated with shutting down, moving away, or moving forward either reactively or defensively, will support us to recognize when this happens, and to find ways of staying present to the experience and the therapeutic relationship.

However no amount of exercises in a training group can build the kind of emotional courage needed for the work of being a therapist. At best these exercises serve to highlight areas of vulnerability, sensitizing students/therapist to their emotional reactivity and helping them to recognize when they are no longer able to remain present and attuned to the experience and needs of their clients. In terms of building emotional courage, I do not believe that there are any shortcuts. It is a willingness on the part of the therapist to engage in therapy that best supports the development of this crucial capacity.

4) Relational Patterns

This section follows from the previous one, but is an invitation to explore the deeper themes or issues that organize how we meet with, and engage with, others. It is directed not so much to the therapist who is at the very beginning of his/her work with clients, but the beginning therapist nearer to the end of his or her training. This is simply because some clinical experience or practicum work is necessary for these relational patterns to become evident. We have to have the experience of tripping over ourselves enough times to be able to begin asking the question of what we are contributing to the process.

There are a number of ways of thinking about these core issues or enduring relational themes. A more traditional Gestalt approach would be to describe these patterns in terms of introjects; beliefs, attitudes and attributions that have been taken in and swallowed whole. Fodor (1998) has criticized this view of introjection, arguing that everything we take in is assimilated in some way. It's not that a certain belief or attitude sits somewhere inside of us as an undigested lump, but rather that everything we take in becomes part of our phenomenal field, and contributes to the organization of our perception and experience. This is an important distinction and helps make clear that the work of undoing these introjects is no simple task. Wheeler (1991) talks about "structures of the ground." I like this, and as a metaphor I think it captures more accurately the nature of the work; less like weeding out the unwelcome exotic plant, and more like a complete restructuring of the landscape.

A more controversial way of discuss these relational patterns would be to use the lens of characterlogical disorders, or to use Johnson's (1994) language, character styles. The diagnostic labels associated with these theoretical frameworks have made if difficult for some Gestalt therapists to engage with the ideas, and there is much debate in the Gestalt literature about the value of this approach. While it is well beyond both the scope and intention of this chapter to address this issue, I do think there are a number of contemporary writers, Johnson (1994) and McWilliams (1994) in particular, who describe these characterlogical processes in ways that are sufficiently consistent with the principles of phenomenological description. Whatever theoretical differences do exist, and I do not want to downplay them, I think they are worth struggling with for the insights into human functioning these differing perspectives offer.

Although the idea of relational patterns feels relatively straightforward, understanding what they are, and how they shape who we are and how we engage with others, feels infinitly more complex. For example, I might have a good understanding of narcissistic processes; however, it is another thing altogether for me to be able to see how my more narcissistically driven needs shape who I am as a therapist. My capacity to do this is in some respects dependent on my being able to step out of the shame that would have me disown my narcissistic appetites entirely, and find a place of compassion for this aspect of myself. Giving up my need to defend against the parts of myself that leave me feeling ashamed, frees me to see more clearly how my work is organized by these key relational patterns.

While I think this work of understanding and engaging with these relational patterns is complex and demanding, it is important, and even the beginning therapist will benefit from some reflection on these issues.

A simple exercise is to make a list of those self-statements or self-judgments that emerge in those moments when we feel most fragile, or distressed. Such judgments typically include things like, "nobody loves me," or "I don't belong," or "my only worth is in what I do for others." A follow on from this is to think about the kinds of contexts or situations in which these judgments are provoked, and the response they evoke. For example, I might have judgment or core issues around having to always be right, know I am vulnerable to feeling this whenever someone disagrees with me or challenges something I say. In response to this feeling I know I am likely to pull away from the other with an air of offended hurt. Having some sense of these key relational themes, what is likely to trigger them, and what response I am likely to make, is invaluable.

What this work points to is the need for the beginning therapist to engage in his or her own process of self-discovery and healing. The work of understanding ourselves is fundamental to our capacity to stay present to our experience and that of our client's. Our awareness and our capacity to know and love ourselves are the things that allow us to attend with exquisite sensitivity to the space that emerges between us and the client.

A Further Point for Reflection

Described above are processes that can be taken up as reflective exercises away from the experience of actually sitting with a client. What it doesn't address is the need to be both aware of, and attentive to, what might be impacting the therapist in a more immediate way as she/he walks into the therapy room. Both are important and contribute significantly to the therapist's capacity to be present with the client.

For example, being able to register the kind of day you have had, or are having, and how that impacts your mood, your energy, or your capacity to think and engage with clarity, and perhaps most importantly your ability to attend to your client, is an important and necessary skill. Knowing how to manage a sense of being tired, or distracted, is equally impor-tant. Counseling textbooks often suggest a range of grounding exercises to support the therapist in this process. Also useful are short physical exercises which can be supportive both in terms of increasing the therapist's energy and sense of vitality, but also in terms increasing awareness in the here and now. They are all resources that are useful for the therapist to have in terms of supporting them to be present with the client and less caught in the vicissitudes of the day.

Conclusion

This reflective model offers a framework that allows therapists to be thoughtful about some of what might shape and organize their experience as they meet with clients and engage in the therapeutic process. As such it is also a framework that will support therapists in becoming more consistently relational in their approach. It is by no means exhaustive, and the differing domains I have described are somewhat arbitrary. Nonetheless, the process of engaging with the question of who we are, and how this shapes our phenomenal field, can only enrich us. I do believe this is crucial in terms of our capacity to stay close to our own experience and that of our clients. I am drawn to the rather poetic idea that 'to know all is to forgive all.' Of course we cannot know all, and even our knowing of ourselves is at best partial. But in our willingness to know ourselves as best as we can, while at the same time accepting our fallibility, we find the freedom to engage with curiosity rather than judgment in all the therapeutic process evokes.

References

Fairfield, M. & O'Shea, L. (2007) *Getting Beyond Individualism.* (Prepublication)

Fodor, I.E. (1996). A woman and her body: The cycles of pride and shame. In R. Lee & G. Wheeler (Eds.), *The Voice of Shame: Silence and Connection in Psychotherapy.* San Francisco: Jossey-Bass.

Hubble, M.A., Duncan, B.L., & Miller, S.D. (1999). *The Heart and Soul of Change: What Works in Therapy.* Washington: American Psychological Association.

Jacobs, L. (2003). Ethics of context and field: The practices of care, inclusion and openness to dialogue. *The British Gestalt Journal, 12*(2), 88-96.

Johnson, S.M. (1994). *Character Styles.* New York: Norton & Company.

Kepner, J. (2003). The embodied field. *The British Gestalt Journal, 12*(1), 6-14.

Lewin, K. (1997). *Resolving Social Conflicts & Field Theory in Social Sciences.* Washington: American Psychological Association.

Mackewn, J. (1997). *Developing Gestalt Counselling.* London: Sage Publications.

McConville, M. (2001). Husserl's phenomenology in context. *Gestalt Review, 5*(3), 195-204.

McWilliams, N. (1994). *Psychoanalytic Diagnosis: Understanding Personality Structure in the Clinical Process*. New York: Guilford Press.

McWilliams, N. (1999). *Psychoanalytic Case Formulation:* New York, Guildford Press.

O'Shea, L. (2000). Sexuality: Old struggles & new challenges. *Gestalt Review, 4*(1), 8-25.

O'Shea, L. (2003). The erotic field. *The British Gestalt Journal, 12*(2), 105-110.

Parlett, M. (1991). Reflections of field theory. *The British Gestalt Journal, 1*, 69-81.

Parlett, M. (1993). Towards a more Lewinian gestalt therapy. *British Gestalt Journal 2/2*, 115-120.

Parlett, M. (1997). The unified field in practice. *Gestalt Review 1/1*, 16-33.

Parlett, M. (2005). Field theory, in A.L. Woldt, & S.M. Toman, (Eds.), *Gestalt Therapy: History, Theory and Practice*. London: Sage.

Roberts, A. (1999). The field talks back. *The British Gestalt Journal, 8*(1), 35-46.

Spezzano, C. (1993). *Affect in Psychoanalysis: A Clinical Synthesis*. Hillsdale: Analytic Press.

Stawman, S. (2009) Relational Gestalt: Four waves. (This text, pp 11-36).

Staemmler, F.-M. (2006). A babylonian confusion?: On the uses and meanings of the term 'field." *The British Gestalt Journal, 15*(2), 64-83.

Wheeler, G. (1991). *Gestalt Reconsidered: A New Approach to Contact and Resistance*. New York: Gardner Press.

Wright, G. (1984). Reflections at the speed of thought. *The Gestalt Journal 7/1*, 75-83.

Yontef, G. M. (1984). Modes of thinking in gestalt therapy. *The Gestalt Journal 7/1*, 33-74.

Zinker, J. (2001). *Sketches: An Anthology of Essays, Art, and Poetry*. Cambridge, MA: GestaltPress.

Dialogue Goes To Work:

Relational Organisational Gestalt

• • • • • • • • • • • • • • • • •

Sally Denham-Vaughan and Marie-Anne Chidiac

W riting is frequently motivated by a passionate interest and involvement in a topic. We would therefore like to introduce this chapter by giving you some background to our shared passion for both relational Gestalt psychotherapy and working in organisations.

I, (SD-V), work as a Clinical Psychologist and Senior Manager in the British National Health system. Here, psychology is closely allied to the medical model and has a focus on individual diagnostic formulations, and personalised "treatment plans." My early acquaintance with Gestalt psychotherapy (some twenty-five years ago), mapped nicely onto this individualistic paradigm. I could "diagnose" myself according to the cycle of experience, notice my "interruptions to contact," be more fully aware of my needs and then aggress upon the environment to meet them.

Recently, I have faced a growing dilemma; empowering individuals to "meet their needs," can lead to a trail of human casualties lying in their wake! Short term personal needs get prioritised resulting in immediate and often individualistic and/or oversimplified solutions to problems, with little regard for long-term relationships.

I initially observed that the emerging discipline of "Gestalt in Organisations" looked very similar to the individually orientated Gestalt clinical paradigm outlined above, with "successful performers" (be they individuals, teams or companies), focussing on a neo-Darwinian approach to competitors. I find attempts to work both clinically and organisationally in this context immensely stressful; rather like running a triage clinic on the front line of a battlefield. I am therefore searching for alternative ways of "being:" solutions that do not create more casualties than survivors, and that optimise health, growth and creativity.

I, (MAC), did not set out to become a Gestalt organisational consultant, I evolved into one. In the early 90's I consulted with organisations wanting to "capitalise on their human assets," with greater emphasis being placed on the relational rather than transactional aspects of the "psychological contract" (D'Annunzio-Green et. al, 2005). Sadly, very few organisations really know what this means in practice. Mergers, for instance, often see the human "asset" walk itself out of the door, as idealised talk of integrity, fairness, or bottom-up-consultations fail to come alive. Motivating staff often meant laughable affairs such as outdoor retreats, bungie jumping or survival tests for executives. This *disconnection* between what people really want or feel and the HR interventions aimed at increasing motivation, (and thereby performance), is what attracts me to Gestalt theory applied to organisations. I am searching for something more "real" and congruent in the way businesses connect with the emotional and personal lives of their employees.

An Increasing Relational Focus in Organisational Life

Within the clinical domain, the emergence of an increasingly relationally based emphasis within the Gestalt psychotherapy literature has already led to changes. These are perhaps best summarised by Lee (2004), who makes the case for a "Relational Ethic." He argues that the need to create specific types of supportive environmental and relational conditions for clients is *directly* proposed by Gestalt psychotherapy's emphasis upon "field phenomena" as formative of the self. In other words, since our surroundings directly affect who we are being and becoming, ignoring the impact of negative environments means that we are ignoring the deleterious effect this has on an individual's functioning. According to Lee, this is theoretically incongruent as well as personally damaging.

This emphasis on the importance of physical and phenomenal surroundings was always highlighted in Paul Goodman's contribution to Gestalt therapy theory, and it seems obvious to us just how essential this is to consider within an organisational context. This relevance has recently also been emphasised by Frew, (2006), who argues that:

> In their "youth," both organisational leadership theory and Gestalt therapy practice were "leader heavy." More attention, research and writing was devoted to the leader/therapist and less attention paid to the followers/clients and aspects of the relational/environmental field in which the leadership and therapy were being practiced (p. 124).

In the last decade, there has been an increasing interest in the place and use of dialogue in management processes (see Isaacs, 1993, Schein, 2003, Jacobs & Heracleous, 2005, to name a few). Bokeno (2007) for instance, stresses that within organisations dialogue should not be viewed as an instrument, but rather involves tough interpersonal work requiring a radical reorientation of how organisations think about human interaction.

A Focus on Support

The continuous drive for performance improvement in organisations, as well as the emergence of data relating to the costs of stress-related problems, has challenged the way change is approached in organisations.

Organisational Gestalt practitioners are focusing on creating supportive field conditions, increasing leadership and presence and maximising working performance, rather than working just to treat the individual casualties of toxic working environments. Writers such as Nevis, (1987), Bentley, (2001), Newton, (2002), and Rainey Tolbert, (2004), have documented this work, often providing a perspective that integrates Gestalt therapy, general systems theory and organisation development.

We believe that the time is now right to develop a radically relational organisational Gestalt approach; one that emphasises core conditions of dialogue, the power of developmental issues, and attends to developing supportive field conditions that will act to reduce shame. Relational Organisational Gestalt, (ROG), is our personal contribution to that project. We begin with some conceptual framework and then move to application.

"Brothers in Arms:" Organisations Are More Than Collections of Individuals

There is an increasing awareness in business of the need to work in partnerships by creating linkages across the value chain (from supplier to customer) and looking at benefits and limitations from a systemic perspective rather than an individual one. Although this is happening more readily and visibly at a macro, organisation-wide level, it is yet to translate to individuals who are still assessed in isolation against mostly individualistic competencies.

Attending to a Gestalt field theoretical perspective, however, brings us into "a state of necessary respect for, and inclusion of, both other people and our environment," (Denham-Vaughan, 2005a, p. 147), which is perhaps most challenging in a working situation. Here, we ask people to transcend their traditional focus on optimising individual functioning and instead also focus on the good of the wider community. This is not a message that many Chief Executives within a commercial setting have wanted to hear, historically, but increasingly whole systems approaches have been shown to bring maximal benefits across the organisation. We believe therefore, that the workplace is now ready to embrace complex, emergent, relational and multi-dimensional change strategies, the "stuff" of a whole systems approach.

So far the challenge of moving relationally oriented Gestalt practice into organisations has not been widely written about. We want therefore to address this here by articulating and demonstrating our developing model of Relational Organisational Gestalt (ROG), as applied to the *coaching* con-text, since this is perhaps the most immediately illuminating example of putting our theory into practice.

The Coaching Challenge

In the mid to late 90's links were starting to be made between "emotionally intelligent leaders" and business performance (Opengart, 2005; Goleman, 2000). Not only are leaders expected to cope with growing complexity and stress, but also an awareness of their personal styles, prejudices and personal impact is now a common leadership requirement in increasingly global and multicultural organisations.

Coaching has become the main form of facilitating this necessary personal development, and companies are investing significant money, time and skill in this area. For example, in two years 17 Melbourne-based HR directors of large companies spent 15 million dollars on coaching programmes to develop their executives (Dagley, 2006). On a global scale, the expenditure therefore is immense. But what is it exactly that people are investing in?

Many coaching techniques try to emulate the fast moving, action-oriented surroundings of businesses, but in this confluence we think they lose sight of the power of relationships and strategies of dialogue to maximise potential. Our experience is that optimal personal growth via coaching is facilitated by authentic presence with our clients. Relational coaching thus requires both backbone and heart (O'Neil, 2000), both rigour and relationship. The business world is ready for coaching that emphasises the need for integrating and developing qualities of both "Will and Grace;" where "will" can be defined as "directed action" and ability to initiate, and "grace" as a quality of "receptivity" and responsiveness (see Denham-Vaughan, 2005b, for a full discussion).

In particular, we believe it is important to move away from coaching based on the deficit, (acquisitional), model. Historically, coaching contracts overstress the need for upfront objectives and demonstrable outcomes; the starting point frequently being what is "wrong" with an individual and/or what needs fixing, and with a gathering of 360° feedback to garner relevant data.

In contrast, the ROG coaching model we develop in this chapter includes the use of a systemic, field-oriented approach, where issues emerging for the coachee are viewed as a function of the current relational context with the coach. The dyadic meeting thereby offers a window to aspects of relational style that could be relevant at work, both in assisting individual performance, and also — through the new relational experience in the dyad — a window to additional relational skills that can be offered to a team. For example, specific elements of relational support that enable a firmer sense of self and mobilise creative potential can be identified, practised and transferred to the working situation. Here, these act not only as a set of competencies the individuals can employ for their own benefit, but also as psychological procedural competencies people can bring to their teams, thereby developing more supportive and person friendly environments.

A wonderful example of the mutuality of relational coaching is put forward by Boyatzis et. al (2006) who contends that when leaders experience compassion through coaching the development of others, they experience psychophysiological effects that restore the body's natural healing and growth processes. This statement is similar to our own conclusion that "presence" (defined as energetic availability and fluid responsiveness), is a potential attribute of *both* coach and coachee (Chidiac & Denham-Vaughan, 2007). With presence, both individuals are affected and changed by the meeting.

ROG coaching assumes that "what needs to happen" will emerge. It is not a context where the coachee needs to arrive with a clear, pre-formed "agenda for change" *or* where the coach sets targets or goals. The most important dimension is considered to be the emergent relational aspect; the evolution of what "we" are going to address *together*. It is however, the *coache's* responsibility and task to take the lead in establishing the relational supports within which this occurs. The coach initiates attempts to understand the coachee's experience and desires. Successful exploration requires a mutual co-regulatory and reciprocal process that is a feature of quality dialogic relational Gestalt clinical work; calibrating the differential elements of "needed" and "repeated" (see note[1]) relationships as they occur here and now between coach and coachee—and paralleling this to the coachee's working context. Elements of this process will now be explained in more detail.

---

[1] 'Needed' relationships refers to relational experiences which, if present, would now provide optional conditions for maximising both current performance and mobilising positive change.

'Repeated' relationships refers to sedimented relational patterns emerging in the present that have been useful as a way of surviving less than optimal environments. Although useful as emergency adaptations, these patterns also tend to reduce a person's range of responsiveness and perceptiveness, and are likely to decrease creativity and performance. In extreme cases, 'repetitions' of particular relational patterns may be traumatising; for example, the experience of being bullied or victimised at work may reflexively trigger memories of being bullied at school. This 'triggering' process can therefore lead to a sudden constriction of contacting possibilities in the current environment, resulting in decreased range of "selfings" or ways of being able to function and respond. Obviously, what is "needed" and what is "repeated" varies according to each person.

A Relational Coaching Framework

ROG coaching aims to develop the coachee's relational competencies by exploring his/her relational needs and then examining how these are met, (or not), with other people. We emphasise, both theoretically and practically, how different ways of being emerge as a function of changing environments, be these physical or relational. In other words, we explore the minute ways in which the self I am here-and-now with you is directly, immediately and constantly affected by who and how you are with me and vice versa. In our contracting process, there is thus an explicit focus on the coaching relationship as the major educational vehicle and context for learning and development.

We identify four key dimensions of ROG Coaching, which we will now briefly describe:

1). The Working Alliance

We have found that in order to create sufficiently safe surroundings for relevant personal, often profound issues to emerge it is vital that the coach attends closely to the coachee's experience of the coaching relationship.

For instance, finding the right balance between challenge and support is crucial, particularly when the coachee is shame prone, or if they work in extremely shaming organisational environments. Too little support from the coach can result in the coachee modulating contact by withdrawing and "hiding;" while an "overdose of niceness" can lead to avoidance of looking at the coachee's contribution to difficult situations. In summary, it is important to create relational conditions where the coachee's issues can emerge, rather than either be hunted down or lost in a wash of overprotectiveness.

Since the coaching situation necessarily involves an exploration of work performance, with either an overt or covert expectation of "improvement," there is often potential for shame. This "evaluative" component, combined with possible exposure of previously hidden and/or unknown developmental relational issues requires considerable psychotherapeutic skill from the coach. Kets de Vries (2005) refers to this process as establishing the "Clinical Orientation" or utilising the clinical paradigm, and states this is vital if coaching is to be beneficial.

2). Dialogic/Interpersonal Dimension

It is outside the scope of this paper to offer a detailed description of the elements of dialogic Gestalt psychotherapy theory and practice. In summary however, "Dialogic Gestalt" refers to the therapeutic application of the philosophy of dialogue developed by Martin Buber, (e.g., 1958). When applied within a relationship, this involves a rhythmic oscillation of both "I – it" and "I-thou" modes of being by the therapist/coach to explore the meeting with the client/coachee at the emerging contact boundary. Four key "dialogic competencies" are required by the therapist and/or coach and are described by Jacobs (1989) as "Presence, Commitment to Dialogue, Inclusion and Confirmation."

Briefly noted, in terms of the philosophical ground of ROG, the interpersonal dimension of coaching builds on existential phenomenology (as opposed to transcendental phenomenology — see Stolorow and Jacobs, 2006, for a full description), a hermeneutic model of self incorporating awareness of the here and now, and a dialogic stance (Hycner and Jacobs, 1995). It is within this interpersonal dimension that the coach aims to spend the majority of their time, and that yields the most noticeable results in the workplace.

3). Developmental Dimension

The use of the word "Relational" within this chapter when referring to the ROG model incorporates additional features to traditional dialogic Gestalt psychotherapy (which is, of course, also "relational"). We used this term to refer specifically to the model outlined fully in Hycner and Jacobs (1995), which features use of Kohut's (1984), "self-object" transferences, together with a methodology originating in contemporary inter-subjective systems theory (see Stolorow, Brandchaft and Atwood, 1987). Intersubjectivists examine the minutiae of relational patterns emerging in the here and now between therapist/coach and client/coachee. In particular, the "inter-subjective" domain is highlighted as revealing interpersonal patterns which can be explored and transformed by the coach's skills of "affect attunement," understanding and embodied and affective responsiveness to the coachee.

These psychodynamic theories add a developmental dimension to the exploration of the here and now dialogue and enable the coach to view the habitual relational patterns that emerge during a coaching process as reflective of archaic relational "lacks," or "needed" relationships. These often present as powerful unfulfilled longings within current relationships. Within an organisational environment, it is our experience that knowledge of, and ability to work with, these relational configurations (self-object transferences), is at least as important as an appreciation of so-called "classic" transference responses created by "repeated" relational situations. We actually see more individuals struggling with the *absence* of key relational supports they need from their leaders/colleagues in order to function optimally, than we do instances of positively damaging behaviours. Hence, the focus on "what is missing" or longed for can be crucial. In practice, we find it helps to identify these Kohutian self-object needs and transferences as they emerge, not only in the *content* of the material, but especially *within* the coaching dyad.

Although we use this clinical paradigm, we are not seeing emergence of these self-object needs as developmental deficits that need to be clinically addressed in therapy, but as evidence of healthy, ongoing longings for mirroring, idealisation and twinship, which support psychic stability, containment and growth. For example, a positive idealised relationship with a leader can create a sense of identify and containment during a change process. Leaders should therefore be able to both recognise their own needs for idealisation and support and tolerate those needs when they are present in others. Similarly, needs for twinship and a sense of belonging, of being part of something, can reinforce self-worth, self-esteem and bring a sense of intimacy and sharing. Within an organisation, this can give a clear sense of an individual's contribution to the whole, and positively reinforce performance. Likewise, being accurately mirrored can give a real sense of competency and self-worth, of being seen as an important individual. We believe that increasing awareness of this developmental dimension of relational experiences provides us with the lens through which to focus on growing edges for coachees.

4). Systemic Dimension

A key difference between Relational Gestalt *Psychotherapy* and ROG *coaching*, (more on this later), is that the latter process is primarily an aspect of an organisational process rather than a private individual initiative. As such, the ethical imperative is not only to the client, but also to the organisation. On occasions, this can lead to conflicted feelings in the coach, which require thorough examination and exploration in supervision. It is vital however that the coach holds this organisational focus, and also has a good understanding of the situational demands of the work system and the inherent challenges it poses to the coachee. It is this knowledge of the organisational field that gives credibility and qualification to practice as a ROG *coach*, as opposed to a psychotherapist.

Two Coaching Examples

The two transcripts that we have provided here offer a window into ROG as it is practiced in a coaching context. It is important to note that the transcripts are also "live experiments" aimed at developing, explicating and articulating Relational Organisational Gestalt coaching principles. As such, they are taken from an ongoing series of "co-coaching" sessions that we, as Gestalt practitioners working both clinically and organisationally, have undertaken in order to support and develop our practice.

We are presenting two excerpts from co-coaching sessions, where one of us is working as the coach and the other is the coachee. The sessions have taken place over approximately the six months prior to writing this paper, and have generally lasted between 20-30 minutes, occurring at approximately 4-week intervals. Sessions have generally taken place face-to-face, but due to travelling commitments, have occasionally taken place on the phone. All sessions are tightly bounded and separated from other contact, which has included course development and also working together as psychotherapy trainers within a Gestalt Psychotherapy Training Institute. Both of us however, have "majority time" careers in other organisations: SDV as a Senior Manager and clinician within the British National Health Service and MAC as an independent organisational consultant/ coach.

The transcripts have been organised in this way in order to provide a direct insight into not only the thinking of the coach, but also the coachee. Previous work, (Chidiac & Denham-Vaughan, 2007) concerning the use of presence and "fit" between individuals, concluded that in a genuinely horizontal and dialogic relationship, the client has presence as well as the therapist/coach. This means that the coachee's insights, opinions and changes throughout the session are as important as the coach's, and that both individuals contribute equally to the ongoing hermeneutic cycle. In addition, we believe that the coachee is likely to need to demonstrate, learn, and acquire skills of dialogic relating in order to maximally benefit from relational coaching. In saying this, we are not only referring to optimising their own personal growth, but also to acquiring essential relational skills for use in the workplace. These skills are central to a transformational leadership style where use of presence and ability to form and sustain a variety of relationships is crucial.

The material that follows is, as has already been stated, taken from two separate coaching sessions. In each, there is the unique opportunity to read the individual formulations of coach and coachee concerning what is going on in the session. These formulations were evolved in isolation from the dyadic partner. Each point of punctuation for commentary also includes theoretical linkage to exemplify the theoretical teaching points that we have already articulated.

Introduction to Transcript One

Coachee: At our previous coaching session, we had worked on my fear and anxiety around a new work opportunity that had arisen for me. The change implied a considerable shift in direction and the need to re-skill myself in certain areas. After that session, I was clearer that what was holding me back wasn't "rational" but a fear of what I didn't know, of what might be. I had chewed on this and had decided to go forward with the new opportunity.

Coach: The previous session had crystallised a figure that had been emerging over the past four sessions: whether to go for a promotion into a specialist area of work, or whether that was going to be "too much." I was aware of "treading carefully" as, although this seemed a relatively simple choice, I judged that the coachee was finding it difficult to make full contact with this figure. Last session I had commented on emotions seeming to "hover" in the background, but I had experienced her as unwilling to get in contact with them. [Transcription of coach's comments in italics.]

Theoretical linkage. The coachee says she "worked on her fear and anxiety," while the coach has found her "unwilling" to contact emotions. This points to several possibilities, which might be clarified in this session. The two members of the dyad may have different contact styles, so that what one experiences as a strong emotion, the other experiences as a "potential emotion." It seems there is a need for a higher degree of affect attunement (see later), by the coach to increase relational support, if this figure is going to be shared.

Transcript One

Coachee: Erm…yeah it's been the dithering that I actually didn't like. It was the uncertainty. (Pause). And I've decided that my wobble is connected to what I don't *know* so I am wobbling…and I won't know until I jump in.

Coach: Mmm, what happened then? There was a little wu-uh?

Coachee: You know, it's like you imagine things that are worse than they will be, and so that holds you back and ...And I was just thinking, "...is what is holding me back my reality or my fear?" [Sigh; Pause]. And so, it almost feels like ...I'm taking a run and I am going to jump off!

Coach: Over here, when you sat down and you said you were in a different place, my experience is that you have already jumped.

Coachee: Yes, maybe it does feel that way. Maybe it has to feel a bit that way. Because I have been jumping in and then I have been going "whooooo" with my wobble. Actually, once I am in the situation, I feel alright.

Coach: You feel alright?

Coachee: Yeah, I feel alright! I feel "Oh yeah" I can cope with this. I can, you know, this is a strange phrase, I can bullshit my way through this.

Coach: You can bullshit your way through this. And how is that – to say that?)

Coachee: Really familiar to me... (Laughs). I know I can manage this. I think what I need to get a handle on, it's not the new job that will be difficult, it's not...it's how demanding I get of me whilst I am doing it.

Coach: Sounds like you're going to set yourself a standard that you don't need to set in order to manage it. How is that?

Coachee: I think it will be a challenge, I don't know if I will manage it. I don't know if that makes sense?

Coach: My experience is that you are going to say you are bullshitting and my bet is I won't know; but you will

*know and feel disappointed or somehow that you could
do better.*
Coachee: Mm, and I will work to do better.

Coachee: I am taken aback by how accurate my coach
is in saying that I *have* already jumped and I felt seen. My
figure however, was around whether I would have enough
resources to cope now that I *have* jumped. Her next
intervention, about her not knowing if I'm bullshitting or not,
makes me focus on a forward direction rather than whether
I will be able to manage. It also takes me out of the intrapsychic and into a more relational frame of reference.

Coach: I am concerned by my sense that she has
already made an important decision to jump in, rather than
making it within the session. I challenge her by bringing her
awareness into the present and to what might be
happening between us. I am exploring the potential for
parallel process; that is, is what she is describing about her
process in relation to work, occurring here? In other words,
might she now "bullshit her way through" our session.

Theoretical linkage: The change of direction by the
coach into an exploration of the "here and now" relationship, begins to raise the idea of a "relational figure." This
move is informed by the coach's awareness that the
coachee seems to be very reliant on self-support and is not
taking much relational support from the coach. The coach
is wondering how this relates to her issue about work, and
is already looking to a potential focus for transformation. If
she took more support, might her sense of "too much" be
reduced? The interventions are future focussed and
also change focussed, as illustrative of Relational Organisational Coaching as opposed to relational Gestalt
Psychotherapy.

Coach: You'll work to do better, even though from out here, you might be doing just fine.

Coachee: Yeah. Somehow it is what I know. It's like I have to be real.....you know? It's something about integrity that comes into it.

Coach: What I notice is that you are describing a system there that is pretty much about you and your standards and your integrity, but somehow also knowing that you will be OK for other people.

Coachee: Yes, and they probably have less integrity?

[Pause].

Coach: You look a bit alarmed that you said that.

Coachee: Because I am imaging how much I am projecting this? My sense of what is out there is that I know that generally I will meet people with less knowledge and less integrity.

Coach: So, where that leaves me is interested in what is happening here and now between you and me, which is of interest to me. There is a really important part of your process that you have done on your own, that I am now witnessing but I have not been part of.

Coachee: Yeah.

Coach: I'm not making a judgment about that. I'm describing how I experience being with you. It feels like you go away and manage yourself.

Coachee: Yes, I guess it's how it is. [Pause]. I am now wondering if I have left you behind? I sort of worry about that but then also go to a familiar place of making decisions on my own. It's like what informs me that it's right.

Coach: Comes from yourself?

Coachee: Yeah, yes, that's it. OK. Does that make sense?

Coach: *Erm, it makes partial sense, because what I hear is that most of your thinking and processing is a one-person event. And when you say you have left me behind... I think it is such a curious configuration of where I am in relation to you...behind, that you have gone on without me.*

Coachee: But is that an interpretation of what you said? because I don't feel that you are behind, I feel that something happened between us last time we met.

Coach: *Absolutely*

Coachee: That you are....I don't feel you now behind.

Coach: *No, I am feeling alongside, and that you had a gap and in the gap, something really important has happened to you. And it just has echoes for me of this process that you are describing about how your wobble will not be about other people; it will be something about you.*

Coachee: About me. Yes. Because I think I found it really affirming, you know, solid, when you said that others won't notice the wobble, you said something like "others won't know."

Coachee: I worried about my coach and whether she felt left behind. For a moment, I wondered if I needed to work harder here and that I hadn't done enough... I felt our relationship was safe enough for me to say that and also to believe that she felt alongside, even though I didn't feel I was making perfect sense...

Coach: I am still struggling to explore how "together" we are. I have a concern about her statement regarding "integrity." Is she commenting on her experience of me? She is correct that I do not have specialist knowledge of her work content. I am struggling to support myself sufficiently to sustain the inquiry about how we are doing relationally, but I sense this inquiry is essential. I was surprised by her formulation of the "gap" I pointed out, as her "leaving me behind" and I felt slightly "put down." I noticed a "frisson" of defensiveness creeping in!

Theoretical linkage. The focus on the current relationship as a window into the coachee's relational patterns at work is beginning to deliver valuable material. There is a sense that the awarenesses are "new," and an indication of archaic and developmental "id" themes emerging. The coach has sustained the dialogic work sufficiently enough through her commitment, to raise a potential "repeating" relational theme: that of being self-sufficient, but concerned for leaving another "behind." Kohut's self-object/narcissistic transferences are now worth considering. The client does not doubt her competency, (mirroring), and exhibits no fears of being able to lead, (idealising): There are doubts however as to whether another will be able to "keep up." This seems more in the realm of a longing for twinship, of being genuinely identified, affiliated and belonging with others who are essentially similar. There is an emerging (healthy) narcissistic concern regarding being "too little or too much," which is commonly encountered when coaching highly successful and competent individuals. Although they suffer from the usual concerns regarding taking on new/more challenges, they have accumulated experience of being able to rise to the occasion adequately. This often leaves them somewhat lonely and unsupported at work, as colleagues may struggle more openly and thereby get more support.

Relationally, this theme is now "lurking" around the dyad. Although initially the coachee was seeking assistance regarding whether she could "manage" her new role, it is the coach who is being "left behind" and is feeling defensive. Thus, the figure of inadequacy has shifted. Theoretically, classic analysts would argue this is via the mechanism of "projective identification," or that the coachee *may* be projecting this issue onto the coach. Relationally, we must hold the possibility that the coachee's attitude may have triggered a repetitive theme in the coach's life which pertains to her worry over her adequacy; or that she may also be accurately *perceiving* that the coach lacks specialist knowledge concerning the coachee's new role. Knowledge/information gaps such as these are common and unavoidable in coaching. The task for the Relational Organisational coaches is not to "skill themselves up" (as is appropriate in "Acquisitional" coaching), but to sustain the availability of their relational presence without defending against, and/or shaming, the coachee.

Coach: *No, I imagine they just won't know that you're wobbling unless you choose to show them. You know that you're less solid than you might be, and that bothers you.*

Coachee: That matters.

Coach: That matters; and your chin goes up.

Coachee: Yes, that matters. Somehow it seems that the integrity is so important; so if you're bullshitting, that matters. I think that is why sometimes I put so much work into things. It's not for the others; it's for myself. [Long exhale]

Coach: I just felt a bit fatigued then.

[Pause]

Coachee: I just think I can't...it's like, do I need to put so much work in on one hand, if what can be achieved can be achieved with less. And then, on the other hand, am I being real and honest enough if I don't?

[Pause]

Coach: I'm noticing you look a bit erm...not upset, but a bit moved. Just wondering whether it is with the content or something.

Coachee: The content is fine, it is just the realisation of this ...I felt drained as I said that.

Coach: I feel a bit drained and around my eyes I feel a sense of strain and pressure. [Pause] It sounds like your definition of "real" is a 100% effort.

Coachee: It means.. to always... how can I always give 100% of more effort?

Coach: That's right, good question. [Pause] So "real" sounds like 100% full-on effort and anything less than that, you somehow wonder if you have let yourself down.

Coachee: Yeah, it's like I've been dishonest.

Coach: With yourself?

Coachee: Yes, I guess so.

Coach: What about...I'm just going to put in a bit of my experience...let's imagine I'm going out for a dinner with you and 100% effort is a three course meal. I only want a sandwich; I have not got appetite for a three course meal.

Coachee: [Sigh] But you need the three courses to choose from!

Coach: Oh, I see. So you have to get it all out and get it all ready.

Coachee: I need to be sure that, if needs be, it will be there because that's what you might need....

Coach: And it sounds like you don't trust me to tell you... or to bring my own....

Coachee: No. No I don't.

Coach: What's it like to say that? No. Like I might not be able to look after myself and my needs as well as you could...

Coachee: I think you can for you, but you are coming to dinner with me so you want something from me, and I need to be ready, because I said I would be.

[Pause]

Coach: Ready to do what sounds like anything at all times, on a state of alert?

Coachee: If you put it in a work context, you know, I protect myself by contracting. I agree and I need to be within those boundaries. I need to feel as fully there as you might have the right to expect, and as I would have the right to expect of me. And it feels….

Coachee: The example of the meal and my coach coming to dinner resonated strongly with me. In realising the state of alertness this puts me in, the issue of how well resourced I am to take this new job is back for me. The difference now is that I am clearer on my responsibility in working in this way.

Coach: I am still insisting on the "we" dimension; highlighting the lack of checking out with me/the other, or being open to the emerging relational domain. I have a very strong embodied sense of how exhausting this might be, maybe a "confluent" moment, but a useful one to support my compassion for her struggle. I was also dimly aware that this was more comfortable for me than sitting with her competence, which potentially triggered feelings of inadequacy in me.

Theoretical linkage. The relational connection seems to contain a great deal of potential for shame for both parties. The coachee is sensing she is doing something "wrong" and the coach is starting to lose her self-support and conviction in her competence. This is evidenced by the increasing amounts of her own material/experience coming in.

The use of "Inclusion" in this way is a helpful strategy for increasing awareness of our own presence, but is potentially more shaming for the coachee due to the differentiation from the "authority figure." The coach does try to minimise the risk of this by sharing her own process (inclusion), in a specific way that shifts the focus from discussion of content to awareness of embodied process. This also strives for connection with developmental ways of relating which precede the verbal self[2] (Stern, 1985). These strategies of affective and embodied attunement can be highly effective in building the interpersonal relationship. The result we see is that the coach does become somewhat "over-identified" with the coachee as evidenced by her sense of fatigue and drop in energy, but has appropriately preferred the risk of confluence to that of shaming the coachee. Later in this section however, while trying to break away from the confluence, she brings in her own image of the meal, but over-differentiates (to bolster her own sense of worth?), and the client does feel

---

[2] Stern (1985) puts forward a view of how infants experience the world around them and how from that they develop a sense of themselves and of their relation to others. He contends that development proceeds through complex 'domains of relatedness' which emerge in succession but do not replace each other. The *Domain of Emergent Relatedness* starts at birth and is the primary experience of an emergent sense of self in the sensory field; the infant is able to take in data across different modes of perception. In the *Domain of Core Relatedness*, the infant develops a sense of self in terms of an experiential sense of agency for his own actions, self-coherence, self-affectivity and a sense of continuity with his own past. In the *Domain of Intersubjective Relatedness*, infants discover that they are able to share their subjective experience with others (e.g. their intentions, affective states), and key to this domain is the affective attunement of the primary carer to the infant. Finally, the *Domain of Verbal Relatedness* begins with the development of a verbal sense of self.

ashamed. Predictably, the client moves swiftly away from the relational focus back into discussing the work contract. The relational figure is temporarily ruptured and although the longing for twinship was met, the coach disrupted it. The coach now needs to work to try and repair this. Overall, not a good moment of mutually reciprocal self-and-other regulation, but such moments are unavoidable and do provide key opportunities for strengthening relationships. A key relational competency therefore for the coach, is to tolerate and be resilient to her/his own shame when these ruptures occur.

Coach: It feels very important and extremely demanding. I am just wondering, I know you said this is about you and your standards, but what do you expect of the other in the contract?

Coachee: (Shudders)....Gosh...It is sort of my realisation that I expect them not to change their mind around the boundaries. But there is part of me that always wants to be ready if they did!

Coach: OK.

[Pause]

Coachee: So, I think ...Whew....this sounds dreadful to say, but probably I don't expect a lot from them....yes.

Coach: It sounds difficult to say.

Coachee: Yes, it is very difficult. It's not that I want to put the others down, but it's like, it's *my* responsibility.

Coach: It's your responsibility and what I heard you say earlier is that they have less integrity.

Coachee: Not all of them actually. I think that was a sweeping generalisation.

Coach: *What if you stayed with it because it just came out as a generalisation. I am just wondering if some-times...Is it what you expect?*

[Pause]

Coachee: Yes. And I don't say it as a bad thing, you know. I am thinking they will change because they have to, because they are a part of a whole system. A part of the whole machine.

Coach: *But you need to be ready for that?*

Coachee: I do get the feeling that I need to be ready, and then my mind says "of course, they change and then I need to change," so I reset the rules of engagement and all the rest. But I think what drives me is that in my gut....yes in my gut I just always need to be ready.

Coachee. I feel ashamed by my comment around integrity as I am reminded of it. On reflection, I wonder if I was referring to my expectation of less reliability from others. Overall, I feel understood in my need to be constantly ready and feel that my coach has a clear idea of the pressures that can exist in the workplace.

Coach. Although I was aware of the relational rupture and her moving away from me back into discussion of her work, I lacked the self-support to directly enquire about this. I was experiencing some of her statements as dismissive, and was not sure if I could support myself if I brought her back into the "Here and Now." What if she did "put me down" or question my integrity?

Theoretical linkage. Within a relational Gestalt psycho-therapy session, it would be imperative that the therapist move to discussion of the here and now emerging relational issues as a focus to explore the "rupture and repair" cycle that is deemed to be essential for healing and growth. Our experience of Relational Organisational Coaching however is that this is a complex choice-point. The overarching emphasis needs to be on the relevance of what emerges for the work context; and whether the relational issues are sufficiently dysregulating in that context to need to be worked with here. In this example, we see the coach playing with whether to let the coachee "return to work," (which is what this process is all about anyway), or confront the relational issues between them. On balance, she settles for the alliance seeming "good enough," since the coachee is becoming animated about insights she is having regarding work. We would judge a direct relational enquiry at this point as having been more needed by the coach than the coachee; and that therefore it was appropriate to "let it go." If the client had seemed de-energised, or withdrawn, the coach would have needed to make a direct attempt at repair. This dyad has sufficient alliance (dimension 1), built up over time to negotiate the rupture without directly addressing it. The shift in focus also neatly offers support to the coachee by discussing realistic pressures of working in a demanding and constantly changing organisation. We judge this a "best option" since it supports her current way of being as one that is appropriate to organisational field conditions, even though it may not be optimal in the here and now relationship. Coaches often need to consider how focusing more overtly on the coach/coachee relationship will play out in a working environment. In this instance, the coachee's style is certainly "good enough" and ethically valid, so it is appropriate not to challenge it here.

Coach: It looks like that, you need to be ready. Be prepared to deliver and you should have known in advance that they might need it.
Coachee: Hmmm... hmm... [Pause]

Coach: What's happening? What happened?

Coachee: Hmm [pause] Yes, I always need to plan. [Pause] I am getting in touch with.... I guess with a very old state of alertness. Phew! [Long exhale] ...And that's OK.

Coach: What does that mean when you say "that is OK?" It feels like every time we hit this place of you being in trouble, you say "that's OK.. Is it a signal to you or a signal to me?

Coachee: Probably a bit of both. It's probably a signal that I don't need to be rescued. It's a signal for you to be OK with me not being OK. [Looks moved and upset, then glances up and laughs.]

Coach: Well I am curious....what I am so struck by is that there is a different rule for me.

Coachee: You're right.

Coach: Yes, in these moments when you look... you look whatever this is, I don't want to say upset, that I'm let off the hook and told not to panic because you're preparing me.....you have been prepared for this and this is fine, no panic! Very much one rule for you and a different rule for other people. It's like in that moment I feel, you come and look after me as well; you have a plan.

Coachee: I think it is interesting that you use the word "panic," 'cos I think it hits it on the spot for me. I think it helps me as well if you don't panic.

Coach: I'm not feeling remotely panicky.

Coachee: I can see that in your face. It is reassuring for me.

Coach: You look like you are doing just fine. OK, you're a bit upset and...

Coachee: ...and so what? [Laughs]

Coach: ...and so what! I am not feeling concerned about you in any major way. I am interested in your process and how that relates to what you are talking about, but I am not having "an alarm" about your fragility.

Coachee: No, and I am not either. But I am taking away how much I work hard for every eventuality.

Coachee. I become aware of how good it feels that I don't need to take care of my coach...or worry about her worrying about me. I'm in touch with how much this is a pattern for me, an old developmental pattern of needing to make sure all is ok around me...one that drains my resources. This is an important take away for me, which I stay with for the months to come; and provides me a new perspective on how I engage with others and how much responsibility I carry.

Coach. I finally "get" that although I have experienced her as a bit distant, she finds our relationship just the right distance. It is the fact that I am able to tolerate her distance and not feel "panicked" by it that has reassured her, and I notice she looks very pleased with the session. I am a bit surprised that I seem to have "got away with" the relational rupture and am very glad that I made the choice not to try and heal it by drawing her back in to *my* concerns about how we were doing. I can see that although I was diagnosing a lack of "twinship," she seems very satisfied. I am pleased I managed to support myself to trust the coachee's process, presence and choice of figure.

Theoretical linkage. This final section is very illustrative of key differences between psychotherapy and coaching. The therapist, particularly when working with fragile clients, is likely to have made choices to directly address the here and now relationship and use that as a vehicle for healing. Working directly with the self-object transferences and countertransferences that emerge is essential.

In contrast, the coach uses her/his experience of the relationship as a diagnostic; only directly addressing that if the working alliance is compromised, or the relational style judged to be highly toxic for the coachee or others they encounter. Instead, the coach allows relational issues to surface in the dialogue, but does this in service of assisting the coachee's performance in very different field conditions, which must be understood. This demonstrates why, although the clinical paradigm is necessary for quality coaching, it is insufficient. The coach must really understand and have an embodied knowledge of organisational field conditions. An absence of this is likely to either offend coachees by being overly "therapeutic" and intrusive, or dysregulate them by leading them to expect from their boss what they get from their coach. In our experience, the absence of a truly integrated knowledge of both these dimensions can have profoundly negative consequences for the coachee.

Transcript Two

Coachee. At our previous coaching session I had dared to tell my coach a very brief dream image I had experienced about 6 weeks earlier. I had mentioned the image before, but had not told her the content. Last session had therefore felt like taking a huge risk in admitting I had dreamt about standing with her and a work colleague. It had emerged that I had been left with a very good and strong feeling from the dream. She had been very nonchalant about me dreaming about her, which had helped me, even saying it was a pretty common event in a coaching relationship. On the basis of that, although I still felt confused, I had decided to take things a bit further.

Coach. During our last session, the coachee brought the figure of a dream in which I figured. Although it was clear the dream held a lot of significance for her, I felt that she was hesitant in exploring it fully with me. I had felt tested and was left with imagining she had needed to see if I could handle her dream and her pushing me away. I felt curious to see if the dream would re-emerge in this session, as it seems to hold connotations of defiance and aggression, while also validating our connection.

Theoretical linkage. With the coachee "taking a huge risk" in admitting to the dream and the coach feeling tested, the previous session seems to have been one in which a foundation was being set for more challenging work to be done. This is an important aspect of building the working alliance, (dimension 1), in coaching and ideally should be made more explicit and named.

Here, we also noted the importance of the calmness of the coach while hearing the dream, and "normalising" dreaming about her, which had regulated the coachee. More intense and focused responses on the part of the coach around the dream may have been too shaming and resulted in the meeting taking on the flavour of a therapy session. This can often be unhelpful and lead to the coachee feeling humiliated and over-exposed.

Coachee: So...I feel in a very different place from when I met you last time because I was feeling quite strong and robust then and I feel a bit more...maybe vulnerable. I don't know, but less defended. (Pause). I would like to start by saying what I was left with.
Coach: I'd like to hear that.
Coachee: It's different. There was this whole thing that I felt embarrassed and awkward about, feeling like a toddler, feeling that somehow I wanted to run off and do things, and yet I wanted somebody also to hold

some limits. I thought "I'm sure this relates to why I don't do certain things at work," "why I don't actually end up running things.." I have run things, but I have sort of made this commitment, "NO MORE!"

Coach: Because if you run things then what?

Coachee: I'd be on my own!

Coach: So there won't be that connection?

Coachee: And nobody will hold me. I won't feel held. And that's the bit that I think. I just feel I've had too much time in my life holding myself, you know, and other people. So I feel a lot of conflict about "well, if I take these next steps up, then it feels like, I am back to holding myself and making my decisions and holding everybody else." It is actually a better position for me to be the second person down in something, even if I don't feel a lot of respect for the person at the top and feel that I should be doing it. That's a lot of conflict and tension ...

Coach: Yes, huge tension.

Coachee: Oh, I can't believe I said this...I've got to breathe in a bit. I can't believe I got that out.

Coach. I experienced the coachee as very present and authentic in putting forward what was going on for her. I was aware of how important and also shaming it was to have described her process so honestly. Although she seemed to have a strong response, I felt confident in the coachee's self-support and wondered about her feeling even more infantilised or "like a toddler"' if I dwelled on, or blatantly avoided, the shame process. I therefore decided to "stay with"' even though I felt anxious and was wondering if she felt too ashamed, whether I would be deflected or pushed away as in our previous session. I felt on delicate ground to get the balance right in order for us to work on what she was bringing.

Theoretical linkage. The coachee seems to have experienced great mobilisation and has a very embodied response. This may suggest a different "domain of related-ness," possibly to do with core self and intersubjective self[3] (Stern, 1985). In working with this, the physical and vocal calmness of the coach is very important. The coachee is highly aware of nonverbal ways of relating, and these tend to be far more important and figural than content issues. The process is suggestive of a longing for an "idealised other" This is potentially a self-object transference that may suggest a problematic archaic issue occurring at work. The relational work gives a very useful diagnostic insight into this. It is hard to see how this would emerge in acquisi-tional coaching. Throughout this section of transcript, the coach trusts the presence of the coachee and their ability to engage in dialogue when there is sufficient relational support. Each coachee will need different types and styles of support and it is the responsibility of the coach to moderate their relational style to facilitate the meeting. This process is established through the formation of the working alliance; dimension (1) in ROG.

Coach: *How is it to have got it out?*
Coachee: I don't feel proud of that, you see. I don't feel proud of it.
Coach: *That you need somehow to be held?*
Coachee: Blughch! You've said it now, that's revolting. I feel patronised and sort of infantilised and er...blugh. I don't like that.
Coach: *Wow I've really said it now. And I notice your reaction and I'm thinking of the times in my life where I couldn't have done a lot of things within organisations unless I knew there was someone behind me. And*

---

[3] See Note 2.

your reaction is how disgusting that you might even need that. "How revolting?"

Coachee: Absolutely. I do feel that. I feel that...I feel ashamed of that...I feel I really don't like you mentioning it. I really don't like that.

Coach: Because you have to do everything on your own?

Coachee: It's just better; it's just better for me.

Coach: How?

Coachee: I don't know, that's the conflict you see. I just hit this point of conflict that I used to do everything on my own and that's why I was successful. To me they go together. However, I felt lonely, envied, erm...lonely is the word that keeps coming out. I don't know what I want to try and say. Because it's like–be more successful, that means I'm going to do it on my own.

Coach: That sounds so clear, the absolute certainty that there is no way that you actually can be successful without absolutely doing it on your own.

Coachee: Yes.

Coachee. I am right at my limit of walking out/ending the session. I imagine she didn't realise how much I disliked all this, but I had a sense that I'd rather have been anywhere else. I imagined there would have been negative consequences to me leaving and I could still see that all this was probably important, but I wasn't enjoying the session. I was impressed again by the fact that she stayed calm and just kept right on going.

Coach. I felt like I was skating on thin ice. On one hand, I was intensely aware of how uncomfortable the session was for the coachee and on the other was worried that she would experience me as having backed away if I didn't stay with what was most figural. I tried to normalise the feelings she was talking about by sharing some of my own process. This was still too much and so in my last intervention I backed away from what felt like an early developmental need to be held and supported discussion of how this manifested and affected her in the workplace.

Theoretical linkage. Both coachee and coach are trusting the process, working as authentically as they can mutually support. There seems to be enormous shame now that the archaic longings have been stimulated and surfaced. Coaching can be potentially less shaming than therapy as the transparent coaching agenda is "performance improvement." This is more acceptable to narcissistically wounded, yet successful individuals, who are commonly encountered near the top of organisations. So much so that "Narcissistic Personality Disorder" was dropped from ICD 10 as it was thought to be an adaptive way of being in our current culture! The systemic dimension (4), is always concerned to bring the figure back to the context of the organisation and the coachee's performance within it. This is an ethical issue in ROG and in this case, also supports the coachee to feel more "acceptable," or at least less "pathologised" and shamed.

Coach: How did you learn that?

Coachee: Hmmm [pause] It's like I manage my team, you know. I know they're behind me and I know that actually they give me a whole lot of support and my deputy is incredibly supportive of me. It's people above me or equal to me that are my problem.

Coach: Let's just check this. You can get support, you can almost ...be held by someone as long as they report to you.

Coachee: Up to a point. I would always expect that come the crunch, I would look after them more. But if they were fine and I wasn't, then yes, I would feel I could get support from them. But when it came to the crunch, I'd feel it was my job to lead them, and I would.

Coach: And that feels lonely.

Coachee: Yes, that's the bit that somehow feels, I would like to have equals...you know I told you about the dream...I think that's about having equals...about having partners and I feel uncomfortable with that ...mistrustful with that... like I'm going to be disappointed in that. I said this thing to you, as well about the image, there is this thing about these people are "other." Not aggressive quite, but stronger...I don't know.

Coach: How? Less pushy, less supportive...?

Coachee: No, standing up, being counted. Yes, standing up and being counted. I feel they probably would and I wouldn't. I'd take the easy way out.

Coach: So the others in your dream...would actually take it on?

Coachee: Yes, they'd take it on and do it. And I wouldn't. But I am not so sure you see, that makes it very black and white. I am not so sure. Because that is one side of the story and then there is the other part of the story, that is ... Uurggh, I don't know. I know I feel I am going into areas that I don't know about so well. No, no, I don't want to, not for today.

Coachee. I'd enjoyed getting back to talking about work and then found myself talking about the dream again. The session felt out of my control, which I am not very used to. I kept being surprised. I wasn't really sure what she was doing because it didn't look like much; and yet I found myself back to saying some quite revealing stuff.

Coach. Looking at the coachee's process in the workplace seemed less shaming and she looked more grounded. I was pleasantly surprised at how quickly the dream re-emerges and felt appreciative of the coachee's presence. She clearly tells me that some parts of the dream are too difficult (shameful?) to go into today. I feel respectful of this and yet wondered at the importance of staying with what felt like an important relational figure. I decide to share some of my sense of the dream and tried to convey some of the support I took away from her previous description.

Theoretical linkage. We are still dealing with Kohut's notion of the "idealising transference;" the need that people have to relax and sink into the competence of admired figures and caregivers. The competence of the coach raises this longing. Although most of the time, it is the coachee who leads the figure, the dialogic dimension of coaching also means that how the coach experiences the meeting in the dyad may potentially hold a new awareness for the coachee. Methodologically, this involves a use of inclusion to build a mutually reciprocal regulatory system, with each party sharing awareness as it emerges.

Coach: OK, not for today. Can I tell you what I remember from our conversation previously about the three in the dream? Somehow although the three were alone they also all stood together.

Coachee: Yes, it was like the Three Musketeers.

Coach: In a way, you were saying that the other two would stand on their own...would go it alone, and yet they are not. There was stability in the three.

Coachee: Yes. I don't know. It's a real dilemma. It is that issue of feeling I back off things because I don't want to lead them on my own. And by "on my own," I mean with a far less competent team. My Team at work I have chosen, I chose and recruited everybody.

Coach: My guess is you feel you have groomed them so they would be in support of you.

Coachee: I feel very embarrassed, very wobbly about that.

Coach: Because you need it?

Coachee: It reminds me when I was talking with a colleague about X and... [pause] and she said "well, you have chosen him very carefully" and I felt very embarrassed about that but it would be...[Pause]...that friendship has not happened by chance. That would be to do with competence and trustworthiness.

Coach: Yes.

Coachee: You look as if that's obvious?

Coach: It feels so obvious, I think every person who goes into a new job, you know, the leader, brings in his or her own team. It's like "why wouldn't you choose them?' Somehow there is a "should' there.

Coachee: There's a "I should be more generous" to people who are less "able," but I think I have had enough of being generous.

Coach: Oh yes, so the "you feel you should be more generous" means that you should have the relationship with someone less able? It feels heavy.

Coachee: It is heavy; its very hard work trying to get people to perform competently at things actually they are just not very good at.

Coach: I'm curious that that's what you need to do, that's what you need to carry with you.

Coachee: I think that this is the bit of my story that I carry with me. I regulate other people in order that they function well.

Coach: [Sigh] I feel sad.

Coachee: I feel sad...and angry actually. Angry and a bit pissed off with it. Because I feel I'm carrying dead weights.

Coach: I get a sense of the dead weights pulling down the possibility of new and exciting stuff. I wonder, how can you have that without having all the dead weight?

Coachee. The same thing happens again. I get to my limit and say stop, she stops and then just carries straight on.....and I let that happen seemingly quite happily. This is all new territory for me; therapy did not have this effect of me opening up so quickly as I always felt the therapist had an agenda of infantalising me and wanting me to show more emotions. I am really surprised that here I am talking about emotions quite happily. That may sound paradoxical, but it felt very genuine and real to me....much more so than some of the scenes in therapy where I would eventually cry/rage a lot just to get her off my back!

Coach. I am pleased that we have managed to stay with the overall figure despite a few difficult, shame filled moments. Her early introject around needing to be more generous with those less able felt at odds to me within an organisational setting and I wonder if somehow naming this in the context of her work facilitated her making the connection with an archaic way of being in the world. As she gets in touch with what must be a very familiar pattern of "having to' regulate others, I experience the heaviness of her struggle and feel saddened by it.

Theoretical linkage. Here we see the healing power of the idealising "needed relationship" being very lightly held by the coach, but used to great effect. The coachee is experimenting with whole new ways of being that involve getting support without feeling totally ashamed and/or inauthentic. This has great potential to make a real difference at work by increasing the coachee's willingness to both lead *and* get support. There is clear evidence of raising material from "Id" self-functions into a much clearer figure so that the ego aspect of self can get hold of and make choices about her need for support for differentiation. The coachee links the figure of the dream back to the organisational context. This illustrates that the systemic dimension (4), is always present in the phenomenal field and that linkages to developmental patterns and figures happen spontaneously, without having to directly explore the past "content" issues. In fact, interventions that do focus on these issues (such as, "tell me about your family of origin," etc.), subtly cross a boundary between coaching and psychotherapy and are generally inappropriate within a coaching context. If the coachee raises such material, it is usually helpful for the coach to confirm the effect such information may have in terms of a "legacy" affecting the present work situation, rather than enquiring into the content of the historical narrative.

Key Issues in the Application of ROG Coaching

We hope you can see how we have used these transcripts to illuminate the theoretical descriptors of ROG coaching that we described earlier. We now want to finish by addressing some key issues relating to the application of ROG coaching as well as trying to "lay to rest' some misperceptions that might be lingering.

Practitioner Skills for ROG Coaching.

Kohut developed the concept of "empathic immersion" as a strategy for interpreting a client's/coach's transferential material but relational Gestalt psychotherapy instead incorporates the Intersubjective method of "sustained empathic enquiry" (see Stolorow, Brandchaft and Atwood 1987, for a full description). Key procedural competencies for relational Gestalt practitioners (clinical and organisational), therefore include competence in skills of dialogue, and *also* familiarity and expertise with concepts and methods of affect attunement.

These skills are neither simple to learn, nor easy to acquire. In particular, there is a requirement for sustained personal work by the therapist/coach in order to fully comprehend the nature of their own "presence;" that is the nature of their "beingness" and the needed and repeated relational configurations phenomena that are most likely to be evoked by their presence, as well as the needed and repeated relational configurations that tend to be evoked repeatedly within the coach's phenomenal field. Additionally, since each coachee needs to be met in a different way, the coach also needs to be capable of evoking self-organisations that might be helpful for the coachee by embodying ways of being that are outside the coach's usual range.

An essential point to make here however, is that in addition to these psychotherapeutic skill sets, the Relational Organisational Gestalt coach and consultant also requires a fully developed sense of a range of organisational field conditions. Regrettably, it is our experience that the combination of highly developed clinical expertise with robust and developed organisational awareness is hard to find. As Kets de Vries (2005) argues, lack of clinical skills can be personally disastrous for the coachee, leading to gross shame, potential traumatisation and personal distress. It is also our experience that lack of the necessary organisational experience and awareness can lead to personal transformation that is dissociated and does not fit the organisational context. This can have disastrous consequences for both the coachee and the employing organisation, as new behaviours disrupt rather than optimise the coachee's experience at work.

Transformational Coaching

Working in a phenomenological, field theoretically informed, relational approach is more likely to access "id' functions that are out of the coachee's awareness. This is different from working solely or primarily with ego functions that are already within the coachee's awareness and which often provide "rational" explanations of behaviour. We agree entirely with Kets de Vries' statement that; "Many incomprehensible active-ties in organizations ("incomprehensible" from a rational point of view, that is) are in fact indicators of what is really going on in the intrapsychic [sic] and interpersonal world of the key players, below the surface of their day-to-day routines. This underlying mental activity needs to be understood in terms of how it resurfaces as fantasies, conflicts, defensive behaviors, and anxieties." (2005, ibid., p. 72).

In our experience, it is in this "underlying" activity that the predominant shapers of behaviour are most likely to be accessed. Yet traditional "acquisitional" coaching, (focused on acquisition of skills, rational competencies, learning key infor-mation or managerial elements of key performance targets), is unlikely to address any of these issues. In contrast, the introduction of a clinically informed methodology (we believe Relational Organisational Gestalt coaching to be the most appropriate, optimally effective and flexible form), can address these underlying, out of awareness elements of performance. We therefore see ROG coaching fitting firmly in the modality of "transformational coaching" described by Summerfield (2006), as being the required, and preferred, organisational intervene-tion style.

Mutuality of Presence

Often the focus in the literature is on the "presence" of the organisational consultant or coach. We view presence as referring to the use of an individual's authentic self to maximise embodied and relational "being" (see Chidiac & Denham-Vaughan (2007), for a full discussion), and not to refer to charisma or "charm." Within a coaching relationship, the coachee's presence is demonstrated in his/her willingness (and ability) to explore new and different "selfings," (ways of being). This is likely to involve raising issues from the background into awareness in order to forge systemic connections to performance at work. The coach's task is to provide a relational environment that supports and enables the coachee to engage fully in this task, for which they are often emotionally unprepared. As such, it is worth outlining the potentially very powerful transformational process of ROG coaching at the contracting phase.

Contracting for ROG Coaching

Irrespective of how the coaching work is presented by the organisation (most often by the HR representative as a means of optimising performance), this preliminary contract needs to be held lightly by the coach. We believe that bringing to awareness transcendent (potential), qualities in a coachee is what ultimately improves the coachee's performance and thereby business results. This means we privilege the coachee's emerging figure of interest in sessions, rather than only focus on the organisation's needs. A key difference therefore in ROG coaching as opposed to other forms of coaching is contracting for the time and space to surface what is not known, what is out of awareness and could be termed an aspect of "id" functioning.

This contrasts with traditional models, where often the initial question: "what do you want to work on" implies that the issue to be worked on is one of "ego functioning," and is already mobilised into the coachee's awareness and shared by the organisation.

As we have emphasised however, it is important to re-member that the coach has a contractual and ethical responsi-bility to the organisation as well as to the individual. In other words, ROG coaching is not a situation where "anything goes" and the coach mindlessly follows the coachee's interests. There is often an explicit demand for some sort of "step-up" in the performance of the person being coached. This "change" will therefore need to be tangible, both to the person being coached and also to the organisation, his/her peers and managers. This can lead to further boundary conflicts for the novice coach! We find that expectations and outcomes do therefore need to be agreed and clarified early in the process, with creativity and flexibility being built into the evaluative processes.

In summary, there is a need for ROG coaches to take a radically field theoretical approach which includes knowledge and experience of organisational demands and realities. This field orientation may be informed by the coach being an internal member of the organisation, or by her/him being grounded in the working realities of many other organisations. In particular, there may be a need to gain information not only from the coachee, but also from colleagues and managers who have dealings with the coachee, and are thereby invested in the coachee's personal transformational process. In practice, this means the contract can look radically different, specifically with regards to issues such as confidentiality, than the contract that exists in a counselling or psychotherapeutic relationship.

ROG Coaching versus
Relational Counselling/Psychotherapy

Finally, we would argue that while both Relational Organisational Gestalt and relational Gestalt psychotherapy involve use
of similar methodology and theoretical epistemology, there are
nonetheless key differences. These are summarised in the table
on the following page. In practice, these differences are in
degrees of emphasis and do not fall into mutually exclusive
categories. Thus, for example, a psychotherapy session may well
address the future and a coaching session the past, but our
experience of typical configurations is described in Table 1, on
the following page.

Conclusion

We have taken this opportunity to evolve and articulate our
model of Relational Organisational Gestalt work and have
offered two transcripts of ROG coaching sessions as live experiments demonstrating our theory in practice. Clearly, there is
much additional work to be undertaken in developing the model
to work with teams, large groups and whole systems. In these
areas, we anticipate that an emphasis on environmental and
phenomenal field factors emerging in the organisational context
will be particularly important. Finally, we hope to have shown
that it is the combination of both clinical and organisational
skills that is essential to the successful practice of ROG.

Table 1 – Relational Organisational Gestalt vs. Relational Gestalt Psychotherapy

Relational Organisational Gestalt	Relational Gestalt Psychotherapy
Temporal focus is present and future.	Temporal focus is present and past.
Situational focus is here and now as it relates to the working environment and situation.	Situational focus is here and now as it relates to any relevant situation.
Sources of information– client/coachee and others.	Source of information-- exclusively client.
Expected knowledge of organisational context.	No prior knowledge of particular context needed.
Key tasks – increased ability to organise "self as instrument" in relation to the working environment.	Key tasks – negotiated by dyad at outset of psychotherapy.
Confidentiality contract – negotiable – requires definition.	Confidentiality contract – agreed between dyad and only broken in situations of clinical risk.
Structure of meetings – negotiable in frequency and length.	Structure of meetings – regular, at least weekly and fixed length.
Length of intervention – usually brief/negotiable.	Length of intervention – negotiable-often lengthy.

References

Bentley, T. (2001). The emerging system: A Gestalt approach to organizational interventions. *British Gestalt Journal. 10*, 13-19.

Bokeno, M (2007). Dialogue at Work? What it is and isn't. *Development and Learning in Organizations, 21*(1), 9-11.

Boyatzis, R. Smith, M.L. and Blaize, N. (2006). Developing Sustainable Leaders Through Coaching and Compassion. *Academy of Management Learning and Education, 5*(1), 8-24.

Buber, M. (1958), *I and Thou.* (R. G. Smith. Trans.). New York: Charles Scribner and Sons (Orig. 1923).

Chidiac, M-A & Denham-Vaughan, S. (2007). The process of Presence: Energetic Availability and Fluid Responsiveness. *British Gestalt Journal. 16*(1), 9-19.

Dagley, G. (2006). Human Resources professionals' perceptions of executive coaching Efficacy, benefits and return on investment. *International Coaching Psychology Review. 1*(2), 34-45.

D'annunzio-Green N., Francis, H. (2005). Human resource development and the psychological contract: Great expectations or false hopes?. *Human Resource Development International, 8*(3), 327-344.

Denham-Vaughan, S. (2005a). Goods and hyper-goods. *International Gestalt Journal, 28*(1), 143-149.

Denham-Vaughan, S. (2005b). Will and grace. *British Gestalt Journal, 14*(1), 5-14.

Frew, J. E. (2006). Organizational leadership theory has arrived: Gestalt theory never left. *Gestalt Review, 10*(2), 123-139.

Goleman, D. (2000). *Working with Emotional Intelligence.* New York: Bantam.

Hycner, R. & Jacobs, L. (1995). *The Healing Relationship in Gestalt Therapy.* Highland, NY: Gestalt Journal Books.

Isaacs, W. (1993). Taking flight: Dialogue, Collective thinking, and Organizational Learning. *Organizational Dynamics, 22*(3), 24-39.

Jacobs, L. M. (1989). Dialogue in Gestalt theory and therapy. *The Gestalt Journal, 12*(1), 25-67.

Jacobs, C. & Heracleous, L. (2005). Answers for questions to come: reflective dialogue as an enabler of strategic innovation. *Journal of Organizational Change Management, 18*(4), 338-352.

Kets de Vries, M. F. R. (2005). Leadership group coaching in action: The Zen of creating high performance teams. *Academy of Management Executives, 19*(1), 61-76.

Kohut, H. (1984). *How does Analysis Cure?* (A. Goldberg, Ed.). Chicago: The University of Chicago Press.

Lee, R. G. (Ed.). (2004). *The Values of Connection: A Relational Approach to Ethics.* Hilsdale, NJ: GestaltPress/The Analytic Press.

Nevis, E.C. (1987). *Organisational Consulting: A Gestalt Approach.* New York: Vintage Books.

Newton, M. (2002). A practitioner's perspective on the applicability of Gestalt orientated organizational development and organizational change. *Gestalt Review, 6,* 101-108.

O'Neill, M. B. (2000). *Executive Coaching with Backbone and Heart.* San Francisco: Jossey-Bass.

Opengart,R. (2005). Emotional Intelligence and Emotion Work: examining constructs from an interdisciplinary framework. *Human Resource Development Review, 4*(1), 49-62.

Rainey Tolbert, M. A. (2004). What is Gestalt OSD? All about the O, the S, the D....and of course, Gestalt. *OD Practitioner, 36,* (4), 6-10.

Schein, E. (2003). On dialogue, culture, and organizational learning. *Reflections: The SoL Journal, 4*(4), 27-38.

Stern, D. (1985). *The Interpersonal World of the Infant.* New York: Basic Books.

Stolorow, R.D. and Jacobs, L. (2006). Critical reflections on Husserl. *International Gestalt Journal, 29*(2), 43-61.

Stolorow, R. D. Brandchaft, B. and Atwood, G. (1987). *Psychoanalytic Treatment: An Intersubjective Approach.* Hillsdale, NJ: The Analytic Press.

Summerfield, J. (2006). Coaching vs Counselling. *The Coaching Psychologist, 2*(1), 23-31.

Scapegoating
from the Inside Out:
A Relational Gestalt Understanding
and Intervention

•••••••••••••••••••

Robert G. Lee

From the Bible (Leviticus 16) the *scapegoat* was a goat in ancient times which would be driven off into the wilderness after being anointed with the sins of the community. The goat escapes death but carries the sins of the people with him to his dying day. Accounts of similar ritual purifications involving goats that were driven from communities carrying the burden of others date at least as far back as the 24th century BC (Wright 1987; Zatelli 1998), perhaps further. The ancient Greeks indulged in a similar practice (Frazer 1922) using humans rather than goats, in which a cripple, beggar, or criminal was stoned, beaten and cast out of the community in response to either a natural disaster (such as a plague, famine or an invasion) or a calendrical crisis (such as the end of the year).

Thus the term *scapegoat* has come to mean an innocent person who is forced to take the blame/load of others. One of the easiest ways for a group of people to attempt to coalesce into a unified body in a time of uncertainty or conflict is for the majority of the members to identify a person or subgroup as being inappropriate, wrong, inferior, dangerous, insane, etc. and cast them out – hence the function of bigotry and discrimination.

Of course this same mechanism, scapegoating, is commonly encountered in therapy and training groups. As therapists and trainers how do we recognize, understand and respond to this phenomenon from a relational Gestalt perspective?

I first learned of the hidden reasons behind scapegoating from a personal experience early in my career – in my Intensive Post Graduate Training Program at the Gestalt Institute of Cleveland (GIC) in 1977. This experience was transformative for me. It taught me about this phenomenon from the inside out, not just that it is wrong/unjust for the scapegoat, but also how it restricts the group that employs it, as well as a first hand experience of the compelling nature of scapegoating and how good people can come to resort unknowingly to scapegoating.

To give you a little background. I was very proud to be attending this program. I had waited four years for this opportunity to develop. In the meantime, I had received Gestalt training and therapy from practitioners where I was living, several hours drive from Cleveland. Now I was able to be trained at the institute where they were trained. For me, Gestalt was about inclusion. So I would not have guessed that I could be part of scapgoating someone.

This intensive program at GIC was designed for clinicians who held an advanced degree in psychotherapy/counseling and who lived out of town. The first phase of the training consisted of four consecutive weeks of being in residence in Cleveland. Relevant to my story here, each evening we participated in a two hour personal growth group. There were eleven people in the personal growth group to which I was assigned.

In the third week of this group, Joseph Zinker became our leader. He was quickly faced with the following situation. The participants in the training program were housed in a multi-story hotel near the institute. About two-thirds of our personal growth group lived together on one floor. The remainder of our group, including me, lived on another floor. People living on each floor shared a kitchen in which they could store and prepare food.

The issue that arose emerged from the people that lived on the other floor from me. It began with Jean and John talking to Ann at the start of group one evening:[1]

Jean: Before we get started today I just wanted to mention something that has become troubling to me. Ann, you have been leaving your dishes in the sink and not washing them. I'd appreciate it if you could wash them after you use them.

Ann: I'm sorry, of course. I have just had some things come up that I had to attend to. I did wash them later.

---

[1] Because this story made such an impression on me I remember a great deal of what happened. At the same time it has been 30 plus years since it happened. At least some of the dialogue given here has been reconstructed to fit with the energy I remember being present in the group. I have changed the names of the group members to respect their privacy.

> John: I understand what Jean is saying. It is a real pain to
>   have to deal with dirty dishes in the sink. So I too
>   would like it if you would wash your dishes after
>   you use them.
> Ann: Again, I'm sorry. I didn't know this had become such
>   an issue.

The group turned to other issues at this point. I didn't think much about what had happened. If anything I was a little surprised and embarrassed. I had left dirty dishes in the sink on my floor, and cleaned them up later. No one on my floor had complained about that to me. I didn't say anything in the group, again perhaps because I was embarrassed. Still, this seemed to be a minor issue between the people who lived on the other floor and wasn't my business.

However, the next evening in group it continued:

> Jean: I again have to say something before we get started.
>   There were dishes left in the sink again today.
>   Were those yours, Ann?
> Ann: Yes, I'm sorry – I got a call from my daughter and got
>   distracted.
> Jean: I have got to say, I am a little more than annoyed.
> Terry: There was also a jar of mustard and a jar of pickle
>   relish left out on the counter.
> Ann: (*with a little irritation in her voice*) Again, I am
>   sorry, as I said I got a call from my daughter.
> John: I just want to say that we all need to be responsible
>   for ourselves here.
> Ann: Look – I am sorry. I do put everything away and
>   clean up later.

Terry: (*in an irritated voice*) This has been going on for a
       while. The space in the kitchen is so tiny. It is just
       so frustrating to have to deal with a mess.

Ann: OK. I get it – it won't happen again.

Although there was a bit of tenseness in the air, the group
turned to other issues. At this point although I was still
surprised about what was happening among the people who
lived on the other floor, it started to make sense to me. Ann was
different from the rest of us. She was older than the rest of us.
She had peroxide-blonde hair that seemed rather "cheap" to me.
Her advanced degree was in education – she had been a teacher
not a therapist. She hadn't taken psychology courses and didn't
speak our language, and frankly she seemed to be a bit empty-
headed to me. I did not understand why the institute had
accepted her to be a participant in this program. I had some
irritation that she was here, although I was somewhat
embarrassed that I felt as such. So I didn't say much about it to
others, except for a couple of small comments to a couple of
other people. Although these exchanges with others were brief,
I got the sense that the people I talked to agreed with me. But I
had not thought of this as an important issue. It was just
something in the background.

Still when others disclosed their growing displeasure and
anger at Ann in our group, I started to "understand" what they
were saying. Although I didn't talk to anyone about it, what was
happening seemed to confirm my initial assessment of Ann.
She just didn't seem to fit in this program.

The issue came to a head the following evening in group.
This time it didn't start right away. It was about two thirds
through the evening when there was a lull in the group that Jean
again spoke:

302 ... RELATIONAL APPROACHES IN GESTALT THERAPY

Jean: I am sitting here seething. (*visibly upset*) I didn't bring it up at the start of group tonight just because – I don't why. I don't like to be complaining; so I thought I could let it pass. But I can't. Ann, you put a huge package in the refrigerator and you are taking up all the space. Where are the rest of us supposed to put anything?

George: (*starting almost before Jean finishes – talking to Ann, contemptuously*) I couldn't believe it. How could you do that? That refrigerator is tiny as it is.

Ann: I am sorry. Today is kind of a special day in our family and my son sent me a cake.

Linda: (*in an annoyed voice*) Well that's nice, but you didn't ask anyone if you could take up that much space in the fridge.

Ann: There wasn't anyone around to ask when it came.

John: (*talking to Ann in an agitated voice*) You consistently don't hear what we are saying. I mean, you didn't ask anyone later either.

Ann: (*near tears*) I'm sorry; I just forgot.

Terry: (*talking to Ann, angrily*) Well, I am sorry. It is just not fair to the rest of us how you forget or get distracted or something else. You always seem to have an excuse.

Ann: (*tears rolling down her cheeks now*) I don't know what to say.

At this point Joseph intervenes:

Joseph: This is obviously a very hot issue that many of you care about intensely right now. Perhaps it would help to look at this through a different lens. It is possible that there might be a larger group issue at work here. It might not be just the refrigerator that is becoming too small for this group. Perhaps the group itself is becoming too small for many or all of you. (*He pauses for a moment.*)

I would like you each to go inside yourself and see if there is some part of you that you don't think would be acceptable in this group, some part of yourself that you haven't shared with the group, maybe not deliberately. Please take a few moments to see if there is such a piece of you. Then if you do find such a part of you, think about how the group would have to change in order for you to feel comfortable sharing/exploring that part of yourself in the group. Please, now take some time and see what you find.

There was silence in the group. For myself, this was new territory. I found that I couldn't even get close to looking at the possibility that there might be a part of me that I believed would not be accepted in the group, although I did have the sense that might be true. I was caught by the idea that a group would change for me – that idea was completely new, and more than a bit scary. I wondered – was it really possible for the group to change for me; would they really want to do that? Didn't I have to conform somehow? I had participated in this group, worked on personal issues, even said things that now seem self-inflated, but had felt that I had contributed to the group. However, I hadn't asked anything of the group in a personal vein. As I say, the idea scared me. I could tell this was very important to me; it represented a whole new sense of belonging that seemed very unfamiliar, although I didn't have that language yet – it was just an unnamed feeling. At the same time, I didn't know how to give voice to that part of me.

Finally Ricardo, who had been one of the most popular group members, and who was not one of the group members that was angry with Ann, broke the silence:

> Ricardo: Joseph is right. There is a piece of me that I have been avoiding sharing with the group. I don't know if this is because I didn't feel safe enough in the group to share this, but possibly – I know to share it I need your kindness. (*Tears form in his eyes.*) I am missing my wife – so so much. (*He starts to cry gently.*) We are in the third week here. But I was on a business trip for two weeks before that. So I haven't seen her for four and a half weeks. I miss her so much. (*He cries more. Mary, who is sitting beside him in the circle, hands him a box of tissues. He pauses, takes a tissue, and wipes the tears from his cheeks.*) I feel like a little kid. (*He laughs slightly.*) I should be able to handle this. But its not enough to just talk to her on the phone.
>
> Mary: Is there anything that we can do?
>
> Ricardo: I know this sounds silly. I feel foolish saying it. (*He pauses.*) I would like to be held by the group. Is that possible?

Without hesitation about half of the group moved to where Ricardo was sitting and together he and they found a position such that he was lying amongst/on them, and they were holding him in various ways. The rest of us moved close to the group holding Ricardo. Ricardo sobed for a while – then said:

Ricardo: We have been away from each other for extended times in the past. I guess it is not just me. She has so much going on right now also. I am worried about her too. (*He cries more, but easier now.*)

The group just stayed with him for a while. After a bit:

Laura: (*to Ricardo*) I am glad you said something. I have been missing my husband. But I only live a couple of hours away; so I have been going home on weekends.

Joseph: (*to Ricardo*) As Laura refers to, you will have this coming weekend free. Is it possible for your wife to join you for the weekend?

Ricardo: I'll check. (*He says quietly and a bit tentatively, but also looking a bit relieved.*)

The group ended soon after this for the evening. My sense at this point was that many of us were dealing with something new, and that Ricardo, although unintentionally, had led the way.

The next night early in the group Jacob suddenly started spraying a can of sparkling water on the people close to him and then threw the can at a person across from him. I was shocked. But the reaction of those close to him was to grab tissue boxes and pillows and start throwing them at him and each other. I finally joined in with the others. There was a lot of laughing and activity and after awhile we all settled down, whereupon Jacob spoke:

Jacob: I don't want to say much, but for me that's what has been missing in this group. I can't be in a group in which I can't play. This group has just been too serious for me.

I don't remember much of the dialogue in the group after this time, that relates to this issue. However, I do remember that this wise, delicately and adeptly administered intervention by Joseph turned the group around. A major transformation occurred that took us on a completely different path that brought a great deal of diversity and personal growth into our group. We became a cohesive unit, not by finding what was wrong with one of our members, but by establishing a tolerance and curiosity for differences in others and in our selves (which was especially helpful during conflict). It was my first learning about the power of support and the importance of the condition of the social field in how we experience ourselves and grow as individuals.[2]

There is a postscript to this story. At the end of our intensive program, from our practicum experience with each other in which we observed each other working as therapists, it became very clear to me (and was supported by what others said to me as well) that Ann had become one of the best therapists in the program.

Some Concluding Remarks with Regard to Theory and Practice[3]

This story is an excellent example of how shame can regulate the social field when there is insufficient perceived support in the field (Lee 1994, 1995, 2001; Lee & Wheeler 1996). Note that shame doesn't necessarily cause the perceived lack of support (although once present in the social field it may contribute

---

[2] My thanks to Joseph Zinker for this and so many other pieces of wisdom that I carry from him.

[3] I want to thank my dear friend Lee Geltman for his collaboration on this section of this article.

extensively to a further sense of insufficient support), it just regulates the field.

A sufficient number of us in the group had begun to believe, without awareness, that there wasn't space enough for us in the group, as Joseph said, that there was some part of us that wouldn't be received by the group. (Of course, even those of us who didn't speak during this process helped set the atmosphere from which scapegoating could emerge – I have tried to indicate my own contribution in this way.) At the same time the group had become important to us, and we wanted to belong. (It is only when we care that we are at risk of experiencing shame.) When people don't experience sufficient support in such instances (external and/or internal), it is the function of shame to pull them back from mobilizing on their yearning for connection. A major task then becomes to attempt to escape/ cope with their shame by camouflaging their yearning for connection. And one common strategy that people use in such situations is to find someone else to carry their shame, scapegoating the person (or subgroup)[4], as priests anointed goats in ancient times.

Selecting someone (or a subgroup) who is different is a common way of facilitating this process. In fact, when our shame gets evoked we will organize in terms of scarcity of resources in the social field, and differences between us and others can stand out as a signal that our belonging will be at risk, which can then trigger the above process. Thus we can use differences to separate us from others rather than to become curious about them and to create an atmosphere that will enrich

---

[4] Of course there are also many other creative strategies that people use to hide their yearning at such times such as withdrawing, stonewalling, dissociating, deflecting, controlling, resorting to addictions, and intellectualizing to name a few.

us all. This is the price that a group that gets caught up in scapegoating pays. Not only do the group members inflict harm on the scapegoat, but as importantly they limit their own possibilities for connection and growth. They buy into an individualistic paradigm sense of the social field condition of reception which then constricts how they can care for and be interested in others and how others can care for and be interested in them. They thus limit their possibilities of connection and growth in so many ways. Again, such is the price of an "us vs. them" mentality, not from just a moral perspective with regard to the scapegoat, but from a deeper/ broader, practical perspective for the whole field.

Note that the risk of scapegoating is highest when the group is going through some change, when group members are more off-balance, or when they are experimenting with forming new conceptions of who they are that reflect the new possibilities of connection that they are encountering or that they wish for in the group. Of course, this means that *the risk of scape-goating in a group is ever-present – the degree being dependent on the perceived lack of reception in the social field.*[5] As group leaders and trainers we must be aware of this possibility and attend not only to the act of scapegoating itself but just as importantly to the perceived lack of reception in the field. In fact, *noticing the beginning emergence of scape-goating is a diagnostic sign that alerts us to members' experienced lack of reception by others in the group, including the group leader.*

What did Joseph notice that clued him into the possibility that what was happening in our group was not just an issue of

---

[5] There will most likely be some low level movements towards scapegoating on an on-going basis as group members struggle with commonly present low levels of uncertainty in the group.

conflict between group members? I am not sure. Perhaps it was the lack of empathy that people displayed for Ann, that no one seemed to be able to understand her situation. Perhaps it was the fact that people were choosing to discuss this in the group instead of outside of the group – that anything brought up in a group can be a sign of the larger perceived condition of the social field. Perhaps it was a lack of connection between group members. Perhaps he noticed how group members were camouflaging their experience, like my over inflating myself.

Whatever Joseph noticed, his intervention was powerful for our group and profound for me. It provided sufficient support for us to become aware of how we were perceiving the possibilities for receptivity in our group and for us to start to explore whether more receptivity, more chances for connection would be welcome. Our group was able to use this support and with Ricardo and Jacob leading the way, the transformation that occurred, which became a foundation for future group development, was truly amazing.

However, if there were more people like me in the group (which I assume Joseph would have noticed and responded to) who did not know how to give voice to their experience, and if Ricardo and Jacob were not present, this probably would have played out slightly differently and the kind of intervention that Joseph chose might not have been sufficient. (Again, I am sure that Joseph would have responded differently in a different situation.)

If you are in a context in which you do not perceive that it is possible for your yearning for connection to be responded to, and you have not had that yearning responded to in the past, then it will be very difficult for you to be aware of your yearning. Such is the protective power of shame. In such a group, asking people to go inside and explore if there is a piece of them that they don't believe would be acceptable in the group might only lead to a collective sense of isolation, further shame, and further camouflaging behavior.

As a group leader and trainer now, I am constantly assessing and reassessing what level of support/connection/challenge the group needs. In cases where I believe more support is needed I might slow the process down, directing attention to the perceived quality of receptivity in the group (with the idea that what is happening between group members might be an indication of a larger group issue), helping people (including myself) to respectfully enunciate their experience, and facilitating a dialogue between group members. In short, I would be trying to move at the group's pace. I might then use an intervention like Joseph's (for people to explore inside themselves) when the group was able to sufficiently define the question.

Or if I sensed the possibility of scapegoating before it reached a peak, I might work with individual group members, helping them test out the level of receptivity that exists in the group by asking them such things as "Would you like to hear how others are responding to what you have said?" Depending on whether I sense that I have to grade the experiment up or down I might also ask, "Who would you like to hear from?" And if the person names someone I would then invite the person to talk to that person. Or if the person somehow indicates that they are somehow shy about asking, I might say "Would you like me to ask if anyone would like to respond to what you have said." As I say, in general I am looking for ways to help people to respectfully test out whether there is interest in them in the group. As they find connection, they usually get a deeper sense of the kind of connection they want in the group. Similarly I might be noticing signs of yearning in such situations like, "The way that you are moving your foot looks playful." If I get back something like, "Yes, I like to play." I might then say, "Would you like to know if there is someone else that would like to play with you." Or "Would you like to know if there are others here who also like to play."

In training groups, I will teach off what happens in the group, drawing people's attention to the differences in how they perceive themselves and others and how they and others act depending on the level of connection they perceive is possible in the group. The lesson is always that we will self-organize dramatically differently depending on the degree of receptivity we perceive in the social field. Shame and belonging will be the primary organizers of the field in these situations. This is the underbelly of scapegoating, which our awareness of as practitioners transforms from a problem into an opportunity.

References

Frazer, J. (1922). *The Golden Bough: A Study in Magic and Religion.* New York: MacMillan.

Lee, R. G. (2001). Shame & support: Understanding an adolescent's family field. In M. McConville & G. Wheeler (Eds.). *Heart of Development: Gestalt Approaches to Working with Children and Adolescents. Vol II - Adolescence* (pp. 253-270). Hillsdale, NJ: Analytic Press/GestaltPress.

Lee, R. G. (1995). Gestalt and shame: The foundation for a clearer understanding of field dynamics. *The British Gestalt Journal, 4*(1), 14-22.

Lee, R. G. (1994). Couples' shame: The unaddressed issue. In G. Wheeler & S. Backman (Eds.), *On Intimate Ground: A Gestalt Approach to Working with Couples* (pp. 262-290). San Francisco: Jossey-Bass.

Lee, R. G., & Wheeler, G. (Eds.). (1996). *The Voice of Shame: Silence and Connection in Psychotherapy.* San Francisco: Jossey-Bass.

Wright, D. P. (1987). *The Disposal of the Impurity: Elimination Rites in the Bible and in Hittite and Mesopotamian Literature*. Atlanta: Scholars Press.

Zatelli, I (1998). The origin of the Biblical scapegoat ritual: The evidence of two Eblaite text. *Vetus Testamentum 48*(2), 254-263.

Surviving Group:

Rupture and Repair in Group Dialogic Process

• • • • • • • • • • • •

Judith Matson, in collaboration with fellow group members[1]

O ther authors have discussed the attributes of relational Gestalt therapy and its reliance on dialogue as an essential tool for healing. These authors suggest that the field conditions that allow and facilitate dialogue include: a commitment to the dialogical process, inclusion, emotional attunement, compassion and confirmation. Most discussions of dialogue have

---

[1] Liz Bentley, Sally Denham-Vaughan, Mark Fairfield, Janice Gerard, Liz Holloway, Lillian Norton, Jan Ruckert, Katy Steinkamp, Carol Swanson. Judith especially appreciates each member of the group at the Winter Residential, which provided the dialogue from which this chapter evolved. It has been a pleasure to midwife this dialogue and to share with a larger audience the depth and power of our work together.

focused on a two-person system, most often the therapist-patient dyad. In this dyad, the responsibility for creating the conditions for dialogue rests primarily with the therapist, although as the therapy develops, the patient often joins the therapist in holding these conditions.

This chapter explores what can happen when dialogue between two individuals occurs within a group setting. It asks: How are the conditions for dialogue held when it is a shared task among group members? What issues might arise when the group represents what was present in early family life, both supportive and traumatic? Without an identified therapist to assume responsibility for creating dialogic conditions, what will result from a collective ownership of establishing these conditions in the small group context?

What follows is our attempt to deconstruct a disruptive event that occurred within a group, triggered by a misunderstanding between two individuals. We explore the incident from multiple perspectives in our desire to provide insight into the ways groups can co-create with individuals the conditions for dialogical work. Each group member shared responsibility for contributing to the field conditions and for the group figures that emerged, as opposed to the notion that the individual has sole responsibility for personal figures of interest. In this way the group bears witness to Perls, Hefferline and Goodman's (1951) organizing principle that the self emerges as a function of the field and that individual/dyadic work necessarily arises from within the group, rather than just affecting the group.

The group itself was part of a week-long training sponsored by the Pacific Gestalt Institute (PGI). Since the founding of PGI in 1999, a Winter Residential program has been offered each year, drawing therapists from the U.S. and abroad. The program focuses on theory-building and experiential learning; it challenges individual growth and development. With its emphasis on community, the Winter Residential provides a place for therapists to live their values and theory, to explore cutting-edge ideas, and to tease out theoretical subtleties. Our experience occurred within the context of therapists coming together in community to support each other in exploring/ encountering their growing edge, the edge where safety is challenged and risk resides.

The confrontation unfolded among ten Gestalt therapists during an afternoon process group, scheduled to last two-and-a-half hours. Although a member of the training faculty was present, she was not expected to facilitate the interaction. Instead, the members of the group shared ownership of the group process; through their presence and engagement, they took responsibility for establishing the conditions for dialogue. It was a hologram experience; each piece of work, whether individual, dyadic, or group, was owned by the group. Each group member contributed to and contained the whole.

The rupture occurred between Linda and Maggie, long-time friends who for years had traveled and roomed together as they attended various Gestalt trainings and conferences. As Linda's interests had expanded to include studying with another institute and Maggie had completed her training, the two women had lost that travel-together connection. Both, however, acknowledged their sense of aloneness in their community as Gestalt therapists and their wish for more on-going contact. Their lives had grown very much apart, and they seldom saw each other. Their sense of disconnection and their longing for more connection was a part of the emotional field, and Maggie asked the group if it would support her in addressing this issue with Linda during a group session. Linda and the group agreed.

The interaction between Maggie and Linda, which had been supported and encouraged by individuals as well as by the cohesiveness and caring of the group as a whole, exploded into a major disruptive incident. The power of this interaction touched each group member and left each questioning just what had occurred. In keeping with our theory, which suggests that reality is perspectival and that any event can best be understood through dialogue and the unique contributions of each person's perspective, we decided to write of our experience. Our purpose was to demonstrate how the field conditions for dialogue might be held by group members, as well as to explore the possible ways the presence of the group might shape or contribute to the emerging figures.

What follows is not an actual transcript of the disruption: it is the remembered words of Linda and Maggie and of the group participants, as shared in writing done at the time, and in subsequent emails. Actual words as remembered are in *italics*. (Repetitive themes were edited out of the transcript for ease in creating dialogue with our readers, and not every voice is heard. With the exception of Jan Ruckert, (faculty), the names used in the transcripts are pseudonyms, and identifying details have been changed.)

The Disruption

Maggie has asked for time to address an issue with Linda during the afternoon session. It is now afternoon, and the group turns its attention to the two. Jan Ruckert, faculty, joins the group; although there is no expectation that Jan will "lead" the group, the transcript indicates the importance of her presence.

Maggie reflects:

> This is why I am here at this training. I want this relationship. "Breathe, Maggie, breathe," I tell myself. My mind is both blank and a jumble of words. Fear, edging on terror, blanks out everyone in the group. No! I must have them for support in order to put my need for Linda out there. Without them, I could fall into the abyss of terror that lies between Linda and me. My body is tight, held tautly, energy radiating out from my belly to my fingers and toes. I cannot move. I want to stay present with my experience and hear hers. The terror comes in waves.

Linda reflects:

> Maggie wants to work something out, and I am fearful. I can feel the "light-headedness" that signals dissociation. I will stay here and be present.

Jan:

> Do you need anything from me or the group?

Maggie:

> I hear the comforting, warm invitation from Jan. I look at the faces around me. I need them here in order to say what I want to say. I've always imagined them with me. Otherwise I know I will not find the courage to persevere. As for what I want?
>
> *Please help me stay present and not get lost in my terror and anxiety. If I panic, I will go away. I don't want to do that.*

Jan:

> *How will we know if you panic and go away?*

Maggie*:*

> *You will be able to see it in my body and breath. I will*
> *become rigid and cease breathing.*

The group agrees to help me, and I hear them.

Linda:

> As Maggie starts talking, I hear her words but have no
> feelings. I am not numb in my usual way. I am trying to
> stay here, and to some degree I am succeeding. So
> much going on, and I can't capture anything to speak
> to, so I wait and am intent on focusing on trying to
> connect with something she is saying. I want it to
> register. I have a conflict about allowing it to register.
>
> I wonder, is this all my fault? Is this more shame and
> humiliation to bear because of how I am hurtful and
> inconsiderate of others? I don't want to go in that
> direction; I want to stay grounded and report out what
> I am experiencing. But I am experiencing so many
> things – which to choose? This is a good place to do
> this; the others in the group will not take sides. I think
> this to myself to soothe and support myself.

Maggie:

> I think I hear Jan asking Linda if she needs anything. I
> don't know if she replies. I am immersed in my fear.
> "Be careful, Maggie. Be very careful," I say to myself.

Linda:

> Somebody asks me what I want. I don't know. I can
> only say something about what I don't want – to be
> humiliated. I say something about what I don't want. I
> think it matches what I think and feel, but I'm not sure
> if it matches.

Maggie:

> I take a deep breath and direct my eyes to Linda's eyes. I want to SEE her, not just look at her. And I want to be seen by her.

> The anxiety is building, and I cannot tolerate another minute of it. I dive into words. I struggle to make the words match my feeling and longing for her. My words tumble out as if I must rush or they won't get said.

Linda:

> *I want to know if you care about me. I don't know if you care about me. I'll call you and you don't return my calls. I know you are busy. I know you are working, and you are in graduate school with lots of reading and writing to do. I know that you are working with the training groups, but I feel like I don't matter to you, and I want to know you care about me.*

> Maggie starts to talk, and I listen, but more than the words, I listen to the other messages from her, especially from her eyes. She looks sincere; she really wants to resolve this. I can see that, but I'm afraid, afraid to get my hopes up and have them dashed again. Can I stay in this conversation without expectations? For moments I listen intently; then I drift away, caught in the turmoil that is stirred by my fears. I must trust this process. That is what I hang on to. I do trust this process, and I want also to have some assurance of a good outcome. I want this tough part to be over and everything to be OK. So stay with what is happening.

Reflections from the group:

- Linda and Maggie, whom I thought were best friends, are sitting opposite each other across the room. Maggie has been sitting very still for awhile. Her face is unusually red, and I imagine that she is breathing fast. She keeps looking at Linda. Maggie suddenly leans forward in her chair and says to Linda: *Linda, this is really hard for me to say to you, but I have to. I want to have a relationship with you. I want to be your friend. I miss you and feel that we are so far away from one another.*

- Maggie and Linda are attempting to heal their broken relationship. Both are clearly disappointed in the other, hurt, and needing to defend themselves, and both seem confused as to how this came about.

- Maggie learns forward, with her hands on her knees as she tells Linda, her friend, that she misses her. *I miss you, and I feel more distance between us. I leave messages, and nothing comes back.*

- Maggie's first words are quite clear. She says she wants a more satisfying relationship with Linda. She goes on to talk about their past relationship, what isn't satisfying now, some of the disappointments she has experienced, how much she misses Linda. I hear the longing under the words, but the emotion is not expressed directly. As Maggie continues, I follow the words but find myself confused. What is it Maggie wants now, in this moment/this interaction now? And what does she want from Linda in the on-going relationship?

- I am rooming with Maggie this week. We have talked a great deal, and I am feeling energetically protective. There is nothing I need to say or do, but to tune in as best I can. I watch her breathing, and when I note it is restricted, I breathe deeply myself, wondering if on some level she picks up that support. Maggie has stopped speaking. What seems like a very long silence greets her words.

- Maggie is explaining her sense of loss that Linda is retreating from contact. Maggie owns that her own style of contacting is contributing to the current situation, and she expresses her distress at the separateness that is increasing.

Linda:

> I feel stony and cold and am appalled by my own distance. How are we ever going to get resolution if I stay this detached?

> I start speaking as best I can, and as I speak, I feel the tears beginning to well up and feelings rising from deep inside. C'mon feelings, don't stop, don't go away, stay with me. What anguish! Am I going to be again this stony cold statue, or am I going to risk being human?

Maggie:

> A torrent of emotion floods me, and I can feel myself weeping and struggling with my shame. Do I have the right to ask? And what if she doesn't care?

Linda:

> C'mon feelings. I don't have any control, they are going to come, or not. Then as I release these thoughts and relax into the kind of frustrated despair I feel, they surface. Now I have feelings, and I can speak of them, clumsily, I'm sure.

Reflections from the group:

- I hear Linda responding to Maggie: You call me, Maggie, and we make a date to do something. I get really excited about seeing you, and then either you don't show up or you cancel. You have done that so many times in the past year. I just can't do that anymore.

-Linda echoes Maggie's words back to her. I reach out to you, Linda, and nothing comes back to me. I feel dropped.

- I watch Linda closely. I am afraid of what she might say to Maggie. I am relieved to see her look at Maggie, and I feel so sad for her when she says to Maggie, *I feel dropped by you, Maggie.*

- Now my attention is with Linda. I have watched her grow and evolve over the years, and I know something of her fragile places. I wonder how it is for her to be on the receiving end of Maggie's words. I wonder if she can, or will, respond. All eyes are on Linda. The silence lengthens. When Linda speaks, I hear in her voice that she is solidly present. As she continues, there is color and expression in her face. She speaks of her own hurts and disappointments in the relationship. Like Maggie, she has phoned and left messages and received no response. Like Maggie, she has been disappointed – there have been plans to meet at the dog park, or to come by the house, that never materialized. Like Maggie, she wants more from their connection and misses the relationship they once had. As Linda continues to speak, I experience a sense of deepening, a moving into a place that has directly expressed emotion.

- I feel the ground slowly sliding away from underneath me as Maggie and Linda continue to do what seems to me like battle with each other, throwing arrows from their defense lines. I breathe. Time stands still and seems like no time.

- I'm conscious that there are ten of us present and that I am one part of this present field of support and goodwill. The tension is palpable. I can feel my whole body alive, attentively sensing each unfolding moment. Maggie and Linda go on and on expressing their hurt and disappointment. I care dearly about them both and notice how much I want them to resolve their difficulties, and yet nothing seems to be moving forward.

Linda:

> Several people in the group speak up trying to support both of us. That is so comforting; I am not alone. I can speak more now. I am more in touch with myself and with the people in the group. I am still wary of Maggie, and I speak of what is happening for me. I am not looking at anyone, and I am aware they are all there and listening.

Maggie:

> I hear Linda as though through a long tunnel:

> *I feel like I can't trust you. I call you and you don't return my calls. You call and invite me somewhere and then cancel at the last minute.*

> I am confused. Linda is saying to me what I have said to her. My heart stops. I cannot breathe. I am holding myself very still, my fists clenched.

Linda continues to speak of her struggle with me: She is interested, and then I disappear, and she is dashed against the rocks by me. She is disappointed by me, over and over again. She tells me she doesn't trust me anymore. *There is no follow through,* says Linda. *I get excited and then you disappoint me.*

Oh my God! What have I done? I hear a comforting voice from the group. Someone says, *Are you panicked and disappearing?* The question brings me back from the edge, and I answer, *No! I am here.* The group is holding us, carefully, attentive, waiting. I wonder if they are holding their breath.

Linda's words fill me with sadness and longing – a deep, primal, archaic pain and longing. I hear her say that I have hurt HER. I struggle to hold on. How is that possible? Did my mother teach me this, to dazzle with excitement and the sweet promise of love, then to dash people against the rocks? Am I my awful mother? Another truth begins to break through my muddled mind; I have hurt Linda with my attempts to maintain my worthlessness to her. If I remain worthless, I do not have the power to hurt another. I am confused, and I press on with my anger. I don't see that Linda is excited about me. I feel my anger surge. I tell her of my most recent pain, in an attempt to let her see how I am hurt, too!

Ann is speaking now. I hear her voice and she is saying something about a lack of fore-contacting and how that contributes to our lack of understanding of each other. I am lost in my feelings of hopelessness right now, here, between us.

Reflections from the group:

- Linda talks about how her excitement builds when she thinks she will be seeing Maggie and then how her hopes get dashed on the rocks when Maggie doesn't appear. Linda has learned to block that building excitement, so as to be less hurt by the dashing, but she still hurts. Linda is now in tears. It is palpable to me how much desire there is on the part of both women to have a friendship that works for them both. I hear a deep yearning for relationship and time together. For a moment I feel into my own deep longing for more friends with whom I can share my own emotional reality.

- Although Maggie seems physically very still, I can sense from the tremor in her voice that she is full emotionally. I feel tearful and moved by the depth of commitment present and think how much they must both care about their friendship to be willing to stay in this difficult place. I notice Linda, flushed and drawn around her mouth, her eyes dark with what looks to me like fear. Nothing changes. I feel the weight of the impasse as I notice I'm holding my breath and then remember to breathe. I look around the group and feel the whole container of our presence. I, too, feel held and supported in my place as part of what's happening, part of the group, my group, and feel easier and able to relax.

- Linda's shoulders begin hunching in, and her chin drops down. She's folding in on herself in front of us. Linda's voice is tight as she says, *This is that familiar place of my being the toxic agent, and I'm fucked up and better get myself fixed.* My breathing is deeper as I fully exhale this feeling of affection for Linda at this moment. "Hang in there, Linda," I'm saying to myself. "Don't go to that damn old archaic place with your sadistic mother."

Maggie:

> Linda appears to collapse in front of me. I see her struggling, and I imagine this is too painful for her. I have asked too much. I am too much. I start to leave, and my mind is confused, and my sadness threatens to overwhelm me. Shock! What?! I hear Linda say: *This is so familiar. I can't do this anymore. You are fucked up, and you better go away and get yourself fixed!'*
>
> My response is instant. *Fuck you, Linda! I am NOT broken, and I don't need to be fixed! I am tired of being the one who has to fix myself to be in this relationship.*

Reflections from the group:

- My reverie on Linda is suddenly broken when Maggie yells across the room, Fuck you! I am so pissed with you, Linda. Fuck you! I'm tired of being the one who has to fix myself.

- Shit, Maggie misheard Linda. Oh God, what's going to happen?

- The disruption is fast and acute. I am too jolted to know if I remember the words. I remember the feelings: horror, confusion, fear. The words went something like this: Linda says, *I don't want you to feel like I'm broken, a broken thing that you need to fix or be careful of.* Maggie's response is instantaneous and angry. *'Don't try to fucking fix me. I don't need any fixing from you!'*

- Maggie bursts out: I'm angry and want to say fuck you. I'm tired of being the one who has to fix myself.

- I'm relieved I'm not in this dialogue. Two friends drifting away from each other, hurting each other and longing to connect. "Make a pact to tolerate getting by, and not go for the sustenance of life," I say to myself. I'm so glad I'm not sitting in either of those chairs. But I am sitting in their chairs. I'm witnessing their fear, shame, anger, anguish, anxiety. I'm breathing these feelings in this group and creating the space to allow this emerging dialogue. Maggie and Linda need me, and I need them to go on speaking.

Linda:

> Maggie is attacking me, saying, *Fuck you.* She is raging and yelling at me. I'm thinking, to myself, "I HAVE TO GET OUT OF HERE. THIS IS NOT GOING TO WORK."

Reflections from the group:

- Linda looks terrified and pushes her chair almost out of the group. Something has gone askew. I think Maggie has misheard Linda, and her backlash sends Linda reeling somewhere.

- Linda thrusts back her chair and starts to her feet, as if to leave the room.

- Linda is a panther springing from her chair, about to leave the room. In her vulnerable state, an arrow has pierced her body.

- *Linda, stay with us, stay with us, we're here with you. Take your time. Take your time."*

- *Don't leave, Linda.*

- Breathe.

- I'm hearing Mary shout to Linda, Stay, Linda, just stay. Stay Linda, just sit down, it will be OK. Just stay. Ann is calling out to her and says, Linda, stay with us, stay with us, we're here for you. I have never heard Jan raise her voice, ever, but she just keeps saying in the loudest, clearest, most loving voice, Linda, Linda, Linda.

- For a second I feel some confusion as to what has happened until it becomes clearer that words have been misheard. I'm shocked by the speed with which this happened.

Maggie:

> I see the group mobilizing, all reaching for us. I'm watching in horror as Linda leaps up, fighting to stay in the room. I hear someone in the group say to me, *No, Maggie, Linda was telling us how SHE is broken and must fix herself, how SHE is toxic!*
>
> Shame and humiliation threaten to overwhelm me! I must run away! My worst nightmare, here, now. I have wounded her beyond words! I am watching a caged animal, terrified, looking for an escape hatch! Look, Maggie. See what you have done! Oh, my God! Linda was talking about herself, not me. What have I done? I can't run away; I can only see the group surround her, quietly talking her down. I hear someone whispering to me, *Stay with us, Maggie. Stay with us. Don't panic. Stay.*
>
> I cannot breathe. I want to go. I can go away where I can take care of myself. I want to stay, and I want to go. I notice the care of the group. They are scared, and

they are holding us. I need them to be here. I need to be here.

Reflection from the group:

- Linda seems to deflate. She is in her chair and looks smaller, frightened, uncertain – mostly very frightened. It seems an eternal moment as everyone focuses on Linda; how will she manage this assault? *Maggie misunderstood what you said, Linda,* says Eric.

- Maggie looks stunned and confused and terrified. Clearly she heard something different from what I heard. I see a battle going on within her. Can she stay, or is she leaving by way of dissociating? I can't rescue her from what has happened. I don't even know what has happened. All I know is that I trust her goodness and her intentions.

- Whatever has happened here is a horrible mistake. I want to support Maggie. Should I touch her physically? No, too much stimulation I think. I touch her with my voice and say softly, *Stay, Maggie. It's going to be OK. Don't leave.*

Maggie:

> Linda is gone. I've dissociated. I don't know what's happening. I have seen her do this before. I know she is gone. I've ruined us. I am stunned. I can't think. I hear Jan saying we have time. I am reassured.

Reflections from the group:

- Linda stops moving and slowly comes back to her seat and sits down. Wow, I thought, I've never seen Linda able to respond before to being called back, to belong. As Linda sits in her chair, she lifts her head. Her eyes are cloudy and unseeing. She says to us, *I've left. I'm dissociating. I'm not here anymore. I don't know what happened. I don't remember. Maybe you can remember for me.*

- Linda looks up and says: *I've lost this. I've disassociated. I don't know what happened.* I say: *It's OK, we'll take our time, and pick up the details later.* Jan is leaning forward, and her gentle, warm voice says we have a lot of time together. There's no hurry. Her warmth is holding Linda.

- Everyone's attention is riveted on Linda. I am looking across the room to Maggie. I feel torn. I'm concerned about Linda, about how Maggie's reaching out to her and her sudden outburst is public and out there. Linda is raw and vulnerable. At the same time I am upset for Maggie. She is so alone on the other side of the room. Maggie's face looks horrified. She is burying it in her hands. I want to reach out to her, but I can't find my voice. I have no words for her or Linda. I am at a loss and feel ashamed that I can't come up with anything.

Maggie:

> Shame. The group waits. They know me. I chose them. We built this together. I matter to them! Something new is evolving. I slow down, and I say what I feel.
>
> *I didn't mean to hurt you! I misunderstood! I thought you were saying I was too fucked up and needed to fix myself. I didn't understand. Please don't leave me. Please don't run away. I don't want to hurt you. Please don't leave me alone.*
>
> I am seeing Linda, looking into her eyes. I am grounded again, and it is painful. I see her.

Linda:

> *I needed to hear that.*

Maggie:

> Linda replies, *I needed to hear you say that.* And I see the group again, holding us as we struggle. And the walls recede.

Reflections from the group:

- Maggie is looking at Linda and sees her tears. She says: I don't want to hurt you. I'm sorry I hurt you. I'm sorry I hurt you.

- Maggie says to Linda, I didn't mean to hurt you. I made a mistake, a terrible mistake. I misheard you, Linda. I thought you were talking about me, not about you. I am so sorry. I didn't mean to hurt you. The group has pulled itself together. We are silent, patient and present. We try to hold Linda and Maggie in our embrace.

- Linda looks up and says, *I needed to hear that.* The way we're holding Linda and Maggie, with words and in silence, helps me know why I come here to be with these people.

- I let go of my breath with relief from the intensity of Linda and Maggie's work and notice how exhausted I feel. Maggie apologizes, and Linda says, *I needed to hear that.* I sit back in my chair, wanting an end to the tension in my body where I hold other painful memories of conflict. I'm imagining that Linda and Maggie feel satisfied, as nothing more is said, and in that pregnant moment when seconds move by, an opportunity for closure seems to arrive. I am assuming that all is well and feel comforted in my belief as each of us moves. The moment is gone, and the days pass by until goodbyes are said.

-That there would be an aftermath was completely out of my awareness until emails came, firstly from Linda and then Maggie. Our thoughts that all was well were based on a false assumption which precluded any awareness of unfinished business.

Aftershocks

Although the group thought the encounter was complete, two months later Linda opened a discussion of unfinished business via email. All the group members were involved in the email discussion, though only Maggie's and Linda's thoughts are included below.

Linda:

> Something was not right for me. I was extremely hurt and needed to protect myself in any way I could. When I said something like - *I needed to hear you say that* - it felt hollow and false in my ears, and it was all I could come up with.

Maggie:

> At the point in our session when I apologized to Linda, I was gone. I had dissociated from my loss of control. Saying, *I'm sorry I hurt you, Linda*, was rote. I heard Linda say, *I needed to hear you say that*. Those words, and the look on Linda's face, felt and sounded threatening to me, but I also used them to get out of the room.

Linda:

> I think that my statement was seen as a sign of closure, and that I derived some comfort and support from it. I was manipulating to find some relief for myself. It was not a statement of closure. It was an extremely retroflected statement of anger, hurt and retaliation, uttered in a way to try to preserve my existence, and a way to escape what was then an unbearable, painful experience. In that moment what I retroflected was my desire to hurt and humiliate Maggie, and I did not want to do that.

Maggie:

> I was so past my support. After my interruption, I no longer had the courage or energy, so I gave up. Something, some part of me, was terribly wounded by the whole process. Something like a promise was held out, then taken away.

Maggie questions:

> What was the purpose of my outburst? We never addressed the violence of my outburst, other than it was a mistake. Why was I screaming? Why was I so quick to lash out? What was under the fury? I violently lashed out! We didn't have time to address that.

Linda questions:

> Is there a lesson to be learned about apparent closure during a very emotional experience? Can a simple statement be trusted at face value? What did Maggie and I need for support which was not provided?"

Linda is not done with using this experience to deepen her understanding of self, nor is Maggie. Both women continue an email discussion, which they share with the entire group.

Linda:

> The idea that I may have something to offer is a major transformation for me. It is emerging in the context of a very supportive group, and it has been a long process. This emergence is not the aha! experience so often cited but a slow, painful metamorphosis. The image of a snake shedding its skin comes to mind. A significant moment in this event came about in my dialogue with Maggie in front of the group. Maggie asked, and I was willing to participate. What is significant for me right now is the moment when Maggie misunderstood what I was saying and lashed out at me in a rage. I froze, then bolted, although not physically. I heard some others – Ann and Mary -- say to Maggie that she had misunderstood what I was saying. The significance of that for me is enormous. Somebody cared, and somebody did something!!

> In my childhood experiences there was no one for me. I felt alone and had to deal with the physical and verbal lashings on my own. I was often confused about what had happened. What did I do or say that evoked such rage and violence? It must be me; I am a bad and toxic person. Now for the first time (that I remember) in the moment, someone saw and did something!!! They got it! They were involved!! This awareness comes several days after the fact, after we have processed and I have heard others' accounts of what had happened. At the time I was terrified with a life-threatening terror and had to get out. I could barely contain my desperate attempt to flee, and through that thick haze of terror I could hear words - *Stay - breathe – it is o.k.* I trusted

those words enough to struggle with my primitive impulse to bolt to safety

Maggie:

Linda, as I sat with you that day in the group, I was so past my support. I was filled with anxiety and was struggling mightily to describe my experience without revealing too much about me and my anger with you. The point in our session where I mis-heard you interrupted what I now believe was an opportunity, had I had the courage, to really make contact with you, acknowledging my anger. After my interruption, I no longer had the courage, or the energy, so I gave up. Was that the purpose of my outburst?

I have been in awful anxiety. I felt so "unfinished" and so shamed by my response to Linda in the group.

I was the middle of five children with an alcoholic, bi-polar, borderline mother and a narcissistic, violent father. My home was chaotic and crazy. I learned to hide in the middle. I would observe and hide and suck my thumb. I never really existed, except in my internal terror – and I was both grateful and lonely as hell. I would sit in the corner with my blanket, sucking my thumb and watching. As I look back on those times now, I think that I was terrified of being seen, and filled with longing to be seen! These became the organizing rules of my life. And I know they served me well while watching my father beat my mother, or my mother beat my sister, or all the permutations of that scene you can imagine – and rarely was I the victim of physical violence. Everyone else was! Not me, because I knew how to hide. I knew how to trim myself to fit even into the tiniest cracks of a wall in order to see yet not be seen. Or perhaps I wasn't the target because I didn't matter.

But I am terrified of conflict and of being seen, because either one in my family could get you killed...at the very least, beaten. So I learned to hold emotion tightly, and every once in a while I would explode in a fury of temper. The explosions would allow an almost orgasmic relief for a while, and in the betweens I would smile.

I thought I heard Linda say something like...well, this is your problem and you need to go away and fix it...and there I was...my reactiveness took over...I was a child again, lost in fury.

Over the next three years, Maggie and Linda continue their friendship, hesitantly at first, then more trustingly. No longer haunted by the terror of this traumatic encounter, they are often able to laugh, play, discuss, argue, and enjoy themselves. Looking back, they can see this group experience as one that highlighted their hopes, their longings for connection and relationship and, at the same time, plunged them into dread and humiliation, exposing their longings and vulnerabilities.

Discussion

The transcript poignantly illustrates the interplay between a longed-for/needed relationship and a dreaded/repeated relationship, as experienced by both Linda and Maggie. Each woman spoke clearly of her desire for a more satisfying connection with the other and of her pain when this is not forthcoming. Their mutual longing was palpable, as each reached towards her friend and spoke of her desire to be important to the other. Each woman carries a legacy of trauma from her family of origin, ready to be triggered, so that dreaded repeated experiences of the past interrupted the present moment, rupturing the desire for connection. What role, then, did the group play in both supporting the longed-for reach and in evoking the dreaded disruption?

We first see the role of the group in supporting dialogue when both Maggie and Linda initially spoke of the importance of the group's presence. Maggie acknowledged her longing for this important connection with Linda, but it can't be spoken without the presence of the group: "I must have them for support in order to put my need for Linda out there. Without them, I could fall into the abyss of terror that lies between Linda and me." Linda, too, acknowledged the importance of the group and used its presence to help ground and support herself: "This is a good place to do this; the others in the group will not take sides. I think this to myself to soothe and support myself."

The group reflections hint at the involvement and engage-ment of individual members. Certainly their sustained presence indicated a commitment to the dialogical process, as they dem-onstrated patience with a time-consuming process, tolerance for intense affect, mutual encouragement to stay with difficult content and unfailing honesty. The commitment continued long after the disruptive incident, starting with the decision to gather in the evening to write of the experience. Although there had been perceived closure during the afternoon, the evening writing, the ongoing emails, and Linda's initiation of the "aftershocks" discussion give testimony to the shared sense of dialogue as an ongoing, complex process.

Individual engagement, as reflected in the flurry of e-mails containing heart-felt responses, continued over the next several months. The group called a half-year meeting, in part to continue processing this event. Each individual continued to own membership in the group and to offer support. The following year at the Winter Residential, memory of the disruption and its effect on trust and care contributed to the field conditions. The dialogic process continued.

At no time was group involvement lackadaisical. Volumes of reflections were edited out, and what remains represents only a small portion of what was written. One group member reflected the thoughts of many when she wrote: ". . . I am one part of this present field of support and goodwill. The tension is palpable. I can feel my whole body alive, attentively sensing each unfolding moment."

In addition to support, the group as a group likely evoked early experiences of trauma. Both Linda and Maggie wrote of trauma in their family of origin and they feared re-experiencing such trauma – disconnection, pain, shame, humiliation – in this group. Both being vulnerable to a traumatized state of mind (Jacobs, 2007 lecture), we can assume that it was the whole of the situation – Maggie's initial confrontation, Linda's response, and the presence of the group – that triggered each woman. Options suddenly evaporated, and Maggie could only hear what she had heard as a child – blame, accusation, and danger; Linda could experience herself only as toxic and collapse into shame and an attempt to escape the group. Both reported dissociation, the childhood form of protection that had best served them.

What role did this group play in the rupture and the premature closure? Did the group collude with a need that seemed to be figure in order to find some partial relief from the tension? While these questions cannot be answered in absolute terms, our theory holds that meaningful experience is co-created through interaction between individuals and their immediate contexts – in this case, the presence of the group. We can therefore assume the group influenced and shaped the disruption as well as aided in its repair. In the sense that the group re-constellated a sense of family, the presence of the group made each woman vulnerable to re-experiencing her early trauma. At the same time, the group provided enough support and containment that this traumatic experience could move toward a resolution different from resolutions in the past. The process continued – imperfectly, painfully, and awkwardly – until both women had an experience that moved them in the direction of healing: neither was left entirely alone with her trauma; neither was judged nor punished for the disruption.

Within the reflections of the group, along with those of Maggie and Linda, we have an opportunity to glimpse inclusion as it occurs within a group. If we use Hycner's definition of inclusion as "putting oneself as much as possible into the experience of the other without losing one's own sense of self" (1991), we can explore the group's attention to self and other. We see the swing between self and other, even when the swing is imperfect and/or incomplete. As group members reflected, they focused on what may have been happening with/for Maggie and Linda, even as they noticed how they were affected by the encounter. One member stated, "I'm concerned about Linda. . . .Linda is raw and vulnerable. At the same time I am upset for Maggie. She is so alone on the other side of the room. . . .I want to reach out to her, but I can't find my voice. . . . I am at a loss and feel ashamed that I can't come up with anything."

Likewise Linda's and Maggie's reflections indicated a profound sense of self and other – other as represented by the group and each other. Reading their dialogue, one can see them move from awareness of self – tightness in the body, anxiety, dissociation, terror – to the other. Maggie wrote, "I want to stay present with my experience and hear hers." Linda reflected:

"Maggie starts to talk, and I listen, but more than the words, I listen to the other messages from her, especially from her eyes. She looks sincere; she really wants to resolve this. I can see that, but I'm afraid, afraid to get my hopes up." This awareness of other includes awareness of the group members. Maggie wrote, "I notice the care of the group. They are scared, and they are holding us. I need them to be here. I need to be here."

Reflections on Group Dialogue and Closure

The group setting provides challenges to the practice of inclusion and emotional attunement, both essential in the dialogical process. Inclusion depends in part on subtle emotional attunement to the other; validation for the accuracy of one's attunement in a group setting can only be approximated. Unlike in individual therapy, when the patient often responds, "Well, not exactly. . ." to the therapist's reflection or interpretation, the group setting limits the mutual refinement of emotional nuances and experiences. But not entirely, for instance as Maggie wrote, "Someone says, *Are you panicked and disappearing?* The question brings me back from the edge, and I answer, *No! I am here.* The group is holding us, carefully attentive, waiting."

Validated or not, the attempt at emotional attunement and inclusion is seen in multiple reflections, even if the words are not spoken out into the group. As an example, one member wrote, "I notice Linda, flushed and drawn around her mouth, her eyes dark with what looks to me like fear. Nothing changes. I feel the weight of the impasse."

The group reflections also provide an example of compassion as practiced within a group setting. The transcript is far more than a report of who said what to whom. It illuminates the process of group members' reaching to understand what was occurring, attempting and desiring to support both Linda and Maggie, expressing care and concern for each woman and her emotional reality. Whether it is the whispered, *Breathe, Maggie, breathe,* or Jan's voice projecting lovingly across the room, *Linda, Linda, Linda,* the quality of engagement and care resonated throughout the reflections. This care and engagement was articulated by one group member: ". . . I am one part of this present field of support and goodwill. The tension is palpable. I can feel my whole body alive, attentively sensing each unfolding moment."

Jacobs' (Hycner & Jacobs, 1995) discussion of confirmation suggests that confirmation is far more than acceptance; it is acceptance of the other as he or she is now, with acknowledgement of the potential for the individual to become something other in the future. An attitude of confirmation holds the space for something new to evolve – in the individual, in the relationship. Maggie's raising her issue with Linda within the group indicated intrinsic trust in the dialogic process and trust that confirmation would be forthcoming. An attitude of confirmation pervaded the group members' reflections. "Maggie looks stunned and confused and terrified. . . I can't rescue her from what has happened. . . All I know is that I trust her goodness and her intentions." "Linda's shoulders begin hunching in, and her chin drops down. . . My breathing is deeper as I fully exhale this feeling of affection for Linda at this moment. 'Hang in there, Linda,' I'm saying to myself. 'Don't go to that damn old archaic place with your sadistic mother.'"

Given that the transcript and reflections indicated the group's commitment to the dialogic process and apparent ability to establish appropriate field conditions for dialogue, we might expect a sense of closure and completion at the end of the afternoon. That did not occur. While a good deal of group support was present, both Linda and Maggie were left with an intense sense of shame, vulnerability, and lack of resolution. What happened?

In the dyadic relationship, the individual has but one other to mirror and reflect back on her; the group includes many. While this provides potential for support, it also evokes vulnerability and the potential for shaming. It spreads the risk – surely one person will understand – as it increases vulnerability through being so widely exposed. Perhaps it was inattention to this vulnerability at the end of the encounter that left Maggie and Linda feeling so raw and ashamed. The group accepted too blithely Maggie's words, *I didn't mean to hurt you! I misunderstood!* and Linda's response, *I needed to hear that.* While both women acknowledge in later reflections that this was not actually closure for either of them, perhaps it was as complete as it could be at that moment, more than two hours after the dialogue began. Yet perhaps the group could have provided additional support rather than dashing off to dinner and away from this intense, highly emotional encounter. Perhaps at least it could have been acknowledged that what seemed like the best closure possible in the moment might need a closer look later.

In hindsight, a few moments to reestablish supported contact – to allow Linda and Maggie to have their experience mirrored and to receive care from the group on a one-to-one basis – might have allowed them to leave feeling somewhat more nourished, accepted as imperfect in this moment, and confirmed for their courage and for who they were becoming. In hindsight, we wonder what sort of support the group members needed in order to stay more fully present and not to yield to the notion that a few closing words meant closure.

An additional hypothesis – evoked by the ongoing engagement of the group members – would be that the premature closure served a function for the group. Deeply touched on many levels and not yet ready to disengage, the group remained active for the next year. Closure, a satisfying equilibrium, would have made future engagement unnecessary. Fairfield (2004) says it well: ". . . . equilibrium is sometimes the optimal state. But this is not always the case, especially when what is needed is to reach something new, to grow, to learn."

A Rilke line comes to mind: "Perhaps all the dragons of our lives are princesses who are only waiting to see us once beautiful and brave. Perhaps everything terrible is in its deepest being something that wants help from us."

References

Fairfield, M., (2004). Gestalt groups revisited: A phenomenological approach. *Gestalt Review, 8*(3), 336-357.

Hycner, R. (1991). *Between Person and Person: Toward a Dialogical Psychotherapy*. Highland, NY: The Gestalt Journal Press.

Hycner, R., & Jacobs, L. (1995). *The Healing Relationship in Gestalt Therapy: A Dialogic/Self psychology Approach*. Highland, NY: The Gestalt Journal Press.

Jacobs, L. (2007). Lecture: Trauma. Campion Mental Health Center, Santa Monica California, February 2007.

Perls, F., Hefferline, F.R., & Goodman, P. (1951). *Gestalt Therapy: Excitement and Growth in the Human Personality*. New York: Julian Press.

Appendix
Co-published Inclusions

The chapter, "Relational Gestalt: Four Waves," was written for this volume. An edited version appeared in the *Gestalt Journal of Australia & New Zealand*, (2008), *4*(2), 37-55.

The chapter, "The Relational Attitude in Gestalt Therapy Theory and Practice," first appeared in the *International Gestalt Journal*, (2002), *25*(1), 15-36.

The chapter, "The Willingness to Be Uncertain: Preliminary Thoughts About Interpretation and Understanding in Gestalt Therapy," first appeared in the *International Gestalt Journal, (2007), 29,* 11-42.

A revised version of "Exploring the Field of the Emerging Therapist," first appeared in the *Gestalt Journal of Australia and New Zealand*, (2005), *1*(2), 47.

Sections of "Attunement and Optimal Responsiveness" were first published in H. Bacal (Ed.). (1998). *Optimal Responsiveness: How Therapists Heal Their Patients.* Lanham, MD: Jason Aronson. Reprinted here with permission from Jason Aronson. The case study was first published in the *International Gestalt Journal* as "The inevitable intersubjectivity of selfhood." *International Gestalt Journal*, (2005), *28*(1), 43-70.

The chapter, "Scapegoating from the Inside Out," first appeared in *Studies in Gestalt Therapy: Dialogical Bridges, 3*(1).

Selected Titles from GestaltPress

Transforming the way we live
and work in the world

Gestalt International Study Center

GISC is a diverse worldwide learning community based on trust, optimism and generosity. We study and teach skills that energize human interaction and lead to action, change and growth, and we create powerful learning experiences for individuals and organizations.

- **Leadership Development**
  - **Leadership in the 21st Century**
  - **Leading Nonprofit Organizations**
  - **Graduate Leadership Forum**
- **Professional Skill Development**
  - **Cape Cod Training Program**
  - **Introduction to the Cape Cod Model**
  - **Executive Personality Dynamics for Coaches**
  - **Applying the Cape Cod Model to Coaching**
  - **Applying the Cape Cod Model in Organizations**
  - **Finding Your Developmental Edge**
  - **Women in the Working World**
  - **Advanced Supervision**
- **Personal Development**
  - **The Next Phase: A Program for Transition & Renewal**
  - **Optimism & Awareness Essential Skills for Living**
  - **Couples Workshop**
  - **Building Blocks of Creativity**
  - **Nature & Transitions**
- *Gestalt Review*

Launched in 1977, Gestalt Review focuses on the Gestalt approach at all systems levels, ranging from the individual, through couples, families and groups, to organizations, educational settings and the community at large. To read sample articles, or to subscribe, visit:

www.gestaltreview.com

For more information about any of GISC's
offerings or to read our newsletter, visit:

www.gisc.com